KRAKEN LATIN 1
STUDENT EDITION

More Latin from Canon Press

Latin Primer: Book 1, Martha Wilson
Latin Primer 1: Student Edition
Latin Primer 1: Teacher's Edition
Latin Primer 1: Flashcard Set
Latin Primer 1: Audiō Guide CD

Latin Primer: Book 2, Martha Wilson
Latin Primer 2: Student Edition
Latin Primer 2: Teacher's Edition
Latin Primer 2: Flashcard Set
Latin Primer 2: Audiō Guide CD

Latin Primer: Book 3, Martha Wilson
Latin Primer 3: Student Edition
Latin Primer 3: Teacher's Edition

Latin Primer 3: Flashcard Set
Latin Primer 3: Audiō Guide CD
KRAKEN LATIN for the Logic Years: Book 1, Natali H. Monnette
KRAKEN LATIN 1: Student Edition
KRAKEN LATIN 1: Teacher Edition

KRAKEN LATIN for the Logic Years, Book 2, Natali H. Monnette
KRAKEN LATIN 2: Student Edition
KRAKEN LATIN 2: Teacher Edition

KRAKEN LATIN for the Logic Years, Book 3, Natali H. Monnette
KRAKEN LATIN 3: Student Edition (forthcoming)
KRAKEN LATIN 3: Teacher Edition (forthcoming)

Orbis Pictus 1: The Natural World, Timothy Griffith

Published by Canon Press
P.O. Box 8729, Moscow, Idaho 83843
800.488.2034 | www.canonpress.com

Natali H. Monnette, *Kraken Latin for the Logic Years 1: Student Edition*
Second edition. Copyright © 2015, 2019 by Natali H. Monnette. First edition 2015.

Cover design by Rachel Rosales (orangepealdesign.com). Cover illustration by Forrest Dickison. Interior design by Phaedrus Media and Valerie Anne Bost. Typesetting by Laura Storm and Valerie Anne Bost.

Printed in the United States of America.

Library of Congress Cataloging-in-Publication Data

Monnette, Natali, author.
Kraken Latin 1: student / Natali Monnette.
Second edition. | Moscow : Canon Press, 2019.
2019021326 | ISBN 9781947644342 (paperback)
Latin language--Grammar. | Latin language--Textbooks.
Classification: LCC PA2080.2 .M66 2019 | DDC 478.2421--dc23
LC record available at https://lccn.loc.gov/20190213267

19 20 21 22 23 24 25 26 27 28 29   10 9 8 7 6 5 4 3 2 1

BOOK 1

Kraken Latin
for the
Logic Years

STUDENT EDITION

by NATALI H. MONNETTE

canonpress
Moscow, Idaho

CONTENTS

Introduction. vi
Pronunciation Guide vii

Unit 1: Lessons 1–8   1

Lesson 1: First Conjugation Verbs & Present Active Indicative 3
Lesson 2: First Declension Nouns / Introduction to Case Usage—
      Nominative, Dative & Accusative 10
Lesson 3: Verbs: *Sum* / Nouns: More Case Usage—Genitive & Ablative /
      Prepositions 18
Lesson 4: Second Declension Masculine 28
Lesson 5: Second Declension Neuter 36
Lesson 6: Verbs: First Conjugation, Imperfect & Future Active Indicative /
      Principal Parts. 43
Lesson 7: Adjectives 53
Lesson 8: Review & Test 63

Unit 2: Lessons 9–16   73

Lesson 9: Second Conjugation: Present, Imperfect & Future Active
      Indicative / Substantive Adjectives 75
Lesson 10: Verbs: *Sum*, Imperfect & Future 84
Lesson 11: Verbs: *Possum*—Present, Imperfect & Future / Complementary
      Infinitives / Imperatives; Nouns: Case Usage—Vocative Case 92
Lesson 12: Nouns: Third Declension Masculine/Feminine 101
Lesson 13: Nouns: Third Declension Neuter. 110
Lesson 14: Verbs: Perfect Active Indicative 118
Lesson 15: Pluperfect & Future Perfect Active Indicative. 130
Lesson 16: Review & Test 140

Unit 3: Lessons 17–24   153

Lesson 17: Personal Pronouns 155
Lesson 18: Third Declension i-stems 165
Lesson 19: Third Declension Adjectives 173
Lesson 20: Verbs: Present, Imperfect & Future Passive Indicative 185
Lesson 21: Numerals / Review of Present Passive System 196
Lesson 22: Perfect, Pluperfect & Future Perfect Passive Indicative 206
Lesson 23: More Numerals: Ordinals 216
Lesson 24: Review & Test 225

Unit 4: Lessons 25–32   239

Lesson 25: Fourth Declension Nouns 241
Lesson 26: Verbs: Third Conjugation Active & Imperative 249
Lesson 27: Verbs: Third Conjugation Passive 258
Lesson 28: Nouns: Fifth Declension / Time Constructions 268
Lesson 29: Verbs: Fourth Conjugation, Active, Passive & Imperative /
       Irregular Verb *eō* 277
Lesson 30: Demonstratives 291
Lesson 31: Verbs: Third -*io* Conjugation, Active & Passive /
       Irregular Verbs *faciō* & *fiō* 304
Lesson 32: Review & Test 318

Appendices   331

Chant Charts 332
English-Latin Glossary 344
Latin-English Glossary 356
Grammatical Concept Index 365
Sources & Helps 367
Verb Formation Chart 369

INTRODUCTION

Avē, imperator, moritūrī tē salutant!
"Hail, emperor, they who are about to die salute you!"

Discipulī Discipulaeque,

Perhaps you are familiar with the Latin phrase quoted above. Suetonius, a Roman historian, recorded that captives and criminals uttered these words to Emperor Claudius just before they were forced to fight to the death in a mock naval battle.* And perhaps you, just as other Latin students before you, feel that these words appropriately describe your mental state as you approach this year of Latin! Some of you have never studied Latin before, and may be approaching this book with some trepidation. Some of you have already spent several years learning this language, and have the battle scars to prove it. Take courage. Although the study of Latin may seem daunting at times, you will survive and be all the better for it. I won't pretend that Latin is easy for everyone, because—as with any other language—you will need to study hard in order to master it.

This primer is the first in a series that will guide you through some major basics of Latin grammar. The goal is not merely to revel in these grammatical delights (although you are certainly welcome do so), but to equip you to translate and then read "real" Latin.

And so welcome to Kraken Latin. Whether Latin feels like a battle or a journey, may you prosper in your endeavors!

Avēte atque valēte,
Natali H. Monnette,
Magistra Discipulaque

---

* Suetonius, *Dē Vitā Caesārum, Dīvus Claudius* 21.6.

PRONUNCIATION GUIDE

When approaching Latin for the first time, many teachers are concerned that they pronounce the words correctly. Due to the many schools of thought on Latin pronunciation (classical, ecclesiastic, Italian, English, and any hybrid thereof), I would advise teachers not to worry, but to simply choose a pronunciation and stick with it. Spoken Latin has been dead so long that no one can be sure what a "proper" pronunciation would sound like, and there is no point in straining at gnats (or macrons). In this book, classical pronunciation is used.

Vowels

Vowels in Latin have only two pronunciations, long and short. When speaking, long vowels are held twice as long as short vowels. Long vowels are marked with a "macron" or line over the vowel (e.g., ā). Vowels without a macron are short vowels.

When spelling a word, including the macron is important, as it can clarify the meaning of the word (e.g., *liber* is a noun meaning "book," and *līber* is an adjective meaning "free").

	LONG VOWELS			SHORT VOWELS	
ā	like a in father: frāter, suprā		a	like a in idea: canis, mare	
ē	like e in obey: trēs, rēgīna		e	like e in bet: et, terra	
ī	like i in machine: mīles, vīta		i	like i in this: hic, silva	
ō	like o in holy: sōl, glōria		o	like o in domain: bonus, scopulus	
ū	like oo in rude: flūmen, lūdus		u	like u in put: sum, sub	
y	like i in chip: gryps, dygnus				

Diphthongs

A combination of two vowel sounds collapsed together into one syllable is a diphthong:

ae like ai in aisle: caelum, saepe

au like ou in house: laudō, nauta

ei like ei in reign: deinde

eu like eu in eulogy: Deus

oe like oi in oil: moenia, poena

ui like ew in chewy: huius, huic

Consonants

Latin consonants are pronounced like English consonants, with the following exceptions:

c	like c in come	never soft like city, cinema, or peace
g	like g in go	never soft like gem, geology, or gentle
v	like w in wow	never like Vikings, victor, or vacation
s	like s in sissy	never like easel, weasel, or peas
ch	like ch in chorus	never like church, chapel, or children
r	is trilled	like a dog snarling or a machine gun
i	like y in yes	when used before a vowel at the beginning of a word or between two vowels within a word (otherwise it's usually a vowel)

UNIT ONE

UNIT 1 GOALS

Lessons 1–8

By the end of Unit 1, students should be able to . . .

- Understand the five attributes of a verb: person, number, tense, voice, and mood

- Chant from memory the endings for the present, imperfect, and future active indicative verbs

- Identify and conjugate a first conjugation verb in the present, imperfect, and future active indicative

- Understand the three attributes of a noun: gender, number, and case

- Chant from memory the endings of first and second declension nouns

- Decline any first or second declension noun

- Decline first and second declension adjectives and know how to use them

- Translate basic sentences

- Know all vocabulary from Unit 1

- Write out from memory the *Pater Noster* (Lord's Prayer) in Latin

LESSON 1

First Conjugation Verbs & Present Active Indicative

Word List

VERBS

1. ambulō, ambulāre, ambulāvī, ambulātum: *I walk*

2. amō, amāre, amāvī, amātum: *I love*

3. cantō, cantāre, cantāvī, cantātum: *I sing, play (music), predict*

4. clāmō, clamāre, clamāvī, clamātum: *I shout*

5. dō, dare, dedī, datum: *I give*

6. laudō, laudāre, laudāvī, laudātum: *I praise*

7. līberō, līberāre, līberāvī, līberātum: *I set free*

8. necō, necāre, necāvī, necātum: *I kill, slay*

9. pugnō, pugnāre, pugnāvī, pugnātum: *I fight*

10. spectō, spectāre, spectāvī, spectātum: *I look at, watch*

11. stō, stāre, stetī, statum: *I stand*

12. vocō, vocāre, vocāvī, vocātum: *I call, summon, invite*

13. vulnerō, vulnerāre, vulnerāvī, vulnerātum: *I wound*

ADVERBS

14. bene: *well*

15. male: *badly, ill, wrongly*

16. nōn: *not*

17. nunc: *now*

CONJUNCTIONS

18. aut: *or*

19. et: and, even, *also*
    et...et: *both...and*

20. sed: *but*

Memorization

Pater noster, quī es in caelīs,

Our Father, who is in heaven

Grammar

Present Active Indicative

In this chapter you'll begin learning about how Latin verbs function. We'll start with the present active indicative of First Conjugation verbs.

	SINGULAR	PLURAL
1ST	-ō	-mus
2ND	-s	-tis
3RD	-t	-nt

This chant by itself doesn't really mean anything, but once you attach these endings to a verb stem, you can know the person and number of your verb. -ō means "I do something," -mus means "we do something," -s means "you do something," -tis means "you all do something," -t means "he, she, or it does something," and -nt means "they all do something." Thus, each verb form tells us **number** (-ō, -s, and -t are singular, and -mus, -tis, -nt are plural) and **person** (-ō and -mus are first person, -s and -tis are second person, and -t and -nt are third person).

Make sure you chant this chart every day until you have it memorized.

Look at the verbs you have to learn in this lesson. You should notice that all of them have an "a" in the second, third, and fourth endings. This is because they are all First Conjugation verbs. Latin verbs, like people, are "born" into certain families called **conjugations** that partake of similar features. Each conjugation will have its own stem vowel shared by all verbs belonging to it. In time you will learn about all five Latin conjugations and their allotted stem vowels, but for now, all you need know is that First Conjugation verbs all have a long -ā- in their stem.

Let's take a verb from this family (*necō, necāre, necāvī, necātum*) and add the endings we have learned to it. To do that we need to find the stem. To get the stem, we go to the second principal part (*necāre*) and remove the *-re*. That leaves you with the stem *necā-*. When we add the endings we get this.

	SINGULAR	PLURAL
1ST	necō	necāmus
2ND	necās	necātis
3RD	necat	necant

Some of you may be wondering why the first person singular form is *necō* and not *necāō*. This is because the *ā* and *ō* have contracted. You can think of it as though the *ō* has swallowed up the *ā* (try saying *āō* over and over and you will see how easily this happens).

What do these words mean? *Necō* is in the first person singular box. **Person** refers to the person performing the action. First person refers to either "I" or "we," second person is "you" or "you all," and third person refers to "he, she, it" or "they." Each of these pairs is either singular (as in "I," "you," "he, she, it") or plural ("we," "you all," "they."). Since the first person singular is *I*, *necō* must mean "I kill."

Note that it is in the present tense, active voice, and indicative mood. **Present tense** means that the action being performed is happening now, in the present. **Active voice** means the action is being performed by the subject (in this case "I kill"). **Indicative mood** means that this word is a statement, either of fact ("I kill krakens") or a question ("Do you kill krakens?") or even an exclamation ("He is killing the kraken!"). We will learn about other kind of verbs later, but for now, just note that we are learning present, active, indicative verbs.

Moving down, *necās* is second person singular, present active indicative. Thus, it means "you kill." The complete Latin chart with English meanings would look like this:

	LATIN SINGULAR	ENGLISH SINGULAR		LATIN PLURAL	ENGLISH PLURAL
1ST	necō	I kill		necāmus	we kill
2ND	necās	you kill		necātis	you all kill
3RD	necat	he/she/it kills		necant	they kill

Depending on the sentence these verbs are in, they can also be translated with the helping verb "do/does" (for questions like "*Does* he *kill* krakens?" and negatives such as "No, he *does* not *kill* them."). Another acceptable way to render them is with an "is/are" plus the verb with an "-ing" at the end: "We *are killing* many krakens this year"; "He *is killing* the kraken right now!" In English we need those helping verbs, but in Latin we can just use the one word. If you had trouble understanding any of this, go back to the Latin Grammar Basics and pay special attention to the verb section, or ask your teacher to help you understand. Don't move on until you understand what the endings mean.

Lesson 1 Worksheet

A. Vocabulary

Translate the following words from Latin to English or English to Latin as appropriate. For the verbs, also fill in the missing principal parts.

1. now: _____

2. clāmō, _____, _____, clamātum: _____

3. I call, summon, invite: _____, _____, _____, _____

4. stō, stāre, _____, _____: _____

5. aut: _____

6. necō, _____, necāvī, _____: _____

7. I walk: _____, _____, _____, _____

8. laudō, _____, laudāvī, laudātum: _____

9. but: _____

10. _____, vulnerāre, vulnerāvī, _____: _____

11. līberō, līberāre, līberāvī, līberātum: _____

12. not: _____

13. I fight: _____, _____, _____, _____

14. male: _____

15. cantō, _____, _____, _____: _____

16. spectō, spectāre, spectāvī, spectātum: _____

17. amō, _____, amāvī, _____: _____

18. well: _____

19. dō, dare, _____, _____: _____

20. et: _____

B. Grammar

Find the stem of the following verbs.

1. amō: _____   4. ambulō: _____

2. stō: _____   5. spectō: _____

3. clāmō: _____   6. līberō: _____

7. Write out the present active indicative verb endings.

	SINGULAR	PLURAL
1ST		
2ND		
3RD		

Conjugate the following verbs in the Present Active Indicative with their English meanings.

8. *cantō*

	LATIN SINGULAR	ENGLISH SINGULAR	LATIN PLURAL	ENGLISH PLURAL
1ST	cantō			
2ND				
3RD				

9. *vulnerō*

	LATIN SINGULAR	ENGLISH SINGULAR	LATIN PLURAL	ENGLISH PLURAL
1ST	vulnerō			
2ND				
3RD				

10. *dō*

	LATIN SINGULAR	ENGLISH SINGULAR	LATIN PLURAL	ENGLISH PLURAL
1ST	dō			
2ND				
3RD				

C. Memorization

Write out the first line of the Lord's Prayer in Latin.

D. English to Latin Translation

1. Now you (pl.) are loving, but I am fighting.

   _____

2. We do not sing.

   _____

3. She gives well.

   _____

4. They stand and now they are walking.

   _____

5. He sings badly, but you all sing well.

   _____

6. He fights, he wounds, and he slays.

   _____

7. I shout and sing, but you (sg.) do not love.

   _____

8. You (sg.) are fighting and now you (sg.) set free.

   _____

9. We watch and praise.

   _____

10. I fight, but I do not kill wrongly.

    _____

E. Latin to English Translation

1. Cantant aut clāmant.

   _____

2. Male pugnās, sed stō et bene pugnō.

   _____

3. Līberāmus, sed necātis.

   _____

4. Nōn amās; vulnerās.

   _____

5. Male pugnant et nōn līberant.

_____

6. Stat, sed ambulant.

_____

7. Bene amāmus et bene cantāmus.

_____

8. Vocātis et clāmātis, sed stat et spectat.

_____

9. Laudant et nunc dant.

_____

10. "Nōn bene," clāmō, "cantātis!"

_____

Lesson 2

First Declension Nouns / Introduction to Case Usage—Nominative, Dative & Accusative

Word List

NOUNS

1. aqua, -ae (f): *water*

2. bēstia, -ae (f): *beast*

3. corōna, -ae (f): *crown*

4. dīvitiae, -ārum (f pl): *riches, wealth*

5. fābula, -ae (f): *story, legend, tale*

6. fēmina, -ae (f): *woman*

7. īra, -ae (f): *anger*

8. lūna, -ae (f): *moon*

9. pīrāta, -ae (m): *pirate*

10. poēta, -ae (m): *poet*

11. rēgia, -ae (f): *palace*

12. rēgīna, -ae (f): *queen*

13. turba, -ae (f): *crowd, mob, throng*

14. villa, -ae (f): *farmhouse, country house*

VERBS

15. cremō (1): *I burn, consume by fire*

16. narrō (1): *I tell, relate, recount*

17. superō (1): *I conquer, defeat*

ADVERBS

18. cūr: *why*

19. hodiē: *today*

20. itaque: *and so, therefore*

Memorization

Pater noster, quī es in caelīs,

Sanctificētur nōmen tuum. Adveniat regnum tuum.

May Your name be made holy. May Your kingdom come.

Grammar

First Declension Noun Endings

Now that you've learned some verbs, it's time to learn some nouns to go with them. Remember, each noun has endings, which tells us how the noun is functioning within the sentence. Is it acting as the subject, an object, or a possessive? Endings, also called **cases**, tell us what a noun is doing within a sentence.

In this lesson, we will be learning a set of endings known as the First Declension endings. A declension is a regular pattern of endings, so that if you know what declension a word is, you can know which ending it needs for any individual case. Declensions, like conjugations for verbs, are simply noun families. Here is the First Declension:

	LATIN SINGULAR	ENGLISH SINGULAR		LATIN PLURAL	ENGLISH PLURAL
NOMINATIVE	-a	a/the *noun* [subject]		-ae	the *nouns* [subject]
GENITIVE	-ae	of the *noun*, the *noun's*		-ārum	of the *nouns*, the *nouns'*
DATIVE	-ae	to/for the *noun*		-īs	to/for the *nouns*
ACCUSATIVE	-am	a/the *noun* [object]		-ās	the *nouns* [object]
ABLATIVE	-ā	by/with/from the *noun*		-īs	by/with/from the *nouns*

Make sure you memorize these endings, because they will be super important later on. Today we will only discuss three of these cases: the **nominative** case, the **accusative** case, and the **dative** case.

A noun in the nominative case will be the subject of the sentence (or a predicate, but that won't be covered till the next Lesson): "*Oswald* sees the dragon." In this sentence, *Oswald* is the subject. Here is another sentence: "*Oswald* is seen by the dragon." Even though the two sentences are very different, *Oswald* is the subject in both sentences, because *Oswald* is the word going with the verb.

A noun in the accusative case denotes the **direct object**: "The dragon sees *Oswald*." In this sentence, *Oswald* is the object that the verb is acting upon. This is different from a sentence such as this: "The dragon is seen by *Oswald*." In this second sentence, there is a preposition before Oswald, so we do not consider it a direct object. The direct object is whatever the verb's action is directed toward. "Oswald" is the thing that the dragon sees.

The dative case indicates the **indirect object**. For example: "The princess gave a sword *to Oswald*." In this example, notice that the verb is directed towards the word "sword." The "sword" is the thing that Oswald is given, and so Oswald is the indirect recipient of that action.

You need to be especially careful when looking for direct and indirect objects, because in English it is sometimes difficult to distinguish them. Consider this example: "The princess gave Oswald a sword." Which is the indirect object? Oswald or sword? Always ask which one the verb is acting on, and in this case, the princess is giving, not Oswald, but the sword (she is not wrapping up Oswald and putting a bow on him and giving him to somebody). Therefore, Oswald is still the indirect object, and sword is the direct object. If you are having trouble distinguishing direct objects and indirect objects, practice making some English sentences until the concepts are crystal clear.

Last time we took our verbs and put different endings from the First Conjugation on them. Today we're going to do a similar thing, but with nouns. We are going to take our nouns and put the endings from the First Declension on them. You are conjugating verbs and declining nouns. Also, notice that the First Declension nouns in the vocabulary list all end with an -a.

In our wordlist, the first form given is the nominative case, the second is the **genitive**, the gender of the noun is given in parentheses, and then the meaning. You will learn more about gender when you get to adjectives, but memorizing the gender of each noun is very important. Most First Declension nouns are feminine, and only a few are masculine.

Again, the dictionary listing of the noun is helpful because it enables us to find the base of the noun. To find the base, we look at the genitive, not the nominative, of the noun. Thus, with the noun *corōna, -ae*, we see that nothing unusual happens and the stem is *corōn-*. Now that you know how to find the stem, add the endings from the First Declension to a few words just for practice.

Nominative and Accusative Cases

Here is a very simple sentence that shows us basic Latin grammar: *Rēgīna pīrātam amat.*

Word order in Latin does not determine what the word is doing (as in English); however, word endings do. Thus, this sentence could be rearranged a number of ways and still mean the same thing: *Pīrātam rēgīna amat. Amat rēgīna pīrātam.*

Usually the Romans would put the subject first and the verb at the end. However, because Latin is a highly inflected language, they could rearrange things for emphasis, for the sake of poetic meter, etc.

Now, whenever you are taking apart a sentence, you should read through the whole sentence, taking note of the verb, the subject noun, and then the direct object. Developing this habit now will pay off later on when things get more complicated.

In this sentence the verb is *amat*. Remembering our endings from last lesson, we know that it is a the third person singular ending, or the ending that goes with *he, she,* or *it*. Also it is present active indicative, so we can parse this verb as a third person singular, present active indicative verb. This is a mouthful, but hopefully you know what each of these words means. It's just a grammatical way of saying this verb means "he/she/it loves."

Now, the verb does not necessarily need a subject. By itself *amat* could actually be a complete sentence, such as "She loves." However, if there is a word in the nominative case, then that word is the subject and it is carrying out the action of the verb. This nominative noun will replace the pronoun subject included in the Latin verb. Not only that, but because the subject is doing the action of the verb, the subject and verb must match in number. In English, we cannot say "The dog run." Neither can we say "The dogs runs." The subject and verb must either both be singular or they must both be plural.

Hopefully you see that the nominative noun here is *rēgīna*. Thus the words *rēgīna amat* mean "the queen loves." If *rēgīna* was nominative plural (*rēgīnae*), then the verb would have to be plural too (*amant*). If the subject and verb do not agree in number, you have made a mistake somewhere. Also notice in our translation that "the queen" has replaced the pronoun "she" that was included in *amat*.

The final word in this sentence is *pīrātam* and it is accusative, which means that it is the direct object of the verb. Whom does the queen love? "The queen loves the pirate." If we had been translating one of the rearranged examples, we might put a little emphasis in our tone as we translated: *Pīrātam rēgīna amat*: "The queen loves *the pirate*." Perhaps the direct object is put first to emphasize that we can't believe she loves a pirate, or this particular one; or, the queen loves him as opposed to someone else. *Amat rēgīna pīrātam*: "The queen *loves* the pirate." Perhaps putting the verb first implies that we thought she hated him, but apparently she loves him. But at the same time, these implications might be incorrect; everything depends on the context.

Let's do a few more examples.

Lūnam spectātis. First look at the verb: *spectātis*. We should parse it as second person plural, present active indicative, and it means, "you all look at." In this case, *you all* is probably going to be the subject, but you should check for any nominatives anyway. There aren't any, so next we can look for any direct objects. Lo and behold, *lūnam* is in the accusative, so our sentence means "You all look at the moon."

It is possible to have a nominative in this type of sentence, but it would function as a description of "you all." If we had had *Pīrātae lūnam spectātis*, our sentence would have meant "You pirates are looking at the moon."

Let's look at one more example: *Fēminae dīvitiās dant*. Again, read through the sentence, mentally noting verbs, subjects (nouns in the nominative), and direct objects (nouns in the accusative), in that order. Our verb *dant* is third person plural, present active indicative, meaning "they give." Now we look for a plural nominative, and we have *fēminae*. Thus, in answer to the question, "Who gives?" we can swap "women" for "they," and have "The women give." What do they give? Why, we look for an accusative (singular or plural), and find *dīvitiās*. Answer: "The women give riches."

Dative Case

While the accusative case indicates a direct object, the dative case is used for the indirect object. In the example "The women give riches," "the riches" is the direct object because they are directly receiving the action of the verb "give." Now if the women were giving the wealth to somebody, then that somebody would be the indirect recipient of the action and thus the indirect object: *Fēminae pīrātīs dīvitiās dant*, "The women give riches *to the pirates*." In English we can also say "The women give the pirates riches" (*pīrātīs* is dative plural).

Now you need to be careful. In the last sentence, *Fēminae dīvitiās dant*, the word *fēminae* could potentially have been in the dative case, since that *-ae* ending does appear three times in the First Declension chant. If we took it as dative singular, then our example sentence of *Fēminae dīvitiās dant* would read: "They give riches to the woman." This also makes perfect sense!

So which is it? "The women give riches" or "They give riches to the woman"? It depends on the context. The word order hints that it's the first one, but in a certain context, the second one could work too. That's why you need to be careful to look at the endings very carefully before you rush to translate. Always double check, and use the process of elimination to find the translation that sounds the best.

Here are a few more examples of the dative case in action:

Poēta turbae fābulās narrat. "The poet tells the crowd stories" (or "tells stories to the crowd"). *Narrat* is third person singular, present active indicative. Since the verb is singular, a nominative subject would have to be singular too. The only word that works is *poēta*. Who is telling? "The poet." What is the poet telling? Our accusative is *fābulās*—stories. To whom is the poet telling stories?—*turbae*, to the crowd.

Rēgīnae corōnam dās. "You give the queen a crown" (or "You give a crown to the queen"). The verb *dās* is second person singular, present active indicative, "you give." The verb requires a singular nominative, but there isn't one, so we keep "you" as the subject and move on to our direct object. What do you give? The accusative is *corōnam*—"a crown." To whom do you give the crown? *Rēgīnae* in isolation could be nominative plural, genitive singular, or dative singular. However, since our verb is singular that eliminates *rēgīnae* as a nominative plural. Although the genitive might work, we will go with the dative since it makes the most sense: "to the queen."

No Definite or Indefinite Articles!

Classical Latin does not have any words for *a, an,* or *the.* Therefore, when translating Latin into English we can use either a definite or indefinite article (or no article at all), depending on the context and on what sounds best. To me at least, in this isolated sentence "The queen loves" sounds better than "A queen loves." The indefinite article might work if we had more to go on, as in, "Once upon a time, there was **a** queen who loved a pirate." However, with "The queen loves **a** pirate" versus "The queen loves **the** pirate," either article sounds fine and the best choice would depend on the overall story in which this particular sentence appeared.

Review

Make sure you are reviewing your verb endings as you do this lesson!

Lesson 2 Worksheet

A. Vocabulary

Translate the following words from Latin to English or English to Latin as appropriate. For the verbs, also fill in the missing principal parts. (There are a few review words mixed in.)

1. dīvitiae: _____

2. today: _____

3. bēstia: _____

4. fēmina: _____

5. crowd: _____

6. nunc: _____

7. īra: _____

8. water: _____

9. narrō, _____, _____,

   narrātum: _____

10. I stand: _____, _____,

    _____, _____

11. poēta: _____

12. itaque: _____

13. palace: _____

14. cūr: _____

15. sed: _____

16. pirate: _____

17. rēgīna: _____

18. fābula: _____

19. farmhouse: _____

20. well: _____

21. clāmō, _____, _____,

    clāmātum: _____

22. lūna: _____

23. I burn: _____, _____,

    _____, _____

24. corōna: _____

25. superō, _____, superāvī,

    _____: _____

B. Grammar

1. Decline *aqua*.

	LATIN SINGULAR	LATIN PLURAL
NOMINATIVE	aqua	
GENITIVE		
DATIVE		
ACCUSATIVE		
ABLATIVE		

2. Decline *fābula*.

	LATIN SINGULAR	LATIN PLURAL
NOMINATIVE	fābula	
GENITIVE		
DATIVE		
ACCUSATIVE		
ABLATIVE		

3. Decline *dīvitiae*.

	LATIN SINGULAR	LATIN PLURAL
NOMINATIVE	—	dīvitiae
GENITIVE		
DATIVE		
ACCUSATIVE		
ABLATIVE		

C. Memorization

Fill in the blanks (but be prepared to recall both lines entirely from memory for the quiz).

_____

Sanctificētur _____ regnum _____.

D. English to Latin Translation

Translate these sentences from English into Latin.

1. The poet looks at the moon and tells the woman a tale.

   _____

2. The beasts are burning the villa and the palace.

   _____

3. The pirates shout, but you (sg.) do not give the pirates wealth.

   _____

4. I love water, but the queen loves crowns.

   _____

5. Why are you (pl.) looking at the moon?

_____

6. We are now singing stories to the pirates.

_____

7. The crowds fight the beast well, but the beast is wounding the crowds.

_____

_____

8. The pirates kill the beast, and so the women love the pirates.

_____

_____

9. The queen summons the women and gives the women wealth.

_____

10. We pirates sing well but love badly.

_____

E. Latin to English Translation

1   Poēta turbae fābulam narrat, et cantat: "Pīrāta rēgīnam amat, sed rēgīna pīrātam nōn amat. Rēgīna corōnās et rēgiam et dīvitiās amat. Pīrāta lūnam spectat, et rēgīnae fābulās cantat, sed fēmina nōn amat. Hodiē rēgīna ambulat, et bēstia rēgiam cremat! Rēgiam et corōnās et dīvitiās cremat, et rēgīnam vulnerat. Sed pīrāta stat, bēstiam pugnat, et bēstiam necat. Rēgīnam līberat et rēgīnae dīvitiās dat. Nunc
5   itaque rēgīna pīrātam amat, et pīrāta rēgīnae et lūnae fābulās cantat."

_____

_____

_____

_____

_____

_____

_____

_____

_____

_____

Lesson 3

Verbs: *Sum* / Nouns: More Case Usage— Genitive & Ablative / Prepositions

Word List

NOUNS

1. agricola, -ae (m): *farmer*
2. harēna, -ae (f): *sand, beach*
3. hasta, -ae (f): *spear*
4. īnsula, -ae (f): *island*
5. nauta, -ae (m): *sailor*
6. patria, -ae (f): *native land*
7. pecūnia, -ae (f): *money*
8. puella, -ae (f): *girl*
9. sagitta, -ae (f): *arrow*
10. sīca, -ae (f): *dagger*
11. silva, -ae (f): *forest*
12. spēlunca, -ae (f): *cave*

VERBS

13. exspectō (1): *I wait for, expect*
14. habitō (1): *I live, dwell, inhabit*
15. sum, esse, fuī, futūrum: *I am*

PREPOSITIONS

16. ā, ab (+ abl.): *from, away from*
17. ad (+ acc.): *to, toward, at, near*
18. ē, ex (+ abl.): *out of, from*
19. in (+ acc.): *into, against*; (+ abl.): *in, on*
20. per (+ acc.): *through*

Memorization

Pater noster, quī es in caelīs,

Sanctificētur nōmen tuum. Adveniat regnum tuum.

Fīat voluntās tua, sīcut in caelō et in terrā.

May Your will be done, as in heaven also on earth.

Grammar

Verb of Being: *sum*

	LATIN SINGULAR	ENGLISH SINGULAR		LATIN PLURAL	ENGLISH PLURAL
1ST	sum	I am		sumus	we are
2ND	es	you are		estis	you (pl.) are
3RD	est	he/she/it is		sunt	they are

Sum, the Latin verb of being, is irregular, which means it doesn't follow the usual or expected verb formation rules. This shouldn't actually be surprising, since it is irregular in many languages. Take English, for example: I *am*, you *are*, he *is*—imagine learning that as a non-native speaker of our language!

However, the endings of the verbs still follow our basic pattern of *-ō, -s, -t, -mus, -tis, -nt*. True, the first person singular ends in *-m*, not *-ō*, but as you will see the first person singular alternates between *-m* and *-ō*. It is also an unusual word because the stem is less consistent than that of regular verbs, so make sure you memorize this word.

Sum or "is" is the verb of being, which means it is a linking verb; that is, it functions like an equals sign. "I am a woman" is saying that *I = a woman*. Thus it is grammatically proper to say "This is she" or "It is I" rather than "This is her" or "It's me." Notice that in English, the pronouns in these last two examples are in the objective case, but technically they should be in the subjective case. In Latin, this means that the words (whether nouns, adjectives, or pronouns) linked to the nominative subject by *sum* will also be in the nominative case. A noun that is linked by *sum* to the subject is called a predicate. Predicates modifying the subject need to be the same case and number as the subject. "I am a woman" should be *Fēmina sum*, not *Fēminam sum*. The women are queens will be *Fēminae rēgīnae sunt*. The two words not only agree in case (both being nominative), but are both plural as well.

Another handy and common usage of *sum* is that in the third person singular or plural, it can mean "There is" or "There are" (rather than "it is" or "they are"). This is especially the case when *est* or *sunt* appears at the beginning of a sentence: *Est rēgīna!* "There is the queen!"

Genitive Case

In this lesson, we are going to learn how to use the remaining noun cases: genitive and ablative. Just to review, the nominative case includes subjects and predicates, the accusative includes direct objects, and the dative includes indirect objects.

The genitive case indicates possession: *Corōnam rēgīnae spectō* can be translated either "I see the queen's crown" or "I see the crown of the queen." You can use either an apostrophe with an *s* or "of," depending on which sounds better.

Now let's look at the genitive in the First Declension Chant:

	LATIN SINGULAR	LATIN PLURAL		LATIN SINGULAR	LATIN PLURAL
NOMINATIVE	-a	a/the *noun* [subject]	-ae	the *nouns* [subject]
GENITIVE	-ae	of the *noun*, the *noun's*	-ārum	of the *nouns*, the *nouns'*
DATIVE	-ae	to/for the *noun*	-īs	to/for the *nouns*
ACCUSATIVE	-am	the *noun* [direct object]	-ās	the *nouns* [direct object]
ABLATIVE	-ā	by/with/from the *noun*	-īs	by/with/from the *nouns*

You may notice that not only are the genitive and dative singular the same, but they are also the same as the nominative plural, *-ae*. You can only tell what case a noun is in through context. For example, in the sentence *Corōnam rēgīnae spectō*, *rēgīnae* cannot be nominative, since the verb is singular, and it cannot be dative, since *spectō* is not a verb that would normally have an indirect object. Therefore, it is a genitive, and since it is next to *Corōnam*, it must possess it.

If we had *Corōnam rēgīnae dō*, it requires a tad more thought. This sentence could mean either "I give the queen's crown" or "I give the queen a crown." Now, taking both of these sentences in isolation, I believe that the latter sounds better; however, there could conceivably be a context in which the former would be the only possible answer. Whenever two or more equally valid translations are possible, I will endeavor to mention them all.

As you practice the genitive, make sure you know how to distinguish between the possessive singular and plural in English. For example, in English, the possessive in *king's cross* is singular. To make it plural, I simply move the apostrophe after the *s*, making it *kings' cross*. The cross does not belong just to one king, but to several kings. Notice that a genitive can be singular or plural, regardless of whether the noun it is modifying is singular or plural. In our example, changing *king's* to *kings'* did not change *cross* to *crosses*, and it would also be fine to say the *king's crosses* or the *kings' crosses*. Confirm that you know how to do this in English as well as in Latin.

Ablative Case and Prepositions

The **ablative** case has many functions, so think of it as one of those multi-tools that has not only a pocketknife, but also a screwdriver, scissors, corkscrew, and so on.

In this lesson, we will focus on two uses: ablative of **means/instrument** and as an **object of a preposition**. When you want to indicate the means or instrument by which an action is done, you simply put that word in the ablative: *Pīrāta bēstiam sicā necat*, "The pirate kills the beast *with* [or *by* or *by means of*] a dagger." In English we have to use a preposition such as "with" or "by" to indicate means/instrument, but in Latin all we need is a word in the ablative.

The ablative can also be used for the object of a preposition, and so, incidentally, can the accusative. Whenever you learn a Latin preposition, you also need to know what case that preposition "takes." The preposition *ex*, for example, means "out of, from" and takes the ablative. This means that the object of the preposition *ex* will be in the ablative case: *ex spēluncā*, "out of the cave."

Some prepositions take the accusative, as with *ad*, meaning "to, toward": *ad spēluncam*, "toward the cave." Prepositions with the accusative often indicate motion toward, whereas those with ablative show rest or separation. This is only a generalization.

This is also a good time to note how some words in English can be translated in different ways in Latin and English. So consider the English word "to." In the last lesson, the sentence

Poēta turbae fābulās narrat can be translated as "The poet tells stories *to* the crowd." There, the English word "to" is considered part of the dative word "turbae." We don't need a Latin preposition for that. However, we translate *Ambulō ad spēluncam* as "I walk to the cave." Here we are translating the word *ad* as "to." Make sure you don't get these two meanings mixed up. If you are having trouble try substituting "to" with the word "toward" and see if the sentence still makes sense. If it does, it's *ad*, and if it doesn't, try the dative, indicating indirect object.

Similarly in Latin, one word can be translated in two ways in English. For example, the word *in* with a noun in the accusative case means "into, against"; *in* plus a noun in the ablative case means "in, on." Thus *In silvam ambulāmus* would mean "We walk into the forest" (showing motion toward), but *In silvā habitāmus* means "We live in the forest" (showing rest). Again, make sure you practice this so that you don't get these two mixed up.

Finally, notice that the First Declension ablative singular ending is only distinguished from the nominative singular by a macron (the line above the vowel). In my personal opinion (no doubt unpopular with Latin purists!), forcing you to memorize all the macrons is overly burdensome. However, in some instances it is quite helpful to notice them, since that little ol' macron can potentially help you figure out what a word is doing in a particular sentence.

Review

Be sure to review First Declension endings in this Lesson so you don't lose track of them!

Lesson 3 Worksheet

A. Vocabulary

Translate the following words from Latin to English or English to Latin as appropriate. For the verbs, also fill in the missing principal parts. For each preposition, include which case(s) it takes.

1. island: _____

2. sīca: _____

3. sum, _____, _____, futūrum: _____

4. native land: _____

5. rēgia: _____

6. agricola: _____

7. per: (+ _____) _____

8. pecūnia: _____

9. arrow: _____

10. itaque: _____

11. nauta: _____

12. silva: _____

13. ex: (+ _____) _____

14. male: _____

15. riches: _____

16. spēlunca: _____

17. ā, ab: (+ _____) _____

18. exspectō, _____, _____, exspectātum: _____

19. hasta: _____

20. I dwell: _____, _____, _____, _____

21. _____, cantāre, _____, _____:

_____

22. to, toward: _____ (+ _____)

23. puella: _____

24. in: (+ _____) _____ (+ _____) _____

25. harēna: _____

B. Grammar

1. Conjugate and translate *sum* in the present active indicative.

	LATIN SINGULAR	ENGLISH SINGULAR		LATIN PLURAL	ENGLISH PLURAL
1ST					
2ND					
3RD					

2. Conjugate and translate *amō* in the present active indicative.

	LATIN SINGULAR	ENGLISH SINGULAR		LATIN PLURAL	ENGLISH PLURAL
1ST					
2ND					
3RD					

3. Decline *sagitta*.

	LATIN SINGULAR	LATIN PLURAL
NOMINATIVE		
GENITIVE		
DATIVE		
ACCUSATIVE		
ABLATIVE		

C. Memorization

Fill in the blanks (but of course be prepared to recall all three lines entirely from memory for the quiz).

_____ noster, _____ in _____

_____ tuum. _____ regnum _____.

_____ voluntās _____ in _____ terrā.

D. English to Latin Translation

1. The beasts are walking from the water to the forest.

   _____

   _____

2. You are sailors and fight the beast with spears and arrows.

   _____

   _____

3. He loves the pirate's girl and walks through the forest to the farmhouse.

   _____

   _____

4. We are not pirates; we are girls and live on a beach on an island.

   _____

   _____

5. The queen summons the farmer away from the native land to the palace.

   _____

   _____

6. I am the queen's farmer and I give riches and money to the girls.

   _____

   _____

7. The poet is telling the crowd tales in the cave today.

   _____

8. The pirates kill the farmer's beasts with daggers and so the farmer does not love the pirates.

   _____

   _____

9. The women are praising the queen's crown today.

   _____

10. The pirates love the women in the native land and so do not burn the women's farmhouses.

   _____

   _____

E. Latin to English Translation

1   Nauta et pīrāta sum, et in īnsulā in aquā habitō. Sunt spēluncae in īnsulā, et bēstiae in spēluncīs habitant. Itaque in spēluncās ambulō et bēstiās sīcīs aut hastīs aut sagittīs necō. Et agricolās pugnō, et villās cremō. Fēminās et puellās līberō, sed agricolās vulnerō aut necō. Fēminam amō; fēmina rēgīna est. In rēgiā in silvā habitat, sed in īnsulā habitō. Rēgīnae pecūniam dō, sed et pecūniam et dīvitiās amō. Bene pugnō,

5   bene superō, bene amō, et bene cantō. Poēta et pīrāta sum, et īnsulam in aquā amō.

_____

_____

_____

_____

_____

_____

_____

_____

_____

_____

_____

_____

_____

_____

_____

_____

F. Crossword Puzzle

Fill in the correct forms of the Latin words, and as appropriate translate the italicized English words into Latin. (Don't use macrons for the Latin words in the puzzle.)

ACROSS

1. *not*

2. ablative singular of *island*

4. *you* (pl.) *are*

5. second person singular present active indicative of *līberō*

8. first person plural present active indicative of the verb meaning *I call*

10. *out of*

13. dative plural of *story*

16. accusative singular of *crown*

17. *today*

18. *cremō* in the first person plural present active indicative

20. *or*

23. genitive plural of the word meaning *pirate*

25. *and so*

26. *the farmers'*

28. *toward*

29. *stō* in the third person plural

31. *sailor* in the nominative singular

32. *bēstia* in the accusative plural

34. *we give*

36. second person singular of *ambulō*

39. *by/with/from the girl*

41. the word for *cave* in the accusative singular

43. *arrow*, if it were the subject of a sentence

45. genitive singular of *poēta*

DOWN

1. 1st principal part of the verb meaning *I kill*

2. *on*

3. accusative plural of *native land*

4. *I wait for*

6. *īnsula* in the accusative singular

7. *you* (pl.) *conquer*

8. 4th principal part of *vulnerō*

9. *why*

11. *well*

12. *now*

14. *we love*

15. accusative plural of *īra*

16. *clamō* in the first person plural present active indicative

19. *of the palaces*

21. *by/with/from the water*

22. *but*

23. *money* in the nominative singular

24. *they love*

27. *for the queens*

30. ablative singular of the word meaning *spear*

33. *you* (pl.) *are walking*

34. nominative plural of the word for *wealth*

35. *forests* (nominative)

37. *badly*

38. *we are*

40. *she does praise*

42. *through*

44. *away from*

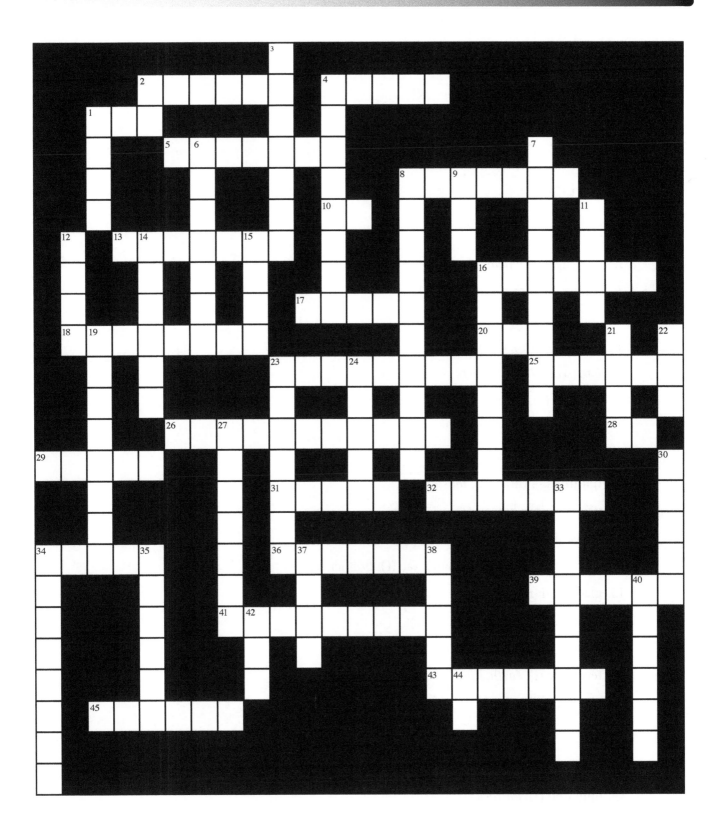

LESSON 4
Second Declension Masculine

Word List

NOUNS

1. ager, agrī (m): *field*
2. alnus, -ī (f): *ship, alder (wood)*
3. camēlus, -ī (m/f): *camel*
4. caper, -prī (m): *(billy) goat*
5. Christus, -ī (m): *Christ*
6. cibus, -ī (m): *food*
7. Deus, -ī (m): *God*
8. deus, -i (m): *a god*
9. dominus, -ī (m): *lord, master*
10. equus, -ī (m): *horse*
11. fīlius, -ī (m): *son*
12. germānus, -ī (m) *or* germāna, -ae (f): *brother, sister*
13. gladius, -ī (m): *sword*
14. ōceanus, -ī (m): *ocean*
15. servus, -ī (m) *or* serva, -ae (f): *slave, servant*
16. terra, -ae (f): *earth, land*
17. vir, virī (m): *man*

VERBS

18. nāvigō (1): *I sail*
19. oppugnō (1): *I attack*
20. portō (1): *I carry*

PREPOSITIONS

21. dē (+ abl.): *from, down from, concerning*

Memorization

Pater noster, quī es in caelīs,

Sanctificētur nōmen tuum. Adveniat regnum tuum.

Fīat voluntās tua, sīcut in caelō et in terrā.

Pānem nostrum quotīdiānum dā nōbīs hodiē,

Give us today our daily bread,

Grammar

Second Declension Masculine Noun Endings

	LATIN SINGULAR	ENGLISH SINGULAR		LATIN PLURAL	ENGLISH PLURAL
NOMINATIVE	-us / -r	a/the *noun* [subject]		-ī	the *nouns* [subject]
GENITIVE	-ī	of the *noun*, the *noun's*		-ōrum	of the *nouns*, the *nouns'*
DATIVE	-ō	to/for the *noun*		-īs	to/for the *nouns*
ACCUSATIVE	-um	a/the *noun* [direct object]		-ōs	the *nouns* [direct object]
ABLATIVE	-ō	by/with/from the *noun*		-īs	by/with/from the *nouns*

In this lesson we will learn the second of the five noun declensions. The chant above is frequently referred to as the Second Declension masculine, because most of the nouns are masculine in gender. The endings of this declension vary slightly with neuter nouns of the same declension, and thus the Second Declension neuter chant will be taught as its own chant in the next lesson. Think of the First Declension as a family with mostly girls and a few boys, and think of the Second Declension as nearly all boys and a few girls.

Certain cities, countries, plants, trees, and a few other random nouns in the Second Declension are feminine. I have included one of these in the vocabulary: *alnus*, meaning "alder(wood)," and by extension, "ship," since alderwood was regularly used in ship-building for its rot-resistant qualities. We will be using *alnus* for "ship" until the more common Third Declension word *nāvis* is introduced.

Make sure you chant through the Second Declension endings a few times. Then compare them to the First Declension endings. First off, we can see that there are two options for a nominative singular ending: *-us* or *-r*. Note that one word cannot have both options. *Puer* is always *puer* and not *pueus*; *equus* always ends in -us in the nominative and does not appear as *equer*. In the plural, the genitive, dative, and ablative are similar or identical to those of the First Declension.

The fabulous thing is that the Second Declension functions exactly like the First Declension. A nominative always acts like a nominative, no matter what declension, and the same is true with the other four cases. Also, a noun is born into a declension and stays there. Thus, *agricola*, though masculine, cannot divest himself of his First Declension identity and become *agricolus*. No, he is born into the First Declension and will always take First Declension endings.

Nouns in the Second Declension will also have the same sort of dictionary listing as First Declension nouns: nominative singular, genitive singular, gender, and definition. The genitive singular is of course where we can find the stem of the noun. Let's start by declining *equus* from your word list. The genitive is listed as simply -ī, so we conclude that the stem is a nice obvious *equ-*. We can then decline our noun thus:

	LATIN SINGULAR	LATIN PLURAL
NOMINATIVE	equus	equī
GENITIVE	equī	equōrum
DATIVE	equō	equīs
ACCUSATIVE	equum	equōs
ABLATIVE	equō	equīs

However, when we move from horses to billy goats, it gets more interesting. The noun *caper* has *-prī* as the genitive. This tells us that the whole genitive is *caprī*, which means that our stem is *capr-*, not *caper-*. The *-e-* has been dropped. The declension of *caper* will then look like this:

	LATIN SINGULAR	LATIN PLURAL
NOMINATIVE	caper	caprī
GENITIVE	caprī	caprōrum
DATIVE	caprō	caprīs
ACCUSATIVE	caprum	caprōs
ABLATIVE	caprō	caprīs

Here are two more examples, one of a noun ending in *-us* and one in *-r*:

	LATIN SINGULAR	LATIN PLURAL		LATIN SINGULAR	LATIN PLURAL
NOMINATIVE	dominus	dominī		ager	agrī
GENITIVE	dominī	dominōrum		agrī	agrōrum
DATIVE	dominō	dominīs		agrō	agrīs
ACCUSATIVE	dominum	dominōs		agrum	agrōs
ABLATIVE	dominō	dominīs		agrō	agrīs

Again, notice that the nominative plural and the genitive singular are the same, and that dative and ablative are the same in the Second Declension singular and plural. Again only context will tells us which case an individual word is. This is why as you translate from Latin into English, you should consider all the possibilities logically to make sure you understand the sentence rightly. For instance, in the sentence *Pīrāta bēstiam gladiō necat*, the word *gladiō* can be either the dative singular or the ablative singular. We need to go slowly and look at the subject and verb first. The rest of the sentence means "The pirate kills the beast." Does he kill the beast "to a sword" or "by means of a sword"? Context alone makes it clear that this is an ablative of means/instrument.

Review

Be sure to review your First Declension endings in this lesson, as well as your verb endings. You might also review the chant for *sum*.

Lesson 4 Worksheet

A. Vocabulary

Translate the following words from Latin to English or English to Latin as appropriate. For the verbs, also fill in the missing principal parts. For each preposition, include which case(s) it takes.

1. Deus: _____

2. portō, _____, _____,

   _____: _____

3. spear: _____

4. lūna: _____

5. Christ: _____

6. fīlius: _____

7. dē: (+ _____) _____

8. ōceanus: _____

9. food: _____

10. terra: _____

11. sister: _____

12. brother: _____

13. ager: _____

14. sword: _____

15. caper: _____

16. alnus: _____

17. I sail: _____, _____, _____, _____

18. _____, līberāre, _____, _____: _____

19. dominus: _____

20. servus: _____

21. camel: _____

22. man: _____

23. per: (+ _____) _____

24. _____, _____, _____, oppugnātum: _____

25. horse: _____

B. Grammar

1. Decline *vir*.

	LATIN SINGULAR	LATIN PLURAL
NOMINATIVE		
GENITIVE		
DATIVE		
ACCUSATIVE		
ABLATIVE		

2. Decline *terra*.

	LATIN SINGULAR	LATIN PLURAL
NOMINATIVE		
GENITIVE		
DATIVE		
ACCUSATIVE		
ABLATIVE		

Translate these verbs into Latin.

3. they sail _____

4. it is _____

5. we are attacking _____

6. we are _____

7. you (sg.) carry _____

8. she shouts _____

9. I walk _____

10. you (pl.) are telling _____

11. I am _____

12. you all dwell _____

C. Memorization

Fill in the blanks, and as usual, be prepared to recall the entire thing from memory for the quiz.

_____ es _____,

_____ tuum. _____ regnum _____.

Fīat _____ tua, _____ in _____ terrā.

_____ nostrum _____ dā _____,

D. English to Latin Translation

1. Christ is the Son of God, and Lord of the earth.

   _____

2. The pirate's brother dwells in the forest and gives food to the beasts.

   _____

3. We love the Lord God, but the pirates love gods.

   _____

4. The camel carries the queen's sister to the palace.

   _____

5. Christ tells stories to the crowds and is now giving the men and women food.

   _____

   _____

6. The billy goat walks out of the field and attacks the farmer's son.

   _____

7. You are pirates; therefore you sail on the ocean and carry men's wealth to the island.

   _____

   _____

8. The poet sings tales to the crowd about women, the queen, and camels.

   _____

9. The slave wrongly attacks the master with a sword, but the master conquers the slave with food.

   _____

   _____

10. Today the horse carries the servant, the camel carries the food, and the goat does not carry.

   _____

   _____

E. Latin to English Translation

1 **Tragoedia[1] Bēstiārum**

Camēlus, caper, et equus in īnsulā in ōceanō habitant. Est cibus in īnsulā, et equus caprō cibum dat, caper camēlō cibum dat, et camēlus equō cibum dat. Equus in agrō, caper in silvā, et camēlus in spēluncā habitat. Hodiē pīrātae ad īnsulam nāvigant, et pecūniam et dīvitiās in spēluncam portant. Sed camēlus

5 spēluncae caprō aut equō nihil[2] dē pecūniā et dīvitiīs narrat. Pīrātae ab īnsulā nāvigant, et camēlus dīvitiās amat et equō cibum nōn dat. Equus agrī et caper silvae ad spēluncam ambulant et dīvitiās camēlī spectant. Īra equī et caprī camēlum spēluncae cremat, et camēlum gladiīs oppugnant et necant. Dīvitiās ex spēluncā portant, sed caper ad silvam portat et equus ad agrum portat. Itaque caper silvae equum agrī oppugnat, et equus caprum pugnat. Equus caprum necat, et caper equum necat. Puella et

10 germānus bēstiās spectant, et dīvitiās ad villam portant. Fīnis.[3]

Glossary
1. *tragoedia*: tragedy
2. *nihil*: nothing [indeclinable noun]
3. *fīnis*: the end

_____

_____

_____

_____

_____

_____

_____

_____

_____

_____

_____

_____

_____

_____

_____

_____

_____

_____

LESSON 5
Second Declension Neuter

Word List

NOUNS

1. argentum, -ī (n): *silver, money*
2. aurum, -ī (n): *gold*
3. auxilium, -ī (n): *help, aid*
4. caelum, -ī (n): *sky, heaven*
5. castellum, -ī (n): *castle*
6. crustulum, -ī (n): *cookie, small cake*
7. discipulus, -ī (m) *or* discipula, -ae (f): *student [male or female], apprentice, disciple*
8. dōnum, -ī (n): *gift*
9. ēvangelium, -ī (n): *good news, gospel*
10. fātum, -ī (n): *fate*
11. gaudium, -ī (n): *joy, happiness*
12. oppidum, -ī (n): *town*
13. perīculum, -ī (n): *danger*
14. puer, puerī (m): *boy*
15. regnum, -ī (n): *kingdom*
16. verbum, -ī (n): *word*
17. vīnum, -ī (n): *wine*

ADVERBS

18. ibī: *there, at that place; then*
19. numquam: *never*
20. semper: *always*

Memorization

Pater noster, quī es in caelīs,

Sanctificētur nōmen tuum. Adveniat regnum tuum.

Fīat voluntās tua, sīcut in caelō et in terrā.

Pānem nostrum quotīdiānum dā nōbīs hodiē,

et dīmitte nōbīs dēbita nostra

and forgive us our debts

Grammar

Second Declension Neuter Noun Endings

The Second Declension neuter is happily just a simple variation of the Second Declension learned in the previous lesson.

	LATIN SINGULAR	ENGLISH SINGULAR		LATIN PLURAL	ENGLISH PLURAL
NOMINATIVE	**-um**	a/the *noun* [subject]	**-a**	the *nouns* [subject]
GENITIVE	-ī	of the *noun*, the *noun's*	-ōrum	of the *nouns*, the *nouns'*
DATIVE	-ō	to/for the *noun*	-īs	to/for the *nouns*
ACCUSATIVE	-um	the *noun* [direct object]	**-a**	the *nouns* [direct object]
ABLATIVE	-ō	by/with/from the *noun*	-īs	by/with/from the *nouns*

Compare the two chants on the board and notice the differences: nominative singular -*um* (not -*us/-r*), and nominative and accusative plurals ending in -*a* (not -*ī* and -*ōs*, respectively).

I can safely say that all Second Declension neuter nouns are neuter, although one can almost never say never or always when discussing language!

There are two rules of thumb for neuter nouns of any declension:

1. The nominative and accusative singular will be the same, and the nominative and accusative plural will be the same.

2. The plural nominative and accusative will end in -*a*.

These rules work for third and Fourth Declension neuter nouns as well as Second Declension neuters.

Nouns in the Second Declension neuter decline and function like the other nouns we have studied. You must go to the genitive to find the stem before declining the noun. Several of these nouns have a stem ending in -*i*, which sometimes gives us a double -*iī*, which is not a problem. Here are a couple of examples, one with the double -*iī* action and one without.

	LATIN SINGULAR	LATIN PLURAL		LATIN SINGULAR	LATIN PLURAL
NOMINATIVE	caelum	caela		gaudium	gaudia
GENITIVE	caelī	caelōrum		gaudiī	gaudiōrum
DATIVE	caelō	caelīs		gaudiō	gaudiīs
ACCUSATIVE	caelum	caela		gaudium	gaudia
ABLATIVE	caelō	caelīs		gaudiō	gaudiīs

Remember that nouns are born into their own particular declensions. Therefore, *gaudia* should never be taken as a nominative singular, because it is not a First Declension noun and never will be. It was born Second Declension, and it was born neuter. (Therefore *gaudia* is either nominative or accusative plural.) This is one of the reasons why it is important to learn each noun's declension in addition to the meaning.

This lesson does not really include any new concepts, just four new forms. If you are having trouble with anything, please go back and carefully review the previous lessons or ask for help if you are struggling with a concept. Know the five cases like the back of your hand.

Lesson 5 Worksheet

A. Vocabulary

Translate the following words from Latin to English or English to Latin as appropriate. For each preposition, include the which case(s) it takes.

1. castellum: _____
2. food: _____
3. always: _____
4. vīnum: _____
5. discipula: _____
6. dē: (+ _____) _____
7. joy: _____
8. ēvangelium: _____
9. fātum: _____
10. native land: _____
11. argentum: _____
12. there: _____
13. crustulum: _____

14. caelum: _____
15. aurum: _____
16. nunc: _____
17. town: _____
18. verbum: _____
19. aqua: _____
20. perīculum: _____
21. gift: _____
22. numquam: _____
23. boy: _____
24. auxilium: _____
25. kingdom: _____

B. Grammar

Decline *dōnum*.

	LATIN SINGULAR	LATIN PLURAL
NOMINATIVE		
GENITIVE		
DATIVE		
ACCUSATIVE		
ABLATIVE		

Identify the gender (Masc., Fem., or Neut.), number (Sg. or Pl.), and case (Nom., Gen., Dat., Acc., or Abl.) of each of the following nouns. Then translate them. If there is more than one option, give all possible answers. The first one is done for you as an example.

	NOUN	GENDER, NUMBER, CASE	TRANSLATION
1.	equōrum		
2.	oppidō		
3.	fāta		
4.	fēminā		
5.	auxilium		
6.	regnī		
7.	discipulās		
8.	puerī		

9.	vinōrum		
10.	terrae		

Identify person, number, and tense of the following verbs and then translate them.

	VERB	PERSON	NUMBER	TENSE	TRANSLATION
11.	portāmus				
12.	sunt				
13.	nāvigō				
14.	necās				
15.	oppugnant				
16.	habitātis				
17.	estis				
18.	laudāmus				
19.	clāmās				
20.	est				

C. Memorization

Say the first five lines of the *Pater Noster* aloud a few times, then fill in the blanks from memory.

_____

_____

_____

Pānem _____ dā _____ hodiē,

et _____ nōbīs _____ nostra

D. English to Latin Translation

Translate each sentence from English to Latin.

1. God gives the kingdoms to Christ the Son of God.

   _____

2. The pirates carry gold and silver and cookies away from the men.

   _____

   _____

3. Christ tells the words of the gospel to the crowds and the disciples.

   _____

4. We are queens and live in palaces, but you farmers never live in castles.

   _____

   _____

5. The servants carry food and wines and cookies to the master's castle.

   _____

   _____

6. Christ is the Word of God and is Lord on earth and in heaven.

   _____

   _____

7. The sailors give gifts and help to the women, and there is joy in the town.

   _____

   _____

8. The boys always tell stories about the moon to the sister's camel.

   _____

   _____

9. They praise and love gold and wealth, but you are servants of Christ.

   _____

   _____

10. You are the farmer's son and are now looking at the horses and goats in the field.

   _____

   _____

E. Latin to English Translation

1   Hodiē germānī et germānae in harēnā ad ōceanum ambulant. Crustula portant et gaudium amant. Sed alnus in ōceanō est, et pīrātae ad harēnam navigant. Germānae perīculum spectant et clāmant. Ōceanō crustula dant et ad oppidum festīnant.[1] Puerī perīculum semper amant et nōn festīnant. Pīrātās spectant. Pīrātae puerōs spectant. Pīrātae puerōs gladiīs oppugnant; puerī pīrātās verbīs pugnant. Pīrātae superant,

5   et puerī pīrātīs crustula dant. Interim,[2] germānae puerōrum ab oppidō festīnant et vīnum portant. Pīratīs vīnum dant, et pīrātās vinō superant. Germānī et germānae aurum et argentum ex alnō ad oppidum portant. Itaque nunc germānī auxilium germānārum amant et perīculum nōn amant.

Glossary
1. *festīnō* (1): I hurry, hasten
2. *interim*: meanwhile

LESSON 6

Verbs: First Conjugation, Imperfect & Future Active Indicative / Principal Parts

Word List

NOUNS

1. dea, -ae (f): *goddess* (dat. and abl. pl. usually *deābus*)

2. fīlia, -ae (f): *daughter* (dat. and abl. pl. often *fīliābus*)

3. magister, magistrī (m): *teacher* (male)

4. magistra, -ae (f): *teacher* (female)

5. mundus, -ī (m): *world, universe*

6. nihil (n, indecl.): *nothing*; (adv.) *not at all*

7. saeculum, -ī (n): *generation; spirit of the age/times*

VERBS

8. cōgitō (1): *I think*

9. creō (1): *I create*

10. mandūcō (1): *I chew, eat*

11. occupō (1): *I seize*

12. ōrō (1): *I pray, speak* (*person* asked takes acc. rather than dat.)

13. pōtō, -āre, -āvī, pōtātum *or* pōtum: *I drink, drink heavily*

14. regnō (1): *I rule, govern, reign*

15. rogō (1): *I ask* (*person* asked takes acc.; *thing* asked for takes either acc. or phrase with *dē*)

16. servō (1): *I save*

17. ululō (1): *I howl, scream*

ADVERBS

18. crās: *tomorrow*

19. herī: *yesterday*

20. ōlim: *once upon a time, formerly, then*

21. saepe: *often*

Memorization

Pater noster, quī es in caelīs,

Sanctificētur nōmen tuum. Adveniat regnum tuum.

Fīat voluntās tua, sīcut in caelō et in terrā.

Pānem nostrum quotīdiānum dā nōbīs hodiē,

et dīmitte nōbīs dēbita nostra

sīcut et nōs dīmittimus dēbitōribus nostrīs.

just as we also forgive our debtors.

Grammar

After several lessons focusing on nouns, it's high time we added to our verb knowledge. Besides, stories told solely in the present can get wearisome. In this lesson, you will learn two more tenses: the imperfect and the future.

Imperfect Active Indicative Verb Endings

	SINGULAR	PLURAL
1ST	-bam	-bāmus
2ND	-bās	-bātis
3RD	-bat	-bant

The present, imperfect, and future are the three tenses in the present system; that is, they are all formed off of the present stem. Remember that to find the present stem, you go to the infinitive (second principal part) and take off the *-re*. To this stem you add the present endings for the present tense, imperfect endings for the imperfect, and the future endings for the future.

Let's start with the imperfect. Looking at the chart, you should see that even though this is a new chant, the standard endings are present: *-m, -s, -t, -mus, -tis, -nt*. (Also, if you are not yet fully confident in your pronunciation, the *-bam* is pronounced more like English "bomb" and not like the sound effect "bam!")

Go back to the sample verb we used in Lesson 1: *necō, necāre, necāvī, necātum*. To find the stem, we simply go to second principle part (*necāre*) and take off the *-re*, yielding *necā-*. If we add the imperfect endings, we get *necābam, necābās, necābat, necābāmus, necābātis, necābant*.

	LATIN SINGULAR	ENGLISH SINGULAR
1ST	necābam	I was killing
2ND	necābās	you were killing
3RD	necābat	he/she/it was killing

	LATIN PLURAL	ENGLISH PLURAL
1ST	necābāmus	we were killing
2ND	necābātis	you (pl.) were killing
3RD	necābant	they were killing

Now, how does the imperfect tense translate? In English we have a special way of emphasizing that an action is ongoing. For example, we can change "I kill" into "I am killing," "I killed" into "I was killing," or "I will kill" into "I will be killing." Latin doesn't really distinguish between these two in the present, so both "I kill" and "I am killing" can be translated by *necō*. However, there are two past tenses in Latin, and the imperfect tense is the one with an extra sense of ongoing, continuous action. In the world of grammar, "imperfect" simply means "incomplete" (not "defective"!). At the same time, the imperfect can be translated in a number of ways. *Necābam* could mean "I was killing," "I killed," "I used to kill," "I kept on killing," "I would kill," and so forth—any variation that depicts this sort of action. This is why it is named imperfect. By contrast, a perfect action is a completed one. We will learn about that tense in Lesson 14.

The time is also ripe to introduce the hero of our text: *Oswaldus* (this name is Second Declension masculine). The sentence *Oswaldus bēstiās necābat* can be translated a number of ways. Perhaps the simplest is "Oswald was killing beasts." This conveys continuous action and allows us to wonder if perhaps he is still on that job.

Context will once again be helpful to us. If we are translating a story about the childhood of Oswald and this sentence appears, we could also translate *necābat* in the following ways:

"[When he was a child,] Oswald *would kill* dragons." Notice this use of the flexible English word "would." In this context, the "would" perfectly expresses the imperfect. In other contexts it can express a polite request ("Would you please pass the salt?") or a hypothetical ("I wouldn't do that if I were you!").

"[When he was a child,] Oswald *used to kill* dragons." This translation could read two ways: either Oswald used to kill dragons and doesn't anymore, or simply he had a habit of killing them in the past and still could be doing that today. The rest of the story would provide us with context.

[When he was a child,] Oswald *killed* dragons. The English "killed" is ambiguous. It can express the continual, habitual action of the imperfect (an added adverb such as *often* would make this more clear). In another context, *killed* can translate a perfect or completed action: "When Oswald was six years old he killed his first dragon." That sentence is describing a one-time, completed event and would be rendered better by the Latin perfect.

Be sure to practice writing example sentences in the imperfect and consider various ways you can translate them.

Future Active Indicative Verb Endings

The future tense shows action taking place in the future, obviously. In English we have several ways to express the future: *Oswald will kill the dragon. Oswald is about to kill the dragon. Oswald is going to kill the dragon. Oswald will be killing the dragon.* Any of these translations will work, provided of course that they work in their context. For our purposes, however, the first option is the simplest and will be the most commonly used in this book.

To conjugate a verb in the Future Active, simply add these new endings to the present stem:

	SINGULAR	PLURAL
1ST	-bō	-bimus
2ND	-bis	-bitis
3RD	-bit	-bunt

Here is our example verb from above, conjugated in the future active indicative:

	LATIN SINGULAR	ENGLISH SINGULAR
1ST	necābō	I will kill
2ND	necābis	you will kill
3RD	necābit	he/she/it will kill

	LATIN PLURAL	ENGLISH PLURAL
necābimus	we will kill
necābitis	you (pl.) will kill
necābunt	they will kill

Although it might go without saying, imperfect and future active verbs function just like present tense verbs: their subjects are in the nominative, they take accusative direct objects, etc.

Verb Synopses

At this point we know enough to do synopses. A verb synopsis is just that—a summary of a verb. Basically, you have a chart asking for a summary of a verb in a specific person and number for all the tenses, voices, and moods you have learned up to this point. For example, I could ask you for a synopsis of the word *necō* in the first person singular in present, imperfect, and future active. The correct answers would be *necō, necābam,* and *necābō.* Practically every quiz and test from here on out will have a synopsis on it, so make sure you are learning your verb endings and can put them on any verb when you are given the principal parts.

Review

Be sure to review your verb endings in this lesson, as well as First Declension noun endings.

Lesson 6 Worksheet

A. Vocabulary

Translate the following words from Latin to English or English to Latin as appropriate. For the verbs, also fill in the missing principal parts. For each preposition, include which case(s) it takes.

1. magister: _____

2. semper: _____

3. saepe: _____

4. I howl: _____, _____, _____, _____

5. fābula: _____

6. through: (+ _____) _____

7. nihil: _____; (adv.) _____

8. cōgitō, _____, _____, cōgitātum: _____

9. mandūcō, _____, _____, _____: _____

10. once upon a time: _____

11. I seize: _____, _____, _____, _____

12. male: _____

13. daughter: _____

14. ōrō, _____, _____, _____: _____

15. herī: _____

16. pōtō, _____, pōtāvi, _____ *or* _____: _____

17. creō, creāre, _____, _____: _____

18. regnō, _____, _____, regnātum: _____

19. goddess: _____

20. servō, _____, _____, _____: _____

21. servus: _____

22. rogō, rogāre, _____, rogātum: _____

23. tomorrow: _____

24. saeculum: _____

25. world: _____

B. Grammar

1. Conjugate and translate *sum* in the present active indicative.

	LATIN SINGULAR	ENGLISH SINGULAR		LATIN PLURAL	ENGLISH PLURAL
1ST					
2ND					
3RD					

2. Conjugate and translate *ōrō* in the imperfect active indicative.

	LATIN SINGULAR	ENGLISH SINGULAR		LATIN PLURAL	ENGLISH PLURAL
1ST					
2ND					
3RD					

3. Conjugate and translate *mandūcō* in the future active indicative.

	LATIN SINGULAR	ENGLISH SINGULAR		LATIN PLURAL	ENGLISH PLURAL
1ST					
2ND					
3RD					

4. Give a synopsis of *servō* in the second person singular.

	LATIN	ENGLISH
PRESENT ACT.		
IMPERFECT ACT.		
FUTURE ACT.		

5. Give a synopsis of *rogō* in the third person plural.

	LATIN	ENGLISH
PRESENT ACT.		
IMPERFECT ACT.		
FUTURE ACT.		

C. Memorization

Say the first six lines of the *Pater Noster* aloud a few times, then fill in the blanks from memory.

_____

_____

_____

Pānem _____ dā _____ hodiē,

et _____ nōbīs _____

_____ nōs _____ dēbitoribus _____.

D. English to Latin Translation

Translate each sentence from English to Latin.

1. The pirates were often eating food and drinking wine and seizing gold.

   _____

   _____

2. Tomorrow you students will summon the teacher and ask about fate and the gospel.

   _____

   _____

3. The daughter was praying to God then for help and He will give the daughter joy.

   _____

   _____

4. Yesterday I was thinking about the world and the ocean and the moon.

   _____

5. We are the queen's servants and will give cookies to the sons and daughters.

    _____

    _____

6. A beast was killing the farmers' horses and goats in the fields yesterday, and so the farmers will wait for the beast tomorrow and will attack [it] with swords.

    _____

    _____

    _____

7. The sailors and pirates were drinking heavily in the town and fighting with daggers.

    _____

    _____

8. Tomorrow the brothers will carry food and cookies into the cave and they will eat in the cave.

    _____

    _____

9. The women were singing tales to the boys and girls and so the beasts were howling.

    _____

    _____

10. God was creating the world and the ocean and is giving [them] to the man and the woman.

    _____

    _____

E. Latin to English Translation

1   Ōlim erat[1] rēgīna, et oppida terrae regnābat. In castellō habitābat et crustula mandūcābat et vīnum semper ibī pōtābat. Erat pīrāta, et rēgīnam amābat sed pīrātam nōn amābat. Agricolam amābat, sed rēgīnam nōn amābat. Fēminās numquam amābat, sed agrōs et villam amābat. Herī pīrāta ab alnō in harēnā ad castellum ambulābat, et rēgīnae, "Tē[2] amō," narrābat. "Tibī[3] aurum et corōnās dabō. Mē[4]
5   amābis?" rogābat. Rēgīna pīrātae, "Numquam," narrābat, "tē amābō. Nihil mihi[5] dabis. Agricolam semper amābō." Itaque pīrāta rēgīnam occupābat et ad alnum portābat. Rēgīna ululābat et clamābat. Erat nauta in harēnā, et pīrātam gladiō et īrā oppugnābat. Nauta pīrātam superābat et rēgīnam servābat. Nunc rēgīna nautam amat. Et rēgīnam et crustula et vīnum amat, itaque in castellō habitābunt et feliciter in aeternum[6] mandūcābunt.

Glossary
1. *erat:* third person singular imperfect of *sum:* he/she/it was, there was
2. *tē:* you (accusative form of *tū,* second person singular pronoun)
3. *tibī:* dative form of *tū*
4. *mē:* accusative form of *ego,* first person singular pronoun: I, me
5. *mihi:* dative form of *ego*
6. *feliciter in aeternum:* happily ever after

E. For Fun: *Litterae Mixtae*

Unscramble the letters to form a Latin verb, then translate it into English.

	UNSCRAMBLE	LATIN VERB	ENGLISH TRANSLATION
1.	istulbiālu		
2.	macōūnd		
3.	āstorgibā		
4.	ōbrāsumā		
5.	stābipo		
6.	tācōbagit		
7.	catucop		
8.	trāvesanb		
9.	narseg		
10.	unbrācet		

LESSON 7

Adjectives

Word List

ADJECTIVES

1. antīquus, -a, -um: *ancient*

2. avārus, -a, -um: *greedy*

3. beātus, -a, -um: *happy, blessed*

4. bonus, -a, -um: *good*

5. caldus, -a, -um: *warm, hot, fiery*

6. ferus, -a, -um: *fierce, wild*

7. fīdus, -a, -um: *faithful, trustworthy*

8. foedus, -a, -um: *horrible, ugly*

9. iūstus, -a, -um: *just, right, fair, impartial, righteous*

10. laetus, -a, -um: *happy, joyful, glad*

11. longinquus, -a, -um: *distant, far away*

12. magnus, -a, -um: *large, big, great*

13. malus, -a, -um: *bad, evil*

14. mīrus, -a, -um: *strange, wonderful*

15. miser, -era, -erum: *unhappy, wretched, miserable*

16. multus, -a, -um: *much, many*

17. parvus, -a, -um: *little, small, unimportant*

18. paucī, -ae, -a: *few*

19. pulcher, -chra, -chrum: *beautiful, handsome*

20. stultus, -a, -um: *foolish*

Memorization

Pater noster, quī es in caelīs,

Sanctificētur nōmen tuum. Adveniat regnum tuum.

Fīat voluntās tua, sīcut in caelō et in terrā.

Pānem nostrum quotīdiānum dā nōbīs hodiē,

et dīmitte nōbīs dēbita nostra

sīcut et nōs dīmittimus dēbitōribus nostrīs.

Et nē nōs indūcās in tentātiōnem, sed līberā nōs ā malō. Āmēn.

And do not lead us into temptation, but deliver us from evil. Amen.

Grammar

First and Second Declension Adjectives

It's time to learn some adjectives! Happily, the Romans loved to reuse all their endings. Thus, even though you technically have a new chant to learn in this lesson, you have already learned all of the endings that you will be using in this lesson.

Hopefully from English grammar you have learned that adjectives modify a noun or pronoun. For example, in the sentence "The gray donkey brays" the word "gray" modifies or describes the word "donkey." In Latin, adjectives signal the noun they describe by matching them in gender, number, and case. This also means that each adjective needs masculine, feminine, or neuter endings in all five cases. If you have a feminine singular ablative noun, you will need to put the adjective in the feminine, singular, and ablative as well.

Just like nouns, adjectives are born into declensions. Here are the endings for adjectives that have First and Second Declension endings:

	SINGULAR				PLURAL		
	MASC.	FEM.	NEUT.		MASC.	FEM.	NEUT.
NOM.	-us / -r	-a	-um		-ī	-ae	-a
GEN.	-ī	-ae	-ī		-ōrum	-ārum	-ōrum
DAT.	-ō	-ae	-ō		-īs	-īs	-īs
ACC.	-um	-am	-um		-ōs	-ās	-a
ABL.	-ō	-ā	-ō		-īs	-īs	-īs

Hopefully you can see that the masculine column follows the Second Declension masculine, the feminine column the First Declension, and the neuter the Second Declension neuter. In this text, I will not ask you to write out the adjective endings in a separate chart, but rather you will have to decline an adjective alongside a noun.

Now, you remember that an adjective matches the noun it modifies in gender, number, and case—not necessarily in declension. As an example, see the declension of "good sailor" below.

Notice that the Word List/dictionary listing of adjectives differs from that of nouns. An adjective is listed as masculine nominative, followed by feminine nominative, and then neuter nominative. You still find the stem by going to the second form—with nouns the second form is the genitive; with adjectives it is the feminine nominative.

Here are a few examples. First off, let's decline "good servant." When you are translating a sentence, always do nouns before adjectives, since adjectives must always match nouns. *Servus* is masculine; therefore, we select the masculine form of the adjective *bonus, -a, -um*.

The stem of *bonus* is simply *bon-*. Thus, our phrase "good servant" will be declined as follows:

	LATIN SINGULAR	LATIN PLURAL
NOM.	servus bonus	servī bonī
GEN.	servī bonī	servōrum bonōrum
DAT.	servō bonō	servīs bonīs
ACC.	servum bonum	servōs bonōs
ABL.	servō bonō	servīs bonīs

Many adjectives, unless the author wishes to emphasize them, will follow the noun they modify. However, having the adjective precede the noun is also permissible. Notice how within each phrase the adjective matches its noun in gender, number, and case.

With the phrase *servus bonus* they also happen to match in declension, but that is only coincidence. For example, consider "good sailor." Our noun, *nauta*, is masculine; therefore, we choose *bonus* again. The phrase will decline as follows:

	LATIN SINGULAR	LATIN PLURAL
NOM.	nauta bonus	nautae bonī
GEN.	nautae bonī	nautārum bonōrum
DAT.	nautae bonō	nautīs bonīs
ACC.	nautam bonum	nautās bonōs
ABL.	nautā bonō	nautīs bonīs

Each of these phrases match in gender, number, and case, but obviously they do not look alike—they do not match in declension. But remember our very important note above—**they do not need to match in declension**. Declension is irrelevant in this context!

You will be tempted to make one of two classic errors when doing noun-adjective matching. The first is that you will use the feminine adjective *bona*, and decline *nauta bona, nautae bonae*, and so on. This is what I call "putting girl clothes on a boy" (or vice versa). Adjectives are the clothes, and although in our day and age it is difficult to tell sometimes which are guy clothes and which are girl clothes, hopefully you get the point. They have just made the poor sailor into a cross-dresser by clothing him in a feminine adjective.

The other error is to rip *nauta* out of the family into which he was born (the First Declension) and attempt to reinstate him as a Second Declension noun: *nautus bonus, nautī bonī*, etc. However, *nauta* was born First Declension and will always be First Declension. He cannot be made into a Second Declension noun.

One more minor note before we leave the masculine noun-adjective combos and move on to the feminine and neuter: just as Second Declension masculine nouns can end in *-us* or *-r* in the nominative, so can some of these adjectives. The words *miser* and *pulcher* in the vocabulary list are good examples of this, which is why you should go to the second form listed to find the stem. For *miser*, since the second form is *misera*, that means the stem is *miser-*. However, for *pulcher* the stem is *pulchr-* (dropping that *-e-*), because we must go to the second form, which is the feminine nominative *pulchra*. Thus, "handsome sailor" would decline *nauta pulcher, nautae pulchrī, nautae pulchrō*, etc.

Let's stick with our adjective "good" as we decline a feminine and then a neuter noun. "Good daughter" is declined as follows (since *filia* is feminine, we select the feminine adjective):

	LATIN SINGULAR	LATIN PLURAL
NOM.	fīlia bona	fīliae bonae
GEN.	fīliae bonae	fīliārum bonārum
DAT.	fīliae bonae	fīliīs bonīs
ACC.	fīliam bonam	fīliās bonās
ABL.	fīliā bonā	fīliīs bonīs

These two happen to match in declension, but remember, that is not the important thing. They must match in gender, number, and case.

Although most Second Declension nouns are masculine, we have been using a feminine one: *alnus*, ship, alder (wood). Since it is feminine, we must again use the feminine adjective *bona*. We must not use *bonus*, because they would not match: we would be putting boy clothes on the girl. We also must not try to take *alnus* out of the Second Declension and try to make it into a First Declension noun *alna*, because it was born Second Declension and so shall remain. The correct declension of "good ship" is as follows:

	LATIN SINGULAR	LATIN PLURAL
NOM.	alnus bona	alnī bonae
GEN.	alnī bonae	alnōrum bonārum
DAT.	alnō bonae	alnīs bonīs
ACC.	alnum bonam	alnōs bonās
ABL.	alnō bonā	alnīs bonīs

Finally, we will decline "good kingdom." Since *regnum* is neuter, we must use the neuter form of the adjective *bonus, -a, -um*:

	LATIN SINGULAR	LATIN PLURAL
NOM.	regnum bonum	regna bona
GEN.	regnī bonī	regnōrum bonōrum
DAT.	regnō bonō	regnīs bonīs
ACC.	regnum bonum	regna bona
ABL.	regnō bonō	regnīs bonīs

Here *regnum* and *bonum* do match in declension, but of course the important thing is that they match in gender, number, and case. Later on, we will learn some other declensions and you will be able to match Second Declension neuter adjectives with them, so make sure you understand this concept.

Predicate Adjectives

When adjectives are used with the verb *sum*, they will also match the noun or pronoun they modify in gender, number, and case. We have already touched on this with nouns. When you say, "The queen is a woman," queen and woman are linked by the verb *is*, and are therefore both in the nominative. Similarly, if we have "The queen is good," we are saying that the *queen=good*, and therefore *good* needs to match in gender, number, and case: *Rēgīna bona est* (not *bonam*).

A final note on translating adjectives: Since the Romans did not use commas, they often employed *et* when using multiple adjectives to describe one noun. Thus *puer bonus et fīdus* literally means "the good and faithful boy," but you could also omit the *et* in your translation: "the good, faithful boy."

Adjective Agreement

When you have a plural subject of mixed gender, things get a little interesting. If it is a group of males and females, then the adjective will be masculine plural. I call this the **generic masculine**, similar to older and now politically incorrect English usage where we could refer to men and women as "mankind." (Think of the slang usage of "guys" to refer to males and females—"How are you guys doing?")

Here is an example sentence of how this would play out in Latin: "The men and women are good." *Virī et fēminae bonī sunt.* If you have a group of females and inanimate objects (if for some reason you wanted to say "The women and the towns are beautiful"), then the adjective will agree with the animate noun, the women: *Fēminae et oppida pulchrae sunt.*

Review

Be sure to review your Imperfect and Future Endings as you go through this lesson!

Lesson 7 Worksheet

A. Vocabulary

Translate the following words from Latin to English or English to Latin as appropriate. For each preposition, include which case(s) it takes.

1. bonus, bona, bonum: _____

2. handsome: _____

3. ferus, fera, ferum: _____

4. danger: _____

5. multus, multa, multum: _____

6. beātus, beāta, beātum: _____

7. antīquus, antīqua, antīquum: _____

8. ugly: foedus, foeda, _____

9. or: _____

10. malus, mala, malum: _____

11. often: _____

12. iūstus, iūsta, iūstum: _____

13. happy: _____

14. miser, misera, miserum: _____

15. mīrus, mīra, mīrum: _____

16. distant: _____

17. out of: _____

18. faithful: _____

19. magnus, magna, magnum: _____

20. small: _____

21. caldus, calda, caldum: _____

22. yesterday: _____

23. few: _____

24. avārus, avāra, avārum: _____

25. foolish: _____

B. Grammar

1. Decline *happy farmer.*

	LATIN SINGULAR	LATIN PLURAL
NOM.		
GEN.		
DAT.		
ACC.		
ABL.		

2. Decline *beautiful sister.*

	LATIN SINGULAR	LATIN PLURAL
NOM.		
GEN.		
DAT.		
ACC.		
ABL.		

3. Decline *fiery danger.*

	LATIN SINGULAR	LATIN PLURAL
NOM.		
GEN.		
DAT.		
ACC.		
ABL.		

C. Memorization

Fill in the blanks from memory. (You should know most of this by now, so only a few hints!)

_____

_____

_____

_____

_____

sīcut _____ dīmittimus _____.

Et ____ nōs _____ in _____ lībera _____ ā _____.

D. English to Latin Translation

Translate each sentence from English to Latin.

1. The queen's castle is ancient and beautiful, and many men and women live in the castle.

    _____

    _____

2. A farmer and son were living in a distant land in an ugly farmhouse.

    _____

    _____

3. The male and female students are good, and so the just teacher will now give cookies to the boys and girls.

    _____

    _____

4. We are beautiful women, but you are ugly pirates.

    _____

5. You (sg.) were thinking then about the wretched sailor's small goat.

    _____

6. The horrible beasts are fierce, and a few men will attack the beasts with spears and arrows.

    _____

    _____

7. The foolish sisters were carrying food through the ancient forest, and now they are not happy.

_____

_____

8. I am the master of many servants, and will give nothing to the greedy and wicked servants.

_____

_____

9. The small brother was fighting the big pirate well with bad words and an ancient sword.

_____

_____

10. Christ's disciples are blessed and will always praise the good words of God.

_____

_____

E. Latin to English Translation

1 Ōlim multī virī et fēminae, puerī et puellae, in īnsulā longinquā in mediō[1] ōceanō habitābant. Poetae fābulās dē camēlō antīquō et malō semper narrābant et cantābant. In fābulīs, camēlus in spēluncā foedā in mediā īnsulā habitābat, et parvōs puerōs et puellās mandūcābat. Itaque, puerī et puellae in silvam in mediā īnsulā numquam ambulābant. Nauta stultus oppidō magna verba ōrābat: "Nōn est
5 camēlus in spēluncā in mediā īnsulā! Ambulabō in silvam et mē[2] exspectābitis. Mihi[3] multum aurum dabitis!" Itaque equus nautae stultī nautam in mediam īnsulam portābat. Nauta spēluncam foedam spectābat. Nauta stultus et equus camēlum antīquum et malum spectābant! Ē spēluncā ambulābat. Nauta stultus ululābat. Equus iūstus camēlō nautam avārum et stultum dabat, et ā silvā ad oppidum ambulābat. Nunc multī poētae fīliīs et fīliābus oppidī fābulās dē nautā stultō, equō iūstō, et camēlō
10 malō narrābant.

Glossary
1. *medius, -a, -um,* middle (of), midst (of)
2. *mē*: accusative form of *ego*, first person singular pronoun: I, me
3. *mihi*: dative form of *ego*

_____

_____

_____

_____

_____

LESSON 8

Review & Test

Word List

No new word list this lesson. Review all the vocabulary from Lessons 1–7.

Memorization

No new memorization this lesson. Review the entirety of the *Pater Noster*.

Grammar

There is no new chant this lesson. Review the verb chants for *sum* and the endings for the present, imperfect, and future active indicative. Review the noun chants for the first declension, second declension, and second declension neuter.

Lesson 8 Worksheet

A. Vocabulary

Translate the following words from Latin to English or English to Latin as appropriate. For each preposition, include which case(s) it takes.

1. gift: _____
2. sailor: _____
3. spectō: _____
4. verbum: _____
5. agricola: _____
6. I drink: _____
7. perīculum: _____
8. sīca: _____
9. daughter: _____
10. fābula: _____
11. numquam: _____
12. caper: _____
13. villa: _____
14. castellum: _____
15. gladius: _____
16. ēvangelium: _____
17. dō: _____
18. goddess: _____
19. ager: _____
20. fīda: _____
21. aqua: _____
22. mala: _____
23. puella: _____
24. wonderful: _____
25. through: (+ _____) _____

26. I praise: _____
27. dē: (+_____) _____
28. longinquus: _____
29. I wound: _____
30. nothing: _____
31. gold: _____
32. lūna: _____
33. equus: _____
34. bonus: _____
35. alnus: _____
36. fēmina: _____
37. why: _____
38. ē: (+ _____) _____
39. righteous: _____
40. I love: _____
41. crown: _____
42. Christ: _____
43. magistra: _____
44. vocō: _____
45. portō: _____
46. aut: _____
47. generation: _____
48. necō: _____
49. son: _____
50. hodiē: _____

51. camēlus: _____

52. mandūcō: _____

53. pirate: _____

54. I howl: _____

55. male: _____

56. cave: _____

57. yesterday: _____

58. queen: _____

59. cōgitō: _____

60. discipula: _____

61. servus: _____

62. caelum: _____

63. cantō: _____

64. man: _____

65. rogō: _____

66. stō: _____

67. ā: (+ _____) _____

68. crustulum: _____

69. servō: _____

70. also: _____

71. auxilium: _____

72. town: _____

73. turba: _____

74. ōlim: _____

75. germānus: _____

76. antīqua: _____

77. līberō: _____

78. regnō: _____

79. sagitta: _____

80. argentum: _____

81. ōrō: _____

82. wealth: _____

83. cibus: _____

84. germāna: _____

85. gaudium: _____

86. pecūnia: _____

87. parvus: _____

88. nōn: _____

89. foolish: _____

90. īnsula: _____

91. habitō: _____

92. ōceanus: _____

93. ambulō: _____

94. dominus: _____

95. hasta: _____

96. mundus: _____

97. ad: (+ _____) _____

98. pugnō: _____

99. regnum: _____

100. often: _____

101. patria: _____

102. caldus: _____

103. bēstia: _____

104. I attack: _____

105. creō: _____

106. now: _____

107. ugly: _____

108. fātum: _____

109. anger: _____

110. blessed: _____

111. Deus: _____

112. rēgia: _____

113. ferus: _____

114. superō: _____

115. harēna: _____

116. avārus: _____

117. there: _____

118. clāmō: _____

119. multus: _____

120. semper: _____

121. poēta: _____

122. magnus: _____

123. terra: _____

124. occupō: _____

125. nāvigō: _____

126. crās: _____

127. sed: _____

128. boy: _____

129. pauca: _____

130. narrō: _____

131. wine: _____

132. therefore: _____

133. laetum: _____

134. silva: _____

135. pulchrum: _____

136. bene: _____

137. I wait for: _____

138. I burn: _____

139. wretched: _____

140. in: (+ _____) _____

(+ _____) _____

B. Grammar

1. Decline *foolish generation*.

	LATIN SINGULAR	LATIN PLURAL
NOM.		
GEN.		
DAT.		
ACC.		
ABL.		

2. Decline *handsome pirate*.

	LATIN SINGULAR	LATIN PLURAL
NOM.		
GEN.		
DAT.		
ACC.		
ABL.		

3. Decline *wretched beast*.

	LATIN SINGULAR	LATIN PLURAL
NOM.		
GEN.		
DAT.		
ACC.		
ABL.		

4. Decline *blessed man*.

	LATIN SINGULAR	LATIN PLURAL
NOM.		
GEN.		
DAT.		
ACC.		
ABL.		

5. Do a synopsis of *navigō* in the first person singular.

	LATIN	ENGLISH
PRESENT ACT.		
IMPERFECT ACT.		
FUTURE ACT.		

6. Do a synopsis of *laudō* in the first person plural.

	LATIN	ENGLISH
PRESENT ACT.		
IMPERFECT ACT.		
FUTURE ACT.		

7. Do a synopsis of *habitō* in the second person singular.

	LATIN	ENGLISH
PRESENT ACT.		
IMPERFECT ACT.		
FUTURE ACT.		

8. Do a synopsis of *cremō* in the second person plural.

	LATIN	ENGLISH
PRESENT ACT.		
IMPERFECT ACT.		
FUTURE ACT.		

9. Do a synopsis of *creō* in the third person singular.

	LATIN	ENGLISH
PRESENT ACT.		
IMPERFECT ACT.		
FUTURE ACT.		

10. Do a synopsis of *pugnō* in the third person plural.

	LATIN	ENGLISH
PRESENT ACT.		
IMPERFECT ACT.		
FUTURE ACT.		

C. Memorization

See if you can write out the entire Lord's Prayer in Latin from memory.

_____

_____

_____

_____

_____

_____

_____

D. English to Latin Translation

Translate each sentence from English to Latin.

1. The girls were looking at the ugly goat in the field and were screaming well.

_____

_____

2. God was always giving good words to men and women, but we are wicked.

_____

_____

3. The pirate was seizing the little boys' cookies in the forest and will eat the food there.

_____

_____

4. The wretched farmer was singing tales about joy and fate to the pretty woman, but she will never love the farmer.

_____

_____

5. There are evil sailors and pirates on the beach; therefore the queen is in her castle.

_____

_____

6. The ancient man loves silver and the moon, but you boys love gold and crowns.

_____

_____

7. The horse will carry the teacher or the student to the town, but the camel carries nothing.

_____

_____

8. You (sg.) love much gold and wealth, and so you will always be waiting for happiness.

_____

_____

9. The small sister is greedy and with many words was asking about the cookies.

_____

_____

10. They sailed from a distant island to the good farmers' land, and they will attack many towns with swords.

_____

_____

E. Latin to English Translation

1　Ōlim vir iūstus in magnō oppidō habitābat. Multī virī ab terrā longinquā nāvigābant et oppidum cremābant; itaque vir ab oppidō festīnābat[1] et parvum fīlium servābat. In ōceanō navigābant et multa perīcula, multōs bonōs virōs, et multōs malōs virōs spectābant. In longinquā terrā iūstus vir rēgīnam pulchram amābat. Et rēgīna virum amābat, sed deī virō narrābant: "Nāvigābis ab terrā rēgīnae ad
5　Ītaliam.[2] Ibī magnum regnum regnābis." Itaque vir ab terrā rēgīnae nāvigābat et rēgīna misera sē[3] in pyrā[4] cremābat. Dea iūstum virum nōn amat, et virō multa perīcula dat. Dēnique[5] ad Ītaliam nāvigat, multōs virōs pugnat et superat, et regnum nunc creābit. Cūr est magna īra in deīs et deābus?

Glossary
1. _festīnō_ (1): I hasten, hurry
2. _Ītalia, -ae_ (f): Italy
3. _sē_: himself, herself, itself, accusative reflexive pronoun (points back to the subject)
4. _pyra, -ae_ (f): funeral pyre
5. _dēnique_: finally

_____

_____

_____

_____

_____

2 UNIT TWO

UNIT 2 GOALS

Lessons 9–16

By the end of Unit 2, students should be able to . . .

- Understand how to use both first and second conjugation verbs
- Understand how to form and use imperatives
- Understand how to use the complementary infinitive
- Chant from memory the endings for perfect, pluperfect, and future perfect active indicative verbs
- Conjugate a first or second conjugation verb in any tense in the active indicative: present, imperfect, future, perfect, pluperfect, or future perfect
- Chant from memory the endings of third declension masculine/feminine and third declension neuter nouns
- Decline third declension nouns of any gender
- Form and use the vocative case in first, second, or third declension nouns
- Understand how to use and translate substantive adjectives
- Translate sentences using all of the concepts learned in Units 1 and 2
- Know all the vocabulary from Lessons 9-16
- Write out from memory the *Magnificat* in Latin

LESSON 9

Second Conjugation: Present, Imperfect & Future Active Indicative / Substantive Adjectives

Word List

VERBS

1. dēleō, -ēre, -lēvī, -lētum: *I destroy*

2. doceō, -ēre, docuī, doctum: *I teach*

3. festīnō (1): *I hasten, hurry*

4. habeō, -ēre, -uī, -itum: *I have, hold*

5. iaceō, -ēre, -uī, ——: *I lie (flat), lie down*

6. intrō (1): *I enter*

7. moneō, -ēre, -uī, -itum: *I warn*

8. mordeō, -ēre, momordī, morsum: *I bite, sting*

9. respondeō, -ēre, -spondī, -sponsum: *I answer, respond*

10. rīdeō, -ēre, rīsī, rīsum: *I laugh, smile*

11. salveō, -ēre, ——, ——: *I am well*

12. sedeō, -ēre, sēdī, sessum: *I sit*

13. teneō, -ēre, tenuī, tentum: *I hold, possess*

14. terreō, -ēre, -uī, -itum: *I frighten, terrify*

15. timeō, -ēre, -uī, ——: *I fear*

16. valeō, -ēre, -uī, -itum: *I am well/strong*

17. videō, -ēre, vīdī, vīsum: *I see*

ADVERBS

18. interim: *meanwhile, in the meantime*

PREPOSITIONS

19. cum (+ abl.): *with*

20. sine (+ abl.): *without*

INTERJECTIONS

21. salvē(te): *Good day! (Be well)*

22. valē(te): *Goodbye! (Be well)*

Memorization

Magnificat anima mea Dominum,

> *My soul magnifies the Lord,*

et exsultāvit spīritus meus in Deō salvātōre meō,

> *and my spirit has rejoiced in God my savior,*

Grammar

There's no new verb chant in this lesson. Instead, review the present, imperfect, and future active indicative endings, because you will be adding them to Second Conjugation verbs.

Verbs: Second Conjugation

Recall that a Latin verb conjugation is simply a family of verbs that share a common stem vowel. Do you remember how to determine if a verb is in the First Conjugation? Take our verb *necō*. The principal parts are *necō, necāre, necāvī, necātum*. To find the stem, we go to the second principal part (the infinitive), remove the *-re*, and voilà! The present stem is *necā-*. The stem vowel is *-ā-*, which is the sign of a First Conjugation verb. To our stem *necā-* we can add the present, imperfect, or future endings.

This process works exactly the same way for Second Conjugation verbs. *Deleō, delēre, delēvī, delētum* means "I destroy." We go to the second principal part, *delēre*, chop off the *-re*, and lo, we have *delē-*. This is our stem for the present system. The stem vowel is a long *-ē-*, which tells us that this is a Second Conjugation verb. The Romans were great recyclers. Thus, we do not have to learn any new endings for a Second Conjugation verb: we can just slap the endings we've already memorized onto this stem:

Present Active Indicative of *deleō,* second conjugation verb*

	LATIN SINGULAR	ENGLISH SINGULAR		LATIN PLURAL	ENGLISH PLURAL
1ST	deleō	I destroy		delēmus	we destroy
2ND	delēs	you destroy		delētis	you (pl.) destroy
3RD	delet*	he/she/it destroys		delent*	they destroy

Imperfect Active Indicative of *deleō,* second conjugation verb

	LATIN SINGULAR	ENGLISH SINGULAR		LATIN PLURAL	ENGLISH PLURAL
1ST	delēbam	I was destroying		delēbāmus	we were destroying
2ND	delēbās	you were destroying		delēbātis	you (pl.) were destroying
3RD	delēbat	he/she/it was destroying		delēbant	they were destroying

Future Active Indicative of *deleō,* second conjugation verb

	LATIN SINGULAR	ENGLISH SINGULAR		LATIN PLURAL	ENGLISH PLURAL
1ST	delēbō	I will destroy		delēbimus	we will destroy
2ND	delēbis	you will destroy		delēbitis	you (pl.) will destroy
3RD	delēbit	he/she/it will destroy		delēbunt	they will destroy

Synopses also work the same way with Second Conjugation verbs.

* Notice that, as in the First Conjugation, the third person singular and plural in the present active have a short stem vowel.

Substantive Adjectives

Hopefully, you are becoming more comfortable with adjectives by now. A sentence such as this one will not pose any problems: *Virōs bonōs laudāmus*, "We praise the good men." In Latin (and in English, for that matter), the substantive use of the adjective means that an adjective can stand alone and function as a noun. ("Substantive" comes from a Latin verb meaning "to stand.") We see the English substantive throughout the Beatitudes: "Blessed are the poor" or "Blessed are the meek," when "the meek" is an adjective standing as a noun: "the meek people." In our sample Latin sentence above, we can actually leave out the *virōs* and say *Bonōs laudāmus*, and it means exactly the same thing: "We praise the good men."

Context also matters here. If we have this sentence in isolation, it is safe to translate the masculine plural ending *-ōs* as "men." If it had been *Bonās laudāmus*, we would say "We praise the good women"; and, if it had been *Bona laudāmus*, "We praise the good things." Without a clear context, use "men" as your default masculine substantive, "women" for the feminine, and "things" for the neuter.

However, if the substantive adjective occurs in a story, we must look at the context to see what was the most recent masculine plural entity discussed. If the story were about a bunch of farmers who were working hard and bringing in a big harvest, then the *bonōs* of *Bonōs laudāmus* would probably refer to those farmers. Thus we could translate it as either "We praise the good men," meaning "the farmers," or even just say, "We praise the good farmers."

Review

Again, keep reviewing your adjective endings and don't forget the imperfect and future endings!

Lesson 9 Worksheet

A. Vocabulary

Translate the following words from Latin to English or English to Latin as appropriate. For the verbs, also fill in the missing principal parts. For each preposition, include which case(s) it takes.

1. sine: (+ _____) _____

2. iaceō, _____, _____, _____: _____

3. _____, vidēre, _____, _____: _____

4. I warn: _____, _____, _____, _____

5. habeō, _____, habuī, _____: _____

6. mordeō, _____, _____, _____: _____

7. I teach: _____, _____, _____, _____

8. respondeō, _____, _____, responsum: _____

9. timeō, _____, _____, _____: _____

10. Goodbye! _____ from _____, _____, _____,

    _____

11. with (+ _____) _____

12. _____, ridēre, _____, _____: _____

13. salveō, _____, _____, _____: _____

14. salvē(te) _____

15. I hasten: _____, _____, _____

16. sedeō, _____, sēdī, _____: _____

17. intrō, _____, _____, intrātum: _____

18. meanwhile _____

19. _____, tenēre, _____, _____: _____

20. I frighten: _____, _____, _____, _____

21. dēleō, _____, _____, delētum: _____

B. Grammar

Identify the gender (Masc., Fem., or Neut.), number (Sg. or Pl.), and case (Nom., Gen., Dat., Acc., or Abl.)—any possible options—of the following noun and adjective combinations. Then translate them.

	PHRASE	GENDER, NUMBER, CASE	TRANSLATION
1.	verba fera		
2.	bēstiae pulchrae		
3.	pīrātae antīquī		
4.	foedī castellī		
5.	mundō mīrō		
6.	fīdīs magistrīs		
7.	crustula calda		
8.	alnō malā		

9.	harēna longinqua		
10.	multārum sagittārum		
11.	agrōs beātōs		
12.	stultīs deābus		

13. Conjugate and translate *rīdeō* in the present, imperfect, and future active indicative.

Present

	LATIN SINGULAR	ENGLISH SINGULAR		LATIN PLURAL	ENGLISH PLURAL
1ST					
2ND					
3RD					

Imperfect

	LATIN SINGULAR	ENGLISH SINGULAR		LATIN PLURAL	ENGLISH PLURAL
1ST					
2ND					
3RD					

Future

	LATIN SINGULAR	ENGLISH SINGULAR		LATIN PLURAL	ENGLISH PLURAL
1ST					
2ND					
3RD					

14. Do a synopsis of *intrō* in the third person singular.

	LATIN	ENGLISH
PRESENT ACT.		
IMPERFECT ACT.		
FUTURE ACT.		

15. Do a synopsis of *terreō* in the second person plural.

	LATIN	ENGLISH
PRESENT ACT.		
IMPERFECT ACT.		
FUTURE ACT.		

C. Memorization

Fill in the blanks.

Magnificat _____ mea _____,

et _____ spīritus _____ in ___ _____ meō

D. English to Latin Translation

Translate each sentence from English to Latin. Use substantive adjectives wherever possible!

1. The good (female) teacher teaches the students many things, but the foolish ones answer the good (woman) nothing. [*Remember:* doceō *takes a double accusative*]

   _____

   _____

2. The greedy son of the queen was ruling the faithful men and women badly, and they will warn the wicked man.

   _____

   _____

3. The fiery beast was stinging many goats and camels, and will eat the good and the bad.

   _____

   _____

4. The ugly big brother was frightening the little sisters, and they feared the fierce bad boy.

   _____

   _____

5. The beautiful women enter into the town with the happy daughters and will see many things.

   _____

   _____

6. Men are always evil without the gospel.

   _____

   _____

7. The farmer's daughter is carrying cookies out of the farmhouse; and so you all are happy and are smiling.

   _____

   _____

8. We are faithful horses and were lying down in the field, but the evil goats were hastening into the farmhouse and biting the small boys.

   _____

   _____

9. The fierce pirate saw the handsome sailors and shouted: "You are strong but I will destroy many!"

   _____

   _____

10. The queen has much gold and silver and many crowns, but the wretched woman is not happy.

_____

_____

E. Latin to English Translation

1 Ōlim erat[1] bēstia calda et mala, et fera multōs terrēbat. Virōs et fēminās, rēgīnās et agricolās, equōs et camēlōs terrēbat. Misera in spēluncā sedēbat et miserōs rīdēbat, aut mala verba lūnae ululābat. Interim Oswaldus Magnanimus[2] in oppidum intrābat et rogābat, "Cūr multī timent?" Respondēbant, "Bēstiam caldam et malam timēmus. Oppidum delēbit et cremābit!" Oswaldus Magnanimus respondēbat, "Malam delēbō!"

5 Itaque Oswaldus Magnanimus ad spēluncam foedam in silvā miserā festīnābat. Bēstiam feram vidēbat, et fera Oswaldum spectābat. Calda ululābat, sed Oswaldus nōn timēbat. Bēstiam gladiō bonō et magnō oppugnābat. Nunc bēstia nōn rīdēbat, et dēnique[3] timēbat. Oswaldus malam delēbat, sīcut[4] turbīs oppidī narrābat.

Glossary
1. _erat:_ third person singular, imperfect active indicative of _sum:_ he, she, it was; there was
2. _magnanimus, -a, -um:_ brave, bold, noble
3. _dēnique:_ finally
4. _sīcut:_ just as

_____

_____

_____

_____

_____

_____

_____

_____

_____

_____

_____

_____

_____

_____

_____

_____

LESSON 10

Verbs: *Sum*, Imperfect & Future

Word List

NOUNS

1. āla, -ae (f): *wing*

2. centaurus, -ī (m): *centaur*

3. cervus, -ī (m): *stag, deer*

4. geminus, -ī (m): *twin*

5. cētus, -ī (m): *sea monster, kraken, whale*

6. inimīcus, -ī (m): *(personal) enemy*

7. līberī, -ōrum (m, pl): *children*

8. porcus, -ī (m): *pig*

9. scūtum, -ī (m): *shield*

10. unda, -ae (f): *wave*

11. venēnum, -ī (n): *poison*

VERBS

12. captō (1): *I hunt*

13. dēclārō (1): *I declare, make clear, explain*

14. maneō, -ēre, mansī, mansum: *I remain*

15. obsideō, -ēre, -sēdī, -sessum: *I besiege, remain near*

16. volō (1): *I fly*

ADVERBS

17. dēnique: *finally*

18. repentē: *suddenly*

CONJUNCTIONS

19. -que: *(enclitic) and*

20. quod: *because*

Memorization

Magnificat anima mea Dominum,

et exsultāvit spīritus meus in Deō salvātōre meō,

quia rēspexit humilitātem ancillae suae.

because He has regarded the lowliness of His handmaiden.

Ecce enim ex hōc beātam mē dicent omnēs generātiōnēs,

For behold, because of this all generations will call me blessed,

Grammar

Sum Imperfect and Future

In this lesson, we will learn the imperfect and future of *sum*.

Present Active Indicative of *sum*

	LATIN SINGULAR	ENGLISH SINGULAR		LATIN PLURAL	ENGLISH PLURAL
1ST	sum	I am		sumus	we are
2ND	es	you are		estis	you (pl.) are
3RD	est	he/she/it is		sunt	they are

Imperfect Active Indicative of *sum*

	LATIN SINGULAR	ENGLISH SINGULAR		LATIN PLURAL	ENGLISH PLURAL
1ST	eram	I was		erāmus	we were
2ND	erās	you were		erātis	you (pl.) were
3RD	erat	he/she/it was		erant	they were

Future Active Indicative of *sum*

	LATIN SINGULAR	ENGLISH SINGULAR		LATIN PLURAL	ENGLISH PLURAL
1ST	erō	I will be		erimus	we will be
2ND	eris	you will be		eritis	you (pl.) will be
3RD	erit	he/she/it will be		erunt	they will be

Although *sum* is an irregular verb, notice that the endings are still regular: *-m/-ō, -s, -t, -mus, -tis, -nt.* If you need help distinguishing the imperfect and future, notice that the imperfect *eram* chant has "a" throughout, just like *-bam, -bās, -bat,* and the future *erō* has the same vowel pattern as *-bō, -bis, -bit, -bimus, -bitis, -bunt.* (Also, notice that the *eram* chant has long vowels in the same places as the *-bam* chant: second person singular, first person plural, and second person plural.)

The imperfect and future of *sum* function just like the present does: they are linking verbs, and so nouns, pronouns, or adjectives on either side must be in the nominative. For example, if you wanted to say "Oswald was a just boy," you should say *Oswaldus erat puer iūstus*, not *Oswaldus erat puerum iūstum*. And, just like *est* and *sunt* in the present, if the third person singular or plural appears (especially at the beginning of the sentence), you can translate it as "there" instead of "he/she/it/they": *Crās erunt in villā paucae fēminae*, "Tomorrow there will be few women in the farmhouse." *Ōlim erat rēgīna pulchra . . .*, "Once upon a time there was a beautiful queen . . ."

Lesson 10 Worksheet

A. Vocabulary

Translate the following words from Latin to English or English to Latin as appropriate. For the verbs, also fill in the missing principal parts. For each preposition, include which case(s) it takes.

1. volō, volāre, _____, _____: _____

2. finally: _____

3. captō, _____, captāvī, _____: _____

4. āla: _____

5. because: _____

6. centaurus: _____

7. meanwhile: _____

8. obsideō, _____, _____, obsessum: _____

9. children: _____

10. geminus: _____

11. sine: (+ abl.) _____

12. I declare: _____, _____, _____, _____

13. cētus: _____

14. suddenly: _____

15. inimīcus: _____

16. doceō, docēre, _____, _____: _____

17. porcus: _____

18. cervus: _____

19. with: _____

20. scūtum: _____

21. -que: _____

22. unda: _____

23. rīdeō, _____, _____, _____: _____

24. maneō, _____, _____, mansum: _____

25. poison: _____

B. Grammar

1. Do a synopsis of *sum* in the third person plural.

	LATIN	ENGLISH
PRESENT ACT.		
IMPERFECT ACT.		
FUTURE ACT.		

2. Do a synopsis of *sum* in the second person plural.

	LATIN	ENGLISH
PRESENT ACT.		
IMPERFECT ACT.		
FUTURE ACT.		

3. Do a synopsis of *sum* in the first person plural.

	LATIN	ENGLISH
PRESENT ACT.		
IMPERFECT ACT.		
FUTURE ACT.		

4. Do a synopsis of *sum* in the third person singular.

	LATIN	ENGLISH
PRESENT ACT.		
IMPERFECT ACT.		
FUTURE ACT.		

5. Do a synopsis of *sum* in the second person singular.

	LATIN	ENGLISH
PRESENT ACT.		
IMPERFECT ACT.		
FUTURE ACT.		

6. Do a synopsis of *sum* in the first person singular.

	LATIN	ENGLISH
PRESENT ACT.		
IMPERFECT ACT.		
FUTURE ACT.		

7. Decline *wretched fate*.

	LATIN SINGULAR	LATIN PLURAL
NOM.		
GEN.		
DAT.		
ACC.		
ABL.		

8. Decline *handsome farmer*.

	LATIN SINGULAR	LATIN PLURAL
NOM.		
GEN.		
DAT.		
ACC.		
ABL.		

C. Memorization

Fill in the blanks.

_____ _____ mea _____,

et _____ spīritus _____ in _____ _____ _____,

_____ rēspexit _____ _____ suae.

Ecce _____ ex hōc _____ mē _____ omnēs _____,

D. English to Latin Translation

Translate each sentence from English to Latin. Use substantive adjectives wherever possible.

1. The wild pigs were large but we were hunting the horrible [ones].

   _____

2. Yesterday I was a greedy woman, today I am queen, and tomorrow I will be unhappy.

   _____

   _____

3. The teacher was explaining many things to the students, and so now the children will not be foolish.

   _____

   _____

4. The great man and the fierce centaur were enemies, and the centaur suddenly attacked the great [one] with arrows of poison.

   _____

   _____

5. Because you were small children you were not hunting horrible krakens in the waves.

   _____

6. We were small fiery beasts and used to walk, but we will be great and fly with great wings and will destroy many things.

   _____

   _____

7. We were hunting the ancient stag and finally we were capturing the great beast.

   _____

   _____

8. The enemies were fierce and kept on besieging the good queen's castle with spears and shields.

   _____

   _____

9. The sailors were twins and the brothers were always drinking and fighting.

   _____

   _____

10. The wild deer were lying down in the fields and we looked at the deer and were happy.

   _____

   _____

E. Latin to English Translation

1   Nunc antīquī iūstīque nautae sumus, sed ōlim malī stultīque pīrātae erāmus. Multa oppida et multōs virōsque fēmināsque līberōsque oppugnābāmus. In multīs patriīs manēbāmus et multa castella magna obsidēbāmus. Porcōs ferōs et cervōs in silvīs captābāmus. Ferī inimīcī bēstiārum, servōrum, dominōrum, et rēgīnārum erāmus. Perīcula et bona malaque rīdēbāmus. In spēluncīs in īnsulīs parvīs habitābāmus

5   et cibum mandūcābāmus et multum vīnum pōtābāmus. Semper dēclarābāmus: "Magnī sumus! Laetī et avārī semper erimus! Miserī numquam erimus!" Ōlim in undīs ōceanī nāvigābāmus et repentē bēstiam foedam in aquā vidēbāmus. Erat cētus magnus malusque. Cētus alnum vidēbat et oppugnābat. Bēstiam timēbāmus et sīcīs gladiīsque pugnābāmus. Cētus multōs pīrātās ex alnō necābat mandūcābatque. Dēnique paucī pīrātae ad īnsulam pulchram effugiēbāmus,[1] et dēclarābāmus: "Stultī malīque pīrātī

10   sumus. Bonī erimus et virōs fēmināsque līberōsque nōn oppugnābāmus. Iūstī nautae erimus!"

Glossary
1. *effugiō, -ere, -fūgī, -fugitus*: I escape

LESSON 11

Verbs: *Possum*—Present, Imperfect & Future / Complementary Infinitives / Imperatives; Nouns: Case Usage—Vocative Case

Word List

NOUNS

1. apostolus, -ī (m): *apostle*
2. Biblia Sacra, Bibliae Sacrae (f): *Holy Bible*
3. ecclēsia, -ae (f): *church*
4. liber, librī (m): *book*
5. populus, -ī (m): *people, nation*
6. stella, -ae (f): *star*
7. tenēbrae, -ārum (f, pl): *darkness, gloomy place, shadows*
8. via, -ae (f): *road, way*
9. victōria, -ae (f): *victory*
10. vīta, -ae (f): *life*

ADJECTIVES

11. meus, -a, -um: *my, mine*
12. noster, -stra, -strum: *our, ours*
13. tuus, -a, -um: *your (sg.), yours*
14. vester, -stra, -strum: *your (pl.), yours*

VERBS

15. audeō, -ēre, ——, ausus sum: *I dare*
16. dēbeō, -ēre, -uī, -itum: *I owe, ought*
17. lūceō, lūcēre, lūxī, ——: *I shine, am bright*
18. possum, posse, potuī, ——: *I am able, can*

PREPOSITIONS

19. contrā (+acc.): *against*
20. trāns (+acc.): *across*

Memorization

Magnificat anima mea Dominum,

et exsultāvit spīritus meus in Deō salvātōre meō

quia rēspexit humilitātem ancillae suae.

Ecce enim ex hōc beātam mē dicent omnēs generātiōnēs,

quia fēcit mihi magna,

> *because He has done great things for me,*

quī potēns est,

> *He Who is powerful,*

et sanctum nōmen eius,

> *and His name (is) holy,*

Grammar

Possum and Complementary Infinitives

This lesson includes a nice miscellany of items. First off, we will begin with a compound verb of *sum: possum, posse, potuī, -,* which means "I am able" or "I can." It is irregular, obviously, just as *sum* is. Its stem is basically *pot-,* but whenever that *pot-* runs into an initial *-s,* it is assimilated (absorbed) and becomes another *s.* Thus, *potsum* becomes *possum* and *potsumus* changes to *possumus.* (Try saying *potsum* a bunch of times fast, and you will see how easily that assimilation occurred!) The infinitive *posse* is a condensed form of *potesse.*

You are not really learning a new chant in this lesson: you are merely applying the *sum* chants you have already learned, so make sure you are able to produce *possum* in any requested form.

	LATIN SINGULAR	ENGLISH SINGULAR		LATIN PLURAL	ENGLISH PLURAL
1ST	possum	I am able		possumus	we are able
2ND	potes	you are able		potestis	you (pl.) are able
3RD	potest	he/she/it is able		possunt	they are able

	LATIN SINGULAR	ENGLISH SINGULAR		LATIN PLURAL	ENGLISH PLURAL
1ST	poteram	I was able		poterāmus	we were able
2ND	poterās	you were able		poterātis	you (pl.) were able
3RD	poterat	he/she/it was able		poterant	they were able

	LATIN SINGULAR	ENGLISH SINGULAR		LATIN PLURAL	ENGLISH PLURAL
1ST	poterō	I will be able		poterimus	we will be able
2ND	poteris	you will be able		poteritis	you (pl.) will be able
3RD	poterit	he/she/it will be able		poterunt	they will be able

Note that there are two common ways of expressing the meaning of *possum* in English: "I am able" or "I can." For example, the sentences "Oswald is able to kill the fiery beast" and "Oswald can kill the fiery beast" mean virtually the same thing. English is full of helping verbs such as "can" which don't have an exact Latin equivalent. In our first example, notice how our verb "is able" is followed immediately by an infinitive "to kill."

The main verb is stating Oswald's ability, and this main verb is filled out, or completed, by the infinitive "to kill." We don't usually just say "he is able" and then stop—we must complete the verb: able to do what? This infinitive is called the complementary infinitive, because it complements, or completes, the main verb.

You are actually quite familiar with how the present active infinitive looks in Latin: it is simply the second principal part. The sentence "Oswald is able to kill the fiery beast" in

Latin would then be *Oswaldus bēstiam caldam necāre potest.* We do not add any endings to the infinitive, because of course as an "infinite" form, it is not bound by person and number; we can just plunk it down and it will fill out any verb of any person and number it needs to.

Here are a few more example sentences:

We can sing well. *Bene cantāre possumus.*

We could not sing well. *Nōn bene cantāre poterāmus.*

They will be able to save the girl. *Puellam servāre poterunt.*

Imperatives

In Latin, remember, verbs can have five moods. We have been dealing mostly with indicatives, which function as statements or questions. Just now we learned the infinitive which complements verbs like *possum.* The remaining moods are imperative, subjunctive, and participle, and today we are going to learn about imperatives or commands.

To form a present active imperative, find the present stem by going to the second principal part (present active infinitive) and taking off the *-re.* That stem by itself is the singular present active imperative. If we had *necō, necāre, necāvī, necātum,* then our stem would be *necā-* and thus the singular imperative, "Kill!" would be *necā!* To form the plural, simply add *-te* to the stem: *Necāte!* "Kill!" (talking to a plural audience). This process works the same for all conjugations. *Salvē* and *valē* are actually Second Conjugation imperatives; *necā* is a First Conjugation.

Imperatives, like indicative verbs, can take direct and indirect objects and can be modified by adverbs and so on. If we were to command Oswald to "Kill the fiery beast now!" or "Give gold to the queen!" we would form our imperative and then use accusatives, datives, and adverbs as we have already learned to do: *Nunc necā bēstiam caldam!* and *Dā rēgīnae aurum!* (*Dō* is a bit irregular, and even though its stem vowel a is often short, its singular imperative is *dā.* The plural imperative has a short vowel: *date,* pronounced DAH-tay.)

Vocative Case

Very often when you are commanding someone to do something, you call upon that person by name. This is called "direct address," and a Latin noun used this way takes the vocative case (from *vocō,* "I call"). For most of the declensions, the vocative is the same as the nominative, and you can use the vocative with proper names, common nouns, and even adjectives. If we wanted to say, "Hello, pirate!" we would use *salvē* (since we are speaking to one person) and then put *pīrāta* in the vocative case, which happily is the same as the nominative: *Salvē, pīrāta!* The same is true of the plural: *Salvēte, pīrātae!* "Hello, pirates!" It is a nice optional touch to add an *Ō* in front of the vocative: *Salvēte, Ō pīrātae!* "Greetings, O pirates!" This is why we have been learning five, not six cases.

The vocative for the Second Declension singular is not so simple, unfortunately. We have seen three different nominative options for Second Declension nouns: *-us* (as in *Oswaldus*), *-r* (as in *puer*), and *-ius* (as in *fīlius*). Each of these has a different vocative.

For Second Declension nouns ending in *-us*, the vocative is *-e*. Thus if we were greeting Oswald, we would say, *Salvē, Oswalde!* The way I remember this is with the noun *dominus*, because my school song was taken from Psalm 115:1—*Nōn nōbīs, Domine, sed nominī tuō dā glōriam*, "Not to us, O Lord, but to Thy name give glory." Notice we have both a vocative (*Domine*) and an imperative (*dā*) in this song.

For Second Declension nouns ending in *-r*, the vocative is the same as the nominative: *Salvē, Ō puer!* "Greetings, boy!"

For Second Declension nouns ending in *-ius* in the singular, the vocative is *-ī*: *Salvē, Ō fīlī!* "Greetings, son!"

Conveniently, the vocative plural of all Second Declension nouns, regardless of their nominative singular form, is the same as the nominative plural:

Salvēte, dominī! Greetings, lords!

Salvēte, puerī! Greetings, boys!

Salvēte, fīliī! Greetings, sons! (Note the extra i to distinguish the plural from the singular)

What about the Second Declension neuter, you might ask? Breathe easy—the vocative for both singular and plural is the same as the nominative. If, for some reason, you wanted to speak to a castle, you would say, *Salvē, Ō castellum!* "Greetings, O castle!"

Here is a handy chart setting forth all of the singular vocatives:

	1ST DECLENSION	2ND DECLENSION			2ND DECLENSION NEUTER
NOMINATIVE	-a	-us	-r	-ius	-um
VOCATIVE	-a	-e	-r	-ī	-um
NOM. EXAMPLE	fēmina	germānus	magister	gladius	fātum
VOC. EXAMPLE	Ō fēmina	Ō germāne	Ō magister	Ō gladī	Ō fātum

Vocative of *meus*: Because *me-* + *-e* would give us the awkward *mee*, those two vowels contract to form a long *-ī*: *mī*. Thus you would say *Ō mī fīlī*, "O my son," and in the plural *Ō meī fīliī*, "O my sons." The vocatives of the feminine and neuter forms are completely regular: the vocative of *mea* is simply *mea*, and that of *meum* is *meum*.

Vocative of *meus*: Because *me-* + *-e* would give us the awkward *mee*, those two vowels contract to form a long *-ī*: *mī*. Thus you would say *Ō mī fīlī*, "O my son," and in the plural *Ō meī fīliī*, "O my sons." The vocatives of the feminine and neuter forms are completely regular: the vocative of *mea* is simply *mea*, and that of *meum* is *meum*.

Review
Be sure to practice your adjective endings, as well as the imperfect and future verb endings.

Lesson 11 Worksheet

A. Vocabulary

Translate the following words from Latin to English or English to Latin as appropriate. For the verbs, also fill in the missing principal parts. For each preposition, include which case(s) it takes.

1. book: _____

2. because: _____

3. vester: _____

4. noster: _____

5. apostle: _____

6. audeō, _____, _____: _____

7. wave: _____

8. ecclēsia: _____

9. possum, _____, _____, _____: _____

10. without: _____

11. Biblia Sacra: _____

12. populus: _____

13. trāns: _____

14. star: _____

15. victōria: _____

16. contrā: _____

17. dēnique: _____

18. dēbeō, _____, debuī, _____: _____

19. via: _____

20. tuus: _____

21. vīta: _____

22. I lie down: _____, _____, _____, _____

23. shadows: _____

24. meus: _____

25. lūceō, _____, _____: _____

B. Grammar

Translate these verbs and phrases into Latin.

1. they were able: _____

2. we are: _____

3. O children, love!: _____

4. you (sg.) will be able: _____

5. she can: _____

6. Farewell, shadows!: _____

7. I could: _____

8. I can: _____

9. you (pl.) are able: _____

10. we were able: _____

11. they will be able: _____

12. he was able: _____

13. O star, shine!: _____

14. I will be: _____

15. you (sg.) are: _____

C. Memorization

Fill in the blanks.

_____

_____

quia _____ _____ ancillae _____.

_____ enim _____ _____ _____ mē dicent _____ _____,

_____ fēcit _____ _____,

quī _____ _____,

_____ sanctum _____ eius,

D. English to Latin Translation

Translate each sentence from English to Latin. Use substantive adjectives wherever possible.

1. The disciples and apostles were suddenly daring to speak the gospel to the foolish and wicked crowds.

   _____

   _____

2. The moon and stars are beautiful and are shining in the shadows.

   _____

3. Your son loves our daughter, but she will not love your son because he does not love the church.

   _____

   _____

4. Christ is the way and the life and He shines in the darkness of our world.

   _____

5. The foolish boy cannot conquer the fiery beast and save the queen's daughter, but Oswald can.

   _____

   _____

6. O my son and O my daughter, always love the words of God and the faithful church.

   _____

   _____

7. The faithful teacher was able to teach the Holy Bible to my children.

   _____

   _____

8. The wicked apostle was speaking many things against the church because he loves the gold and silver of the world.

   _____

   _____

9. My master, I am your good servant; therefore, give your help to my wretched children.

   _____

   _____

10. O farmer, your wicked pig is my enemy and you ought to destroy the horrible beast.

   _____

   _____

E. Latin to English Translation

1 Ōlim erant puellae geminae, Iūlia Iūniaque,[1] et in villā ad ōceanum habitābant. Iūlia erat bona sed Iūnia mala erat. Iūlia laeta erat et mundum, agrōs, lūnam, et stellās amābat; et bene cantāre et multīs bestiīs ōrāre poterat. Sed Iūnia avāra erat. Et porcōs et equōs et caprōs lūdere[2] audēbat; itaque Iūniam miseram malamque nōn amābant. Ōlim geminae in harēnā ambulābant, et alnum pīrātārum vidēbant. Iūnia

5 pīrātīs ōrābat: "Dā mihi[3] multum aurum, et germānam meam dabō—serva vestra esse potest." Pīrātae Iūniae ōrābant: "Aurum dabimus, et tuam germanam ad alnum nostram portābimus." Iūlia clāmābat: "Iuvāte!"[4] Oswaldus interim bēstiās ferās in silvā ad harēnam captābat et Iuliam audiēbat.[5] Ad harēnam festīnābat et pīrātās superāre et Iūliam servāre poterat. Iūliam ad villam portābat et parentibus[6] multa ōrābat. Nōn laetī erant sed iūstī, et Iūnia serva nunc est et aquam ad agrōs portābit. Sed porcī et equī

10 et caprī dē poenā[7] cōgitant . . . .

Glossary

1. *Iūlia, -ae* (f) and *Iūnia, -ae* (f) are both first declension names. You can translate them as *Iulia* and *Iunia* or *Julia* and *Junia*.
2. *lūdō, -ere, lūsī, lūsum* (third conjugation): I tease
3. *mihi*: dative singular of the first person pronoun *ego*: I, me
4. *iuvō, iuvāre, iūvī, iūtum*: I help
5. *audiō, -īre, -īvī, -ītum* (fourth conjugation): I hear
6. *parentibus*: dative plural of *parens, -ntis* (m/f) parent
7. *poena, -ae* (f): revenge; penalty, punishment

F. For Fun: *Nōmina Animālium*

How well do you know the scientific names of the following animals? Give it your best shot.

1. _____ cat   a. panthera onca

2. _____ chicken   b. bos prīmigenius

3. _____ cougar   c. panthera leō

4. _____ cow   d. felis catus

5. _____ dog   e. ovis aries

6. _____ donkey   f. equus ferus caballus

7. _____ goat   g. gallus gallus domesticus

8. _____ goldfish   h. sus domesticus

9. _____ horse   i. equus africanus asinus

10. _____ jaguar   j. panthera pardus

11. _____ leopard   k. puma concolor

12. _____ lion   l. carassius auratus auratus

13. _____ pig   m. canis lupus familiaris

14. _____ sheep   n. panthera tigris

15. _____ tiger   o. capra aegagrus hircus

LESSON 12
Nouns: Third Declension Masculine/Feminine

Word List

NOUNS

1. draco, dracōnis (m): *dragon*

2. frāter, frātris (m): *brother*

3. homō, hominis (m): *man, human being*

4. labor, labōris (m): *work, toil, labor, hardship*

5. leō, leōnis (m): *lion*

6. lūx, lūcis (f): *light*

7. māter, mātris (f): *mother*

8. mīles, mīlitis (m): *soldier*

9. pater, patris (m): *father*

10. rex, rēgis (m): *king*

11. sōl, sōlis (m): *sun*

12. soror, sorōris (f): *sister*

13. tigris, tigridis (m/f): *tiger*

14. virgō, virginis (f): *maiden, young woman*

15. virtūs, virtūtis (f): *manliness, courage, strength*

VERBS

16. caveō, -ēre, cāvī, cautum: *I guard against, beware (of)*

17. domō, -āre, domuī, domitum: *I tame, subdue*

ADVERBS/CONJUNCTIONS

18. autem (postpositive conj.): *however, moreover*

19. quandō: *when?, ever; since, because*

20. ubi: *where?, when*

Memorization

Magnificat anima mea Dominum,

et exsultāvit spīritus meus in Deō salvātōre meō,

quia rēspexit humilitātem ancillae suae.

Ecce enim ex hōc beātam mē dicent omnēs generātiōnēs,

quia fēcit mihi magna,

quī potēns est,

et sanctum nōmen eius,

et misericordia eius in prōgeniēs et prōgeniēs timentibus eum.

    and His mercy (is) upon generations and generations of those fearing Him.

Fēcit potentiam in brāchiō suō,

    He has worked power with His arm,

Grammar

Third Declension Masculine/Feminine

In this lesson you will learn a new declension. The Third Declension is merely another family of nouns, and nouns in this declension function just like nouns of the First or Second Declension. A Third Declension noun in the nominative case will act as the subject, just as other nominatives. Third Declension nouns also have gender and number.

	LATIN SINGULAR	ENGLISH SINGULAR		LATIN PLURAL	ENGLISH PLURAL
NOMINATIVE	X	a/the *noun* [subject]		-ēs	the *nouns* [subject]
GENITIVE	-is	of the *noun*, the *noun's*		-um	of the *nouns*, the *nouns'*
DATIVE	-ī	to/for the *noun*		-ibus	to/for the *nouns*
ACCUSATIVE	-em	a/the *noun* [object]		-ēs	the *nouns* [object]
ABLATIVE	-e	by/with/from the *noun*		-ibus	by/with/from the *nouns*
VOCATIVE	X	O *noun*		-ēs	O *nouns*

The Third Declension poses a few new challenges, however. For one thing, the nominative singular is not predictable. If you glance down the Word List, you can see that these nouns end in *-ō, -er, -or, -x, -es, -l, is,* and *-us.* This is why I have put an X in the nominative singular box in the chart above. It does not represent the letter *x*, but rather should be thought of as the *x* in an algebra equation—basically, "whatever-the-nominative ending-happens-to-be."

Because the nominative singular is not predictable, it is even more important for you to learn the genitive singular of these nouns. The genitive singular will tell us not only what declension our noun is in, but also the stem of the noun. In this declension, we find the stem of the noun by removing the genitive singular ending *-is.* Thus, the stem of *draco* is *dracōn-*, and not *drac-*. If we were merely to glance at *frāter* or *pater*, we might assume that they are Second Declension nouns like *puer* or *ager*. However, a look at the genitive singular reveals the folly of such an assumption: *frāter* becomes *frātris*, and that *-is* tells us it is a Third Declension noun. We also see that our stem is *frātr-*. Similarly, you might assume that *virtūs* is Second Declension, but the genitive *virtūtis* tells us otherwise.

Knowing which declension a noun is born into is very important. Again, just as people are born into families and cannot switch families willy-nilly, so Latin nouns are born into particular declensions. If you see the word *rēgum* in a sentence, you may be tempted to read it as an accusative since *-um* can be the accusative singular ending of the Second Declension. However, since *rex* is a Third and not a Second Declension noun, the *-um* is actually the genitive plural: "of the kings" or "the kings'." This is why it's important to memorize your vocabulary carefully and to double check the words so you can consider the different possibilities.

Another unpredictable feature of Third Declension nouns is their gender. In the First Declension, most nouns were feminine with a few masculine vocational nouns here and there. In the Second Declension, most nouns were masculine with the very rare feminine exception. And the Second Neuter comfortingly consisted of all neuters.

However, the Third Declension is a mixed bag of masculine and feminine nouns. (There is a Third Declension neuter consisting of all neuters, and that will debut in the next lesson.) The general rules of gender still apply: a biologically male entity (like *pater* or *frāter*) will be masculine; *māter* and *soror*, feminine; and abstract concepts are almost always feminine: *virtūs*, despite meaning "manliness," is an abstract noun and therefore feminine. The vocative for both masculine and feminine nouns in the Third Declension is the same as the nominative.

Let's decline a few of these.

māter, mātris (f) *mother*

	LATIN SINGULAR	ENGLISH SINGULAR	LATIN PLURAL	ENGLISH PLURAL
NOMINATIVE	māter	a/the mother [subject]	mātrēs	the mothers [subject]
GENITIVE	mātris	of the mother, the mother's	mātrum	of the mothers, the mothers'
DATIVE	mātrī	to/for the mother	mātribus	to/for the mothers
ACCUSATIVE	mātrem	the mother [object]	mātrēs	the mothers [object]
ABLATIVE	mātre	by/with/from the mother	mātribus	by/with/from the mothers
VOCATIVE	Ō māter	O mother	Ō mātrēs	O mothers

rex, rēgis (m) *king*

	LATIN SINGULAR	ENGLISH SINGULAR	LATIN PLURAL	ENGLISH PLURAL
NOMINATIVE	rex	a/the king [subject]	rēgēs	the kings [subject]
GENITIVE	rēgis	of the king, the king's	rēgum	of the kings, the kings'
DATIVE	rēgī	to/for the king	rēgibus	to/for the kings
ACCUSATIVE	rēgem	the king [object]	rēgēs	the kings [object]
ABLATIVE	rēge	by/with/from the king	rēgibus	by/with/from the kings
VOCATIVE	Ō rex	O king	Ō rēgēs	O kings

A note on adjectives: Third Declension nouns can of course be modified by adjectives belonging to the First or Second Declension. Why? Because **adjectives modify nouns in gender, number, and case—but not necessarily in declension**. The nouns declined above are given below with adjectives:

māter laeta, *joyful mother*

	LATIN SINGULAR	LATIN PLURAL
NOM.	māter laeta	mātrēs laetae
GEN.	mātris laetae	mātrum laetārum
DAT.	mātrī laetae	mātribus laetīs
ACC.	mātrem laetam	mātrēs laetās
ABL.	mātre laetā	mātribus laetīs
VOC.	Ō māter laeta	Ō mātrēs laetae

rex bonus, *good king*

	LATIN SINGULAR	LATIN PLURAL
NOM.	rex bonus	rēgēs bonī
GEN.	rēgis bonī	rēgum bonōrum
DAT.	rēgī bonō	rēgibus bonīs
ACC.	rēgem bonum	rēgēs bonōs
ABL.	rēge bonō	rēgibus bonīs
VOC.	Ō rex bone	Ō rēgēs bonī

It is good to practice declining noun-adjective pairs, since you can see the same cases of different declensions working together. Also, notice how helpful adjectives can be in eliminating confusion. You might have been distressed that the *-ae* of the First Declension could be genitive singular, dative singular, or nominative plural? Well, now you can rejoice! If a First Declension adjective is paired with a Third Declension noun, we don't have that ambiguity: *mātris laetae* can only be "of the joyful mother" (genitive); *mātrī laetae* can only be the dative "to/for the joyful mother;" and *mātrēs laetae* must be the nominative plural, "joyful mothers."

This declension is a touch more difficult than the First and Second Declensions, so make sure you learn the noun endings solidly and learn to use them in sentences. Be especially careful with the dative. The nominative and accusative look somewhat similar to the First and Second Declensions, but the Third Declension *-ī* looks like the Second Declension nominative and genitive. Always identify which declension the word is before parsing it ("To parse" a noun or verb simply means to analyze all aspects of it).

Review

Even though you're learning a lot, make sure you review your imperfect and future endings and the new imperatives you've learned to make.

Lesson 12 Worksheet

A. Vocabulary

Translate the following words from Latin to English or English to Latin as appropriate. For the verbs, also fill in the missing principal parts.

1. I am able: _____, _____, _____, _____

2. domō, _____, _____, _____: _____

3. tiger: _____

4. lūx: _____

5. where?: _____

6. homō: _____

7. virgō: _____

8. I fly: _____, _____, _____, _____

9. courage: _____

10. when?: _____

11. mīles: _____

12. cervus: _____

13. frāter: _____

14. pater: _____

15. however: _____

16. sōl: _____

17. lion: _____

18. soror: _____

19. māter: _____

20. I bite: _____, _____, _____, _____

21. liber: _____

22. dragon: _____

23. labor: _____

24. I beware: _____, _____, _____, _____

25. rex: _____

B. Grammar

1. Decline *ancient dragon.*

	LATIN SINGULAR	LATIN PLURAL
NOM.		
GEN.		
DAT.		
ACC.		
ABL.		
VOC.		

2. Decline *beautiful light.*

	LATIN SINGULAR	LATIN PLURAL
NOM.		
GEN.		
DAT.		
ACC.		
ABL.		
VOC.		

3. Give a synopsis of *caveō* in the second person singular.

	LATIN	ENGLISH
PRESENT ACT.		
IMPERFECT ACT.		
FUTURE ACT.		

C. Memorization

Fill in the blanks.

_____

_____

_____

_____

quia _____ _____ magna,

_____ potēns _____,

et _____ _____ eius,

et misericordia _____ _____ _____ et prōgeniēs _____ eum.

Fēcit _____ in _____ suō,

D. English to Latin Translation

Translate each sentence from English to Latin.

1. Dragons and sea serpents are distant brothers but dragons are fiery, have wings, and live in caves.

2. When will the great king besiege and conquer the enemy's castle?

3. God created the fiery sun and it was giving light to humans and beasts.

4. Children, beware of horrible lions and wild pigs when you walk in the Forest of Darkness.

5. The good and faithful mother was giving food and cookies to the little sons and daughters.

6. The greedy tigers were attacking the farmhouses and seizing goats and pigs.

_____

_____

7. We were seeing your sisters in town, where they were speaking words of life to the crowds.

_____

_____

8. The king's brother is great and can tame fierce lions and tigers.

_____

_____

9. Moreover, our fathers were fighting against the evil dragon and finally were able to save the maidens of the town.

_____

_____

10. You all will remain with the disciple's brother because he is a faithful servant of the Lord.

_____

_____

E. Latin to English Translation

1 Ōlim erat regnum pulchrum in patriā trāns ōceanum. Rex antīquus et fīdus et bonus erat, sed fīliōs nōn habēbat—sōlam[1] fīliam pulchram. Rex autem et regnum laetī nōn erant. Draco malus patriam saepe oppugnābat, et bēstiās, multum aurum, līberōs parvōs, et virginēs occupābat. Nunc draco ālīs foedīs ad castellum volābat, et ululābat: "Dā mihi[2] fīliam rēgis aut vestram patriam delēbō!" Rex miser

5 erat, et multōs magnōs ad castellum vocābat: "Pugnāte et malum dracōnem necāte, aut meam fīliam caldō dare dēbēbō. Festīnāte!" Magnī ab castellō ad spēluncam dracōnis malī festīnābant, sed draco nōn timēbat. Draco hominēs aut bēstiās, centaurōs aut cētōs, leōnēs aut tigridēs nōn timēbat. Magnī dracōnem magnum malumque oppugnābant, sed crēmābat. Nunc rex optiōnem[3] nōn habēbat, et fīliam ad spēluncam dracōnis portābat. Sed Oswaldus ad rēgem festīnābat, et clāmābat: "Malum dracōnem

10 necābō, et tuam fīliam servābō!" Oswaldus caldum Gladiō Magnō Virtūtis pugnābat, et malum dracōnem dēnique necābat. Fīlia rēgis laeta erat. Et rex laetus erat, et fīliam Oswaldō in mātrimōniō[4] dabat. Nunc Oswaldus rex regnī laetī pulchrīque erit.

Glossary
1. _sōlus, -a, -um_: only, single
2. _mihi_: dative singular of the first person pronoun _ego_: I, me
3. _optio, optiōnis_ (f): choice
4. _mātrimōnium, -ī_ (n): You should be able to guess this one from the context! (If you can't, look it up in your Latin dictionary.)

LESSON 13

Nouns: Third Declension Neuter

Word List

NOUNS

1. caput, -itis (n): *head*

2. carmen, -inis (n): *song, chant, poem, prophecy*

3. cor, cordis (n): *heart*

4. corpus, corporis (n): *body*

5. flūmen, flūminis (n): *river*

6. grāmen, grāminis (n): *grass, greenery*

7. iter, itineris (n): *journey, road, route, trek*

8. lac, lactis (n): *milk*

9. lītus, lītoris (n): *shore, shoreline*

10. nōmen, nōminis (n): *name*

11. onus, oneris (n): *burden, load, weight*

12. ōra, -ae (f): *shore*

13. ōs, ōris (n): *mouth*

14. tempus, temporis (n): *time*

15. vulnus, vulneris (n): *wound*

ADJECTIVES

16. cārus, -a, -um: *dear, beloved*

17. doctus, -a, -um: *learned, wise, skilled*

18. horrendus, a, um: *dreadful, awful, fearful*

ADVERBS

19. diū: *for a long time*

20. statim: *immediately*

Memorization

Magnificat anima mea Dominum,

et exsultāvit spīritus meus in Deō salvātōre meō,

quia rēspexit humilitātem ancillae suae.

Ecce enim ex hōc beātam mē dicent omnēs generātiōnēs,

quia fēcit mihi magna,

quī potēns est,

et sanctum nōmen eius,

et misericordia eius in prōgeniēs et prōgeniēs timentibus eum.

Fēcit potentiam in brāchiō suō,

dispersit superbōs mente cordis suī;

> *He has scattered the proud in the mind of their heart;*

dēposuit potentēs dē sēde

> *He has put down the powerful from (their) seat*

et exaltāvit humilēs;

> *and has lifted up the humble;*

Grammar

Third Declension Neuter

In this lesson we will add the Third Declension neuter to our noun repertoire.

	LATIN SINGULAR	ENGLISH SINGULAR	LATIN PLURAL	ENGLISH PLURAL
NOMINATIVE	X	a/the *noun* [subject]	-a	the *nouns* [subject]
GENITIVE	-is	of the *noun*, the *noun's*	-um	of the *nouns*, the *nouns'*
DATIVE	-ī	to/for the *noun*	-ibus	to/for the *nouns*
ACCUSATIVE	X	a/the *noun* [object]	-a	the *nouns* [object]
ABLATIVE	-e	by/with/from the *noun*	-ibus	by/with/from the *nouns*
VOCATIVE	X	O *noun*	-a	O *nouns*

If you compare this to the masculine and feminine Third Declension forms, you will notice that they are exactly the same except for the nominative and accusative. When we learned the Second Declension neuter, you learned two guidelines for neuter nouns:

1. The nominative and accusative are the same.

2. The plural nominative and accusative end in -*a*.

Thus our algebraic X ending for the nominative means that whatever the nominative happens to be, that shall the accusative singular be also. *Iter* in the accusative will be *iter*, *grāmen* will be *grāmen*, and so on.

The vocative for the Third Declension neuter is the same as the nominative. Thus you may add to the neuter rules above:

3. The nominative and accusative and vocative of neuter nouns are all the same.

Here are some examples declined.

cor, cordis (n) *heart*

	LATIN SINGULAR	ENGLISH SINGULAR		LATIN PLURAL	ENGLISH PLURAL
NOMINATIVE	cor	a/the heart [subject]		corda	the hearts [subject]
GENITIVE	cordis	of the heart, the heart's		cordum	of the hearts, the hearts'
DATIVE	cordī	to/for the heart		cordibus	to/for the hearts
ACCUSATIVE	cor	the heart [direct object]		corda	the hearts [direct object]
ABLATIVE	corde	by/with/from the heart		cordibus	by/with/from the hearts
VOCATIVE	Ō cor	O heart		Ō corda	O hearts

vulnus, vulneris (n) *wound*

	LATIN SINGULAR	ENGLISH SINGULAR		LATIN PLURAL	ENGLISH PLURAL
NOMINATIVE	vulnus	a/the wound [subject]		vulnera	the wounds [subject]
GENITIVE	vulneris	of the wound, the wound's		vulnerum	of the wounds, the wounds'
DATIVE	vulnerī	to/for the wound		vulneribus	to/for the wounds
ACCUSATIVE	vulnus	the wound [direct object]		vulnera	the wounds [direct object]
ABLATIVE	vulnere	by/with/from the wound		vulneribus	by/with/from the wounds
VOCATIVE	Ō vulnus	O wound		Ō vulnera	O wounds

Review

Make sure you review *sum*, *eram*, and *ero* in this lesson, and that you keep practicing your First/Second Declension adjective endings.

Lesson 13 Worksheet

A. Vocabulary

Translate the following words from Latin to English or English to Latin as appropriate.

1. wound: _____

2. venēnum: _____

3. caput: _____

4. moreover: _____

5. onus: _____

6. grāmen: _____

7. diū: _____

8. carmen: _____

9. journey: _____

10. flūmen: _____

11. ōs: _____

12. ōra: _____

13. lītus: _____

14. wise: _____

15. nōmen: _____

16. immediately: _____

17. suddenly: _____

18. lac: _____

19. tempus: _____

20. interim: _____

21. via: _____

22. heart: _____

23. cārus: _____

24. corpus: _____

25. horrendus: _____

B. Grammar

1. Decline *evil journey.*

	LATIN SINGULAR	LATIN PLURAL
NOM.		
GEN.		
DAT.		
ACC.		
ABL.		
VOC.		

2. Decline *beloved mother*.

	LATIN SINGULAR	LATIN PLURAL
NOM.		
GEN.		
DAT.		
ACC.		
ABL.		
VOC.		

3. Decline *dreadful time*.

	LATIN SINGULAR	LATIN PLURAL
NOM.		
GEN.		
DAT.		
ACC.		
ABL.		
VOC.		

C. Memorization

Fill in the blanks.

_____

_____

_____

_____

_____

_____

et misericordia _____ in _____ et _____ _____ _____ eum.

Fēcit _____ in _____ suō,

_____ superbōs _____ _____ suī;

dēposuit _____ _____ sēde

et _____ humilēs;

D. English to Latin Translation

Translate each sentence from English to Latin.

1. Your journey to the castle will be wretched because the woods of darkness are dreadful.

   _____

   _____

2. The horses were carrying great burdens from the ships across the shore to the town.

   _____

   _____

3. Our goats eat grass and drink water, but our children eat cookies and drink milk.

   _____

   _____

4. You (pl.) were hastening to the town with many soldiers and were singing many songs of victory.

   _____

   _____

5. The evil dragon was wounding the king's body with many wounds of poison, and therefore was able to kill the good king.

   _____

   _____

6. We will hunt lions and tigers across great rivers and in distant caves and through fearful forests.

   _____

   _____

7. The pirates were fighting the soldiers with daggers and bad words; the soldiers were fighting the pirates with swords and arrows.

   _____

   _____

8. O queen, beware of handsome but evil men when you walk from the castle into the town.

_____

_____

9. The evil soldiers seized the Lord's apostles and immediately gave the men large burdens.

_____

_____

10. Will I be able to conquer the ugly king's soldiers and save your town, your children, and your maidens?

_____

_____

_____

E. Latin to English Translation

1   Multī mīlitēs magnī malīque oppidum nostrum diū obsidēbant. Multum cibum aut multam aquam nōn habēbāmus, et timēbāmus. Pugnāre nōn audēbāmus, et tempora mala erant. Dux[1] malus mīlitum nostrō populō clamābat: "Dā mihi[2] vestrum oppidum! Līberī vestrī servī nostrī erunt, et bēstiae vestrae aurumque vestrum erunt nostrae! Sī[3] pugnābitis, oppidum populumque vestrum dēlēbimus."

5   Miserī erāmus et ululābāmus: "Heu![4] Malīs mīlitibus nostrum oppidum dare dēbēmus, aut delēbunt." Fēmina autem pulchra doctaque respondēbat, "Oppidum nostrum malīs nōn dabimus! Deus oppidum nostrum, līberōs nostrōs, et vītās nostrās servābit. Ad inimīcōs ab oppidō ambulābō." Fēmina Deum virtūtem victōriamque ōrābat, et ad ducem inimīcōrum ambulābat. Et multum cibum bonum vīnumque portābat. Ducī dēclārābat: "Mē trādō[5] quod hominēs oppidī diū pugnābunt et oppidum dēlēbis. Bonum

10   cibum vīnumque portō, et serva tua erō." Dux malus pulchram spectābat, et amābat. Multum cibum mandūcābat et multum vīnum pōtābat, et fēminae multa narrābat. Et vīnum pōtābat. Dēnique ēbrius[6] erat et iacēbat. Fēmina gladium magnum virī occupābat et caput gladiō removēbat.[7] Caput inimīcī nostrī ad oppidum portābat, et laetī erāmus. Itaque inimīcōs Deī superāre et oppidum nostrum et līberōs nostrōs et vītās nostrās servāre poterāmus.

Glossary
1. *dux, ducis* (m): leader, guide, general
2. *mihi*: dative singular of the first person pronoun *ego*: I, me
3. *sī*: if
4. *heu*, interjection: alas!
5. *Mē trādō*: "I am surrendering myself"; *trādō* is a compound of *dō*
6. *ēbrius, -a, -um*: drunk, intoxicated
7. *removeō, -ēre, -mōvī, -mōtum*: I remove

_____

_____

_____

LESSON 14
Verbs: Perfect Active Indicative

Word List

NOUNS

1. amor, amōris (m): *love*

2. dux, ducis (m): *leader, guide, general*

3. senex, senis (m): *old man*

4. tellūs, tellūris (f): *the earth, ground, land*

5. vesper, vesperis (m): *evening, evening star*

6. vōx, vōcis (f): *voice*

VERBS

7. āiō (defective): *I say, assert, affirm*

8. errō (1): *I wander, err, am mistaken*

9. exerceō, -ēre, -uī, -itum: *I train, exercise*

10. fleō, -ēre, flēvī, flētum: *I weep*

11. moveō, -ēre, mōvī, mōtum: *I move*

12. nō (1): *I swim*

13. nuntiō (1): *I announce, declare*

14. parō (1): *I prepare*

15. removeō, -ēre, -mōvī, -mōtum: *I remove, take away*

16. reptō (1): *I crawl, creep*

17. vastō (1): *I devastate, lay waste*

Conjunctions/Prepositions/Adverbs

18. nec (neque): *and not, nor*
    nec...nec: *neither...nor*

19. sub (+acc.): *under, up under, close to*
    (+abl.): *below, under(neath), at the foot of*

20. suprā (adv./prep. +acc.): *above, over*

Memorization

Magnificat anima mea Dominum,

et exsultāvit spīritus meus in Deō salvātōre meō,

quia rēspexit humilitātem ancillae suae.

Ecce enim ex hōc beātam mē dicent omnēs generātiōnēs,

quia fēcit mihi magna,

quī potēns est,

et sanctum nōmen eius,

et misericordia eius in prōgeniēs et prōgeniēs timentibus eum.

Fēcit potentiam in brāchiō suō,

dispersit superbōs mente cordis suī;

dēposuit potentēs dē sēde

et exaltāvit humilēs;

ēsurientēs implēvit bonīs

> *He has filled the hungry with good things*

et dīvitēs dīmīsit inānēs.

> *and He has sent the rich away empty.*

Suscēpit Isrāel puerum suum,

> *He has received Israel His son,*

Grammar

Rejoice, for in this lesson you will move on to a new principal part, a new verb stem, and a new tense system. This lesson focuses on the perfect tense, and the next lesson will cover the remaining two tenses, pluperfect and future perfect.

Doubtless, you have been diligently memorizing their principal parts. Let's review all the different moods and tenses we have learned: If we take the word *necō, necāre, necāvī, necātum*, these are the various things we have derived, thus far all from the second principle part:

Infinitive (the second principal part *is* the present active infinitive): *necāre*

Indicative:

>　　Present Active: *necō*, etc.

>　　Imperfect Active: *necābam*, etc.

>　　Future Active: *necābō*, etc.

>　　Imperative: *necā!* (sg.), *necāte!* (pl.)

Perfect Active Indicative

Today, we get to move on to the third principal part, which in our sample verb is *necāvī*. This form is the first person singular, perfect active indicative, "I killed, have killed." To find the stem for the perfect active system, simply remove the *-ī*: *necāv-*. To this stem you can add the perfect active endings:

Perfect Active Indicative Verb Endings

	LATIN SINGULAR	ENGLISH SINGULAR	LATIN PLURAL	ENGLISH PLURAL
1ST	-ī	I *verbed*, have *verbed*	-imus	we *verbed*, have *verbed*
2ND	-istī	you *verbed*, have *verbed*	-istis	you (pl.) *verbed*, have *verbed*
3RD	-it	he/she/it *verbed*, has *verbed*	-ērunt	they *verbed*, have *verbed*

Here is *necō* conjugated in the Perfect Active Indicative:

	LATIN SINGULAR	ENGLISH SINGULAR	LATIN PLURAL	ENGLISH PLURAL
1ST	necāvī	I killed, have killed	necāvimus	we killed, have killed
2ND	necāvistī	you killed, have killed	necāvistis	you (pl.) killed, have killed
3RD	necāvit	he/she/it killed, has killed	necāvērunt	they killed, have killed

Before we get too far ahead of ourselves, we should discuss how to translate the perfect. Recall that the imperfect tense is so called because the action is incomplete, continuous, or habitual. In that sense the perfect tense is the opposite of the imperfect, because it signifies completed action. The perfect can signify a simple past action: *Oswald **killed** the dragon yesterday.* It can also portray action that is completed with reference to the present time: *Rejoice, because Oswald **has killed** the dragon!* You may also say *did kill* for emphasis, or, if you are using a negative word such as "not"—*Oswald **did** not **kill** the dragon.*

One handy aspect of the perfect active system is that it is highly regular, so that even if a verb has wildly irregular principal parts, chances are that the third principal part will end in *-ī* and can therefore be conjugated regularly. Let's take *sum* and *possum* for example. Even though the principal parts of *sum* are *sum, esse, fuī, futūrum*, the third principle part *fuī* does end in *-ī*, and therefore the perfect active stem is *fu-*.

Thus *sum* conjugated in the Perfect Active will look like this:

	LATIN SINGULAR	ENGLISH SINGULAR	LATIN PLURAL	ENGLISH PLURAL
1ST	fuī	I was, have been	fuimus	we were, have been
2ND	fuistī	you were, have been	fuistis	you (pl.) were, have been
3RD	fuit	he/she/it was, has been	fuērunt	they were, have been

Similarly, the principal parts of *possum* are *possum, posse, potuī, -*, and the perfect stem is therefore *potu-*.

The Perfect Active Indicative of *possum* is:

	LATIN SINGULAR	ENGLISH SINGULAR
1ST	potuī	I was able, have been able
2ND	potuistī	you were able, have been able
3RD	potuit	he/she/it was able, has been able

	LATIN PLURAL	ENGLISH PLURAL
potuimus	we were able, have been able
potuistis	you (pl.) were able, have been able
potuērunt	they were able, have been able

We can now add another line to our verb synopsis, which will look like this:

	LATIN	ENGLISH
PRESENT ACT.	necās	you kill
IMPERFECT ACT.	necābās	you were killing
FUTURE ACT.	necābis	you will kill
PERFECT ACT.	necāvistī	you killed, have killed

This is an easy set of endings to learn, but review it thoroughly and be careful to use the third principal part of the verb.

Review

Make sure you review your third declension endings during this lesson, even with all this perfect ending stuff going on. Also, review *possum*, *poteram*, and *poterō* too.

Lesson 14 Worksheet

A. Vocabulary

Translate the following words from Latin to English or English to Latin as appropriate. For the verbs, also fill in the missing principal parts. For each preposition, include which case(s) it takes.

1. darkness: _____

2. nuntiō, nuntiāre, _____, _____: _____

3. I move: _____, _____, _____, _____

4. exerceō, _____, _____, _____: _____

5. king: _____

6. parō, _____, _____, parātum: _____

7. leader: _____

8. suprā: _____

9. vōx: _____

10. I swim: _____, _____, _____, _____

11. vesper: _____

12. reptō, reptāre, reptāvī, reptātum: _____

13. I say: _____

14. for a long time: _____

15. amor: _____

16. neque: _____

17. senex: _____

18. -que: _____

19. I weep: _____, _____, _____, _____

20. sub: _____
    _____

21. vastō, _____, vastāvī, _____: _____

22. however: _____

23. tellūs: _____

24. removeō, removēre, _____, _____: _____

25. I wander: _____, _____, _____, _____

B. Grammar

1. Conjugate *parō* in the perfect active indicative in Latin and English.

	LATIN SINGULAR	ENGLISH SINGULAR		LATIN PLURAL	ENGLISH PLURAL
1ST					
2ND					
3RD					

2. Conjugate *fleō* in the perfect active indicative in Latin and English.

	LATIN SINGULAR	ENGLISH SINGULAR		LATIN PLURAL	ENGLISH PLURAL
1ST					
2ND					
3RD					

3. Give a synopsis of *reptō* in the first person plural.

	LATIN	ENGLISH
PRESENT ACT.		
IMPERFECT ACT.		
FUTURE ACT.		
PERFECT ACT.		

4. Decline *beautiful earth* (use *tellūs*).

	LATIN SINGULAR	LATIN PLURAL
NOM.		
GEN.		
DAT.		
ACC.		
ABL.		
VOC.		

C. Memorization

Fill in the blanks.

_____

_____

_____

_____

_____

_____

_____

_____

_____

dispersit _____ mente_____ _____;

_____ potentēs dē _____

et _____ _____;

ēsurientēs _____ bonīs

et _____ dīmīsit _____.

_____ Isrāel _____ _____,

D. English to Latin Translation

Translate each sentence from English to Latin.

1. Yesterday the dragon flew on great wings over the heads of the crowd.

   _____

2. Many beasts have laid waste our fields, but neither the king nor the leaders will remove the wild [beasts] from the land.

   _____

   _____

3. Oswald was a small boy, but he sailed to a distant island and killed a small kraken there.

   _____

   _____

4. We have wandered to many lands, where we have sung many songs with our beautiful voices to kings and queens, farmers and maidens.

   _____

   _____

   _____

5. Skilled but evil pirates destroyed the general's ship, and so the old man swam to the island and was waiting there for a long time.

   _____

   _____

6. You wept because you gave your love to the beautiful woman, but she has always loved the faithful soldier.

   _____

   _____

7. However, I assert: "I am a great lion, king of beasts, and I have killed many goats and given wounds to many tigers."

   _____

   _____

8. We have prepared burdens for our camels; when will we walk across the sands and look at the evening stars?

   _____

   _____

9. The soldiers were training for a long time in your fields, but finally the general moved the men to the forests.

_____

_____

10. At the foot of the castle sat a small boy, and he was giving grass and milk to the little goats.

_____

_____

E. Latin to English Translation

1   Senex nunc sum, sed mīles magnus ōlim eram. Bene semper pugnāvī, et servus fīdus nostrī ducis rēgisque eram. Inimīcōs spectāvī et nōn timuī, sed timuērunt. Ad īnsulās longinquās nāvī et cum cētīs et bēstiīs ferīs ōceanī pugnāvī. Ōlim ad tellūrem nāvigāvī ubi rex senex erat et populus flēbat. Bēstia foeda horrendaque carmina mīlitum et rēgis et rēgīnae nōn amāvit. Itaque populum oppugnāvit, et
5 multōs necāvit et mandūcāvit. Rex āit, "Servā nostrum populum, Ō mīles magne!" Rēgī āiō: "Tuum populum servābō, et bēstiam malam meīs palmīs¹ nōn gladiō meō necābō!" In tenēbrīs vesperis, bēstiam exspectāvī. In aulam² intrāvit et virum oppugnāvit. Bēstiam palmīs meīs pugnāvī et bracchium³ bēstiae remōvī. Ad palūdem⁴ errāvit et iacuit. Victōria mea fuit, et rex laetus erat. Māter mala bēstiae autem nōn laeta erat, et ab palūde festīnāvit et aulam oppugnāvit. Ab aulā ad palūdem et in spēluncam sub
10 palūde pugnāvimus. Gladium magnum ibī occupāvī et caput matris bēstiae remōvī. Et bēstiam in spēluncā vīdī, et caput gladiō remōvī. Capita bēstiārum ad aulam portāvī. Populus et rex laetī nunc erant. Ad meam tellūrem nāvigāvī, et rex fuī. Nunc draco malus meum populum oppugnat quod servus in spēluncam dracōnis intrāvit et calicem⁵ aurī occupāvit. Senex sum, sed dracōnem necābō et populum meum servābō.

Glossary
1. *palma, -ae* (f): hand
2. *aula, -ae* (f): hall, inner/royal court
3. *bracchium, -i* (n): arm
4. *palus, palūdis* (f): swamp
5. *calix, calicis* (m): goblet

_____

_____

_____

_____

_____

_____

_____

F. For Fun: *Invenī Verba!*

Find the following list of words in the chart below. The words may be forwards, backwards, vertical, or diagonal. If you wish to impress, translate the words as well. If you wish to amaze, translate *and* analyze (parse, etc. as appropriate) the words.

aiunt _____

amorem _____

autem _____

capitis _____

carmina _____

corda _____

corporis _____

cum _____

deleo _____

diu _____

doctorum _____

_____

domuimus _____

_____

draconi _____

dux _____

errabat _____

_____

exercebis _____

_____

festinat _____

flevisti _____

_____

gramen _____

hominem _____

interim _____

intrant _____

iter _____

leoni _____

matre _____

militibus _____

_____

movistis _____

_____

nabat _____

_____

neque _____

nōminibus _____

_____

noster _____

nuntiabunt _____

_____

onus _____

paro _____

pater _____

poteras _____

_____

quando _____

quod _____

reges _____

removet _____

reptavimus _____

_____

rides _____

senex _____

sororem _____

```
N  O  S  T  E  R  F  S  A  R  E  T  O  P  E  X  C  M  U  N  D  A
A  N  E  M  A  R  G  T  G  V  E  S  P  E  R  I  B  U  S  U  B  X
R  F  E  S  T  I  N  A  T  A  I  U  N  T  I  H  V  U  S  N  D  O
I  N  T  R  A  N  T  T  V  S  D  N  U  X  D  B  N  A  U  T  E  M
P  E  L  A  M  O  V  I  S  T  I  S  T  I  E  O  A  R  P  I  E  E
T  P  A  R  O  Q  A  M  C  A  U  B  I  D  S  E  F  E  L  A  R  N
E  M  T  O  R  E  P  T  A  V  I  M  U  S  S  U  B  T  U  B  R  I
L  I  A  E  E  N  R  A  L  E  M  E  B  I  O  Q  T  A  P  U  A  M
L  R  F  M  M  E  R  B  O  R  I  D  E  R  M  E  X  P  U  N  B  O
U  E  C  U  L  P  M  O  T  U  R  U  V  O  A  N  A  B  A  T  A  H
R  T  A  X  U  R  O  S  E  N  E  X  E  P  F  L  E  V  I  S  T  I
I  N  M  S  I  C  T  R  A  T  R  O  B  R  L  A  P  L  U  X  E  S
S  I  B  C  R  E  X  E  L  S  V  L  O  E  X  C  O  R  D  A  U
O  E  N  I  G  R  I  V  Q  U  D  R  A  C  O  N  I  L  I  O  B  B
R  G  D  E  L  E  O  U  U  G  C  U  M  I  N  U  H  R  A  M  O  I
O  R  B  X  U  M  O  L  A  L  I  P  R  M  I  V  G  A  H  U  N  T
R  I  S  O  E  D  A  D  N  A  N  O  M  I  N  I  B  U  S  I  E  I
E  T  P  R  E  G  E  S  D  X  A  E  V  O  T  P  I  L  T  M  P  L
M  A  T  R  E  F  O  D  O  C  T  O  R  U  M  A  X  E  B  U  T  I
A  S  I  T  I  P  A  C  A  R  M  I  N  A  P  I  R  V  A  S  I  M
```

statim _____   vastaverunt _____

sub _____   _____

supra _____   vesperibus _____

telluris _____   _____

tempore _____   virgine _____

tigride _____   vōx _____

ubi _____   vulnera _____

unda _____

_____

LESSON 15
Pluperfect & Future Perfect Active Indicative

Word List

NOUNS

1. amīcus, -ī (m) *or* amīca, -ae (f): *friend*
2. bellum, -ī (n): *war*
3. castra, -ōrum (n, pl.): *camp*
4. cōpia, -ae (f): *supply, plenty, abundance; (pl.) troops*
5. crux, crucis (f): *cross*
6. flōs, flōris (m): *flower*
7. frūmentum, -ī (n): *grain; (pl.) crops*
8. gigās, gigantis (m): *giant*
9. glōria, -ae (f): *fame, glory*
10. laus, laudis (f): *praise*
11. pāx, pācis (f): *peace*
12. proelium, -ī (n): *battle*

ADJECTIVES

13. aeternus, -a, -um: *eternal*
14. īrātus, -a, -um: *angry, wrathful*

VERBS

15. appellō (1): *I name, call*
16. cūrō (1): *I care for*
17. mereō, -ēre, -uī, -itum: *I deserve, earn, am worthy of*

ADVERBS

18. iam: *now, already*
    nōn iam: *no longer*
19. mox: *soon*
20. tum: *then, at that time; next, thereupon*

Memorization

Magnificat anima mea Dominum,

et exsultāvit spīritus meus in Deō salvātōre meō,

quia rēspexit humilitātem ancillae suae.

Ecce enim ex hōc beātam mē dicent omnēs generātiōnēs,

quia fēcit mihi magna,

quī potēns est,

et sanctum nōmen eius,

et misericordia eius in prōgeniēs et prōgeniēs timentibus eum.

Fēcit potentiam in brāchiō suō,

dispersit superbōs mente cordis suī;

dēposuit potentēs dē sēde

et exaltāvit humilēs;

ēsurientēs implēvit bonīs

et dīvitēs dīmīsit inānēs.

Suscēpit Isrāel puerum suum,

recordātus misericordiae,

> *remembering (His) mercy,*

sīcut locūtus est ad patrēs nostrōs,

> *just as He spoke to our fathers,*

Ābraham et seminī eius in saecula.

> *to Abraham and His seed forever.*

Grammar

Pluperfect and Future Perfect Tenses

In this lesson we will add two more tenses: the pluperfect and the future perfect. The pluperfect tense expresses an action that is past the past (think "perfect plus" or "more than perfect"), as in this sentence: *Oswald **had killed** three dragons before he was sixteen years old.*

He was sixteen is already in the past tense, but even before that already past tense time, *he had killed* the dragons.

The future perfect tense is not quite as common and sounds a little funny in isolation, but believe me, you have used it before. The future perfect refers to an action that will be completed in the future, but it will be completed in the past of another future event: *Before he will return to the castle next month, Oswald **will have killed** the evil dragon.* Here we have two future events: 1) the return to the castle and 2) the slaying of the dragon. The slaying will happen before the return. In other words, in the future, another action will be in the past. If you are still having trouble with this, try making a few sentences of your own imitating this example.

These two tenses are formed from the perfect active stem, which is derived by removing the -ī from the third principal part. Conveniently, the pluperfect active indicative endings are identical to the imperfect indicative of *sum*, and the future perfect endings are almost identical to the future indicative of *sum*, with one exception in the third person plural:

Pluperfect Active Indicative Verb Endings

	LATIN SINGULAR	ENGLISH SINGULAR		LATIN PLURAL	ENGLISH PLURAL
1ST	-eram	I had *verbed*		-erāmus	we had *verbed*
2ND	-erās	you had *verbed*		-erātis	you (pl.) had *verbed*
3RD	-erat	he/she/it had *verbed*		-erant	they had *verbed*

Future Perfect Active Indicative Verb Endings

	LATIN SINGULAR	ENGLISH SINGULAR		LATIN PLURAL	ENGLISH PLURAL
1ST	-erō	I will have *verbed*		-erimus	we will have *verbed*
2ND	-eris	you will have *verbed*		-eritis	you (pl.) will have *verbed*
3RD	-erit	he/she/it will have *verbed*		**-erint**	they will have *verbed*

In the third person plural, the future active of sum is *erunt*, but the future perfect active indicative ending is -*erint*. We can't use -*erunt* as an ending for the future perfect because the perfect active third person plural ending is already -*ērunt*. Here is a little saying to help you remember this: "When it's a **word**, it's *erunt*; when it's an **ending**, it's -*erint*." Thus *erunt* means "they will be," *necāverunt* means "they (have) killed," and *necāverint* means "they will have killed."

Here is our sample verb *necō* conjugated in these two new tenses:

Pluperfect Active of *necō*

	LATIN SINGULAR	ENGLISH SINGULAR		LATIN PLURAL	ENGLISH PLURAL
1ST	necāveram	I had killed		necāverāmus	we had killed
2ND	necāverās	you had killed		necāverātis	you (pl.) had killed
3RD	necāverat	he/she/it had killed		necāverant	they had killed

Future Perfect Active of *necō*

	LATIN SINGULAR	ENGLISH SINGULAR		LATIN PLURAL	ENGLISH PLURAL
1ST	necāverō	I will have killed		necāverimus	we will have killed
2ND	necāveris	you will have killed		necāveritis	you (pl.) will have killed
3RD	necāverit	he/she/it will have killed		necāverint	they will have killed

Now that we have all six tenses, our verb synopsis of the active indicative is complete. It will look like this:

Synopsis of *necō* in the second person singular

	LATIN	ENGLISH
PRESENT ACT.	necās	you kill
IMPERFECT ACT.	necābās	you were killing
FUTURE ACT.	necābis	you will kill
PERFECT ACT.	necāvistī	you killed, have killed
PLUPERFECT ACT.	necāverās	you had killed
FUTURE PERF. ACT.	necāveris	you will have killed

One other note: you now know three past tenses. Thus, when you are asked what tense a verb is, and you say "past," that's not enough. Which past? Is it imperfect, perfect, or pluperfect?

Review

Make sure you review the Third Declension endings during this lesson, your imperatives, and the perfect endings. It may seem like a big chunk, but it will help you prepare for the unit test.

Lesson 15 Worksheet

A. Vocabulary

Translate the following words from Latin to English or English to Latin as appropriate. For the verbs, also fill in the missing principal parts. For each preposition, include which case(s) it takes.

1. meanwhile: _____

2. soon: _____

3. laus: _____

4. camp: _____

5. glōria: _____

6. cōpia: _____ (pl.) _____

7. dēnique: _____

8. appellō, _____, _____, appellātum: _____

9. crux: _____

10. war: _____

11. kraken: _____

12. flōs: _____

13. mereō, _____, _____, meritum: _____

14. frūmentum: _____

15. sub: _____

16. then: _____

17. īrātus: _____

18. giant: _____

19. caveō, -ēre, cāvī, cautum: _____

20. proelium: _____

21. cūrō, _____, curāvī, _____: _____

22. eternal: _____

23. iam: _____

24. pāx: _____

25. amīca: _____

B. Grammar

1. Conjugate *mereō* in the perfect active indicative.

	LATIN SINGULAR	ENGLISH SINGULAR		LATIN PLURAL	ENGLISH PLURAL
1ST					
2ND					
3RD					

2. Conjugate *appellō* in the pluperfect active indicative.

	LATIN SINGULAR	ENGLISH SINGULAR		LATIN PLURAL	ENGLISH PLURAL
1ST					
2ND					
3RD					

3. Conjugate *lūceō* in the future perfect active indicative.

	LATIN SINGULAR	ENGLISH SINGULAR		LATIN PLURAL	ENGLISH PLURAL
1ST					
2ND					
3RD					

C. Memorization

Fill in the blanks to complete the *Magnificat*.

_____

_____

_____

_____

_____

_____

_____

_____

_____

_____

ēsurientēs _____ _____

et _____ dīmīsit _____.

Suscēpit _____ _____ suum,

_____ misericordiae,

sīcut _____ est _____ _____ nostrōs,

_____ et _____ _____ in saecula.

D. English to Latin Translation

Translate each sentence from English to Latin.

1. The wise old centaur had hastened from the cave to the town and then sang prophecies there.

_____

_____

2. The boy will give flowers to the girl, but she will have already given [her] love to the sailor.

_____

_____

3. Christ carried the burden of the cross; and so we will give great glory and praise to God.

_____

_____

4. The evil soldiers had burned the crops and then the angry farmers fought the troops in the camp.

_____

_____

5. Soon you (sg.) will have named your faithful servant your son, and you will then give the good man your wealth.

_____

_____

6. The great giants were laying waste many towns and castles; they will even attack the gods in heaven.

_____

_____

7. Because the foolish farmer's evil goats had eaten the woman's flowers, she shouted many bad words and names concerning goats.

_____

_____

8. We will hasten and attack the castle tomorrow, but our leader will have sat and thought about the battle for a long time.

_____

_____

9. You (pl.) moved the troops out of the camp to the beach, where they were able to fight the pirates.

_____

_____

10. My mother and father had often given silver and gold to the church, and food to the wretched.

_____

_____

E. Latin to English Translation

1   Ambulāverāmus et pīrātās malōs in harēnā vidērāmus. Itaque ad oppidum nostrum festīnāverāmus et
virōs fēmināsque līberōsque ibī monuerāmus. Tum omnēs[1] ad castellum festīnāverāmus. Ibī sēderāmus
et mansērāmus, et pīrātae in nostrum oppidum et agrōs nostrōs tum intrāvērunt et cremāvērunt. Miserī
erāmus; et rex noster et rēgīna flēvērunt. Pīrātae āiunt, "Nunc date[2] oppidum vestrum!" Respondimus,
5   "Nōn dabimus!" Tum dux pīrātārum dēclārāvit, "Oppidum vestrum obsidēbimus. Dabitis postquam[3]
vestrum cibum frūmentumque bēstiāsque mandūcāveritis!" Itaque diū flēvimus. Pīrātās nōn superāre
potuimus, quod multum cibum frūmentumque in castellō nōn parāverāmus. Et misera erat fīlia rēgis,
et in turrī[4] castellī ambulābat et deōs ōrābat. Dux pīrātārum virginem pulchram vīdit, et amor in cor
intrāvit. Pīrātīs āit: "Castellum nōn iam oppugnāre dēbēmus. Amō fīliam rēgis!" Pīrātae laetī nōn
10   erant, quod avārī erant et aurum argentumque servōsque amābant. Dux autem pulcher pīrātīs dēnique
persuadēre[5] potuit quod avārīs multum aurum dedit. Tum rēgī in castellō clāmāvit: "Castellum tuum
nōn iam obsidēbimus, quod fīliam tuam amō. Valē." Fīlia rēgis dē verbīs ducis cōgitāvit, et pīrātam
pulchrum spectāvit. Et amor in cor intrāvit, et ab castellō ad ducem festīnāvit. Hodiē pāx est inter[6]
oppidum nostrum et pīrātās.

Glossary
1. *omnēs:* nom. pl. adj. from *omnis:* all, every
2. *date:* in this context, *dō* is better translated "to give up" or "surrender."
3. *postquam:* conj., after
4. *turrī:* abl. sg. of *turris, -is* (f): tower
5. *persuadēre:* infinitive of *persuadeō,* it takes the dative case rather than accusative, and you should be able to guess what it means.
6. *inter:* (+ acc.) between, among

_____

_____

_____

_____

_____

_____

_____

_____

_____

_____

_____

_____

_____

LESSON 16

Review & Test

Word List

No new word list this lesson. Review all the vocabulary from Lessons 9–15.

Memorization

No new memorization this lesson. Review the entirety of the *Magnificat*.

Grammar

There is no new chant this lesson. To prepare for the test, review the following:

- how to form verbs in the second conjugation
- verb chants for the perfect, pluperfect, and future perfect active indicative
- irregular verbs *sum* and *possum*
- how to form imperatives
- noun chants for the third declension and third declension neuter
- it would behoove you to review the first and second declension as well

Lesson 16 Worksheet

A. Vocabulary

Translate the following words from Latin to English or English to Latin as appropriate. Give case(s) for prepositions.

1. autem: _____

2. contrā: (+_____) _____

3. cum: (+ _____) _____

4. finally: _____

5. diū: _____

6. now, already: _____

7. interim: _____

8. soon: _____

9. nec (neque): _____

10. quandō: _____

11. -que: _____

12. because: _____

13. repentē: _____

14. sine: (+ _____) _____

15. immediately: _____

16. sub: (+_____) _____

17. sub: (+_____) _____

_____

18. suprā: (+_____) _____

19. trāns: (+_____) _____

20. tum: _____

_____

21. when?, where?: _____

22. āiō: _____

23. appellō: _____

24. audeō: _____

25. I hunt: _____

26. caveō: _____

27. I care for: _____

28. dēbeō: _____

29. dēclārō: _____

_____

30. dēleō: _____

31. I teach: _____

32. domō: _____

33. errō: _____

34. exerceō: _____

35. festīnō: _____

36. I weep: _____

37. habeō: _____

38. iaceō: _____

39. I enter: _____

40. lūceō: _____

41. maneō: _____

42. mereō: _____

_____

43. moneō: _____

44. mordeō: _____

45. moveō: _____

46. I swim: _____

47. nuntiō: _____

48. obsideō: _____

49. parō: _____

50. possum: _____

51. removeō: _____

52. reptō: _____

53. respondeō: _____

54. I laugh, smile: _____

55. salveō: _____

56. sedeō: _____

57. teneō: _____

58. terreō: _____

59. timeō: _____

60. valeō: _____

61. vastō: _____

62. videō: _____

63. I fly: _____

64. āla: _____

65. amīca: _____

66. amor: _____

67. apostolus: _____

68. war: _____

69. Biblia Sacra: _____

70. caput: _____

71. carmen: _____

_____

72. castra: _____

73. centaurus: _____

74. cervus: _____

75. cōpia: _____

_____

76. heart: _____

77. corpus: _____

78. crux: _____

79. draco: _____

80. dux: _____

81. ecclēsia: _____

82. flower: _____

83. flūmen: _____

84. frāter: _____

85. frūmentum: _____

86. geminus: _____

87. giant: _____

88. glōria: _____

89. grāmen: _____

90. homō: _____

91. cētus: _____

92. inimīcus: _____

93. iter: _____

94. labor: _____

95. milk: _____

96. laus: _____

97. leō: _____

98. liber: _____

99. līberī: _____

100. lītus: _____

101. lūx: _____

102. māter: _____

103. mīles: _____

104. name: _____

105. onus: _____

106. ōra: _____

107. ōs: _____

108. pater: _____

109. pāx: _____

110. populus: _____

111. porcus : _____

112. proelium: _____

113. king: _____

114. scūtum: _____

115. senex: _____

116. sōl: _____

117. soror: _____

118. star: _____

119. tellūs : _____

120. tempus : _____

121. tenēbrae: _____
_____

122. tigris: _____

123. unda: _____

124. poison: _____

125. vesper: _____

126. road, way: _____

127. victōria: _____

128. virgō: _____

129. virtūs: _____
_____

130. vīta: _____

131. voice: _____

132. vulnus: _____

133. meus: _____

134. noster: our, _____

135. tuus: _____

136. vester: _____

137. dear, beloved: _____

138. doctus: _____

139. horrendus: _____

140. aeternus: _____

141. angry, wrathful: _____

B. Grammar

1. Decline *my enemy*.

	LATIN SINGULAR	LATIN PLURAL
NOM.		
GEN.		
DAT.		
ACC.		
ABL.		
VOC.		

2. Decline *wretched farmer*.

	LATIN SINGULAR	LATIN PLURAL
NOM.		
GEN.		
DAT.		
ACC.		
ABL.		
VOC.		

3. Decline *great shield*.

	LATIN SINGULAR	LATIN PLURAL
NOM.		
GEN.		
DAT.		
ACC.		
ABL.		
VOC.		

4. Decline *faithful courage*.

	LATIN SINGULAR	LATIN PLURAL
NOM.		
GEN.		
DAT.		
ACC.		
ABL.		
VOC.		

5. Decline *angry mouth*.

	LATIN SINGULAR	LATIN PLURAL
NOM.		
GEN.		
DAT.		
ACC.		
ABL.		
VOC.		

6. Give a synopsis of *festīnō* in the third person plural.

	LATIN	ENGLISH
PRESENT ACT.		
IMPERFECT ACT.		
FUTURE ACT.		
PERFECT ACT.		
PLUPERFECT ACT.		
FUTURE PERF. ACT.		

7. Give a synopsis of *iaceō* in the first person singular.

	LATIN	ENGLISH
PRESENT ACT.		
IMPERFECT ACT.		
FUTURE ACT.		
PERFECT ACT.		
PLUPERFECT ACT.		
FUTURE PERF. ACT.		

8. Give a synopsis of *timeō* in the second person plural.

	LATIN	ENGLISH
PRESENT ACT.		
IMPERFECT ACT.		
FUTURE ACT.		
PERFECT ACT.		
PLUPERFECT ACT.		
FUTURE PERF. ACT.		

9. Give a synopsis of *possum* in the third person singular.

	LATIN	ENGLISH
PRESENT ACT.		
IMPERFECT ACT.		
FUTURE ACT.		
PERFECT ACT.		
PLUPERFECT ACT.		
FUTURE PERF. ACT.		

10. Give a synopsis of *dō* in the second person singular.

	LATIN	ENGLISH
PRESENT ACT.		
IMPERFECT ACT.		
FUTURE ACT.		
PERFECT ACT.		
PLUPERFECT ACT.		
FUTURE PERF. ACT.		

11. Give a synopsis of *parō* in the first person plural.

	LATIN	ENGLISH
PRESENT ACT.		
IMPERFECT ACT.		
FUTURE ACT.		
PERFECT ACT.		
PLUPERFECT ACT.		
FUTURE PERF. ACT.		

12. Fully conjugate *moneō* in Latin and English.

Present Active Indicative

	LATIN SINGULAR	ENGLISH SINGULAR		LATIN PLURAL	ENGLISH PLURAL
1ST					
2ND					
3RD					

Imperfect Active Indicative

	LATIN SINGULAR	ENGLISH SINGULAR		LATIN PLURAL	ENGLISH PLURAL
1ST					
2ND					
3RD					

Future Active Indicative

	LATIN SINGULAR	ENGLISH SINGULAR		LATIN PLURAL	ENGLISH PLURAL
1ST					
2ND					
3RD					

Perfect Active Indicative

	LATIN SINGULAR	ENGLISH SINGULAR		LATIN PLURAL	ENGLISH PLURAL
1ST					
2ND					
3RD					

Pluperfect Active Indicative

	LATIN SINGULAR	ENGLISH SINGULAR		LATIN PLURAL	ENGLISH PLURAL
1ST					
2ND					
3RD					

Future Perfect Active Indicative

	LATIN SINGULAR	ENGLISH SINGULAR		LATIN PLURAL	ENGLISH PLURAL
1ST					
2ND					
3RD					

C. Memorization

Below is the first word from each line of the *Magnificat*. Fill in the rest.

Magnificat _____

et _____

quia _____

Ecce _____

quia _____

quī _____

et _____

et _____

Fēcit _____

dispersit _____

dēposuit _____

et _____

ēsurientēs _____

et _____

Suscēpit _____

recordātus _____

sīcut _____

Ābraham _____

D. English to Latin Translation

Parse and translate each verb. To parse a verb, list its attributes: person, number, tense, voice, and mood if it is an indicative verb; if it is an infinitive, give tense, voice, and mood only. Then give the first principal part of the verb it comes from. (Abbreviate but keep your meaning is clear.) An example is given below.

	VERB	PERSON	NO.	TENSE	VOICE	MOOD	1ST PRIN. PART	TRANSLATION
	cūrāverās	2nd	Sg.	Plupf.	Act.	Ind.	cūrō	you had cared for
1.	dēbuerāmus							
2.	momordērunt							
3.	audēbātis							
4.	docuerō							
5.	habētis							
6.	flēvit							
7.	āiunt							
8.	manserant							
9.	obsēderis							
10.	dēlēs							
11.	errābimus							

12.	reptāre							
13.	cāvit							
14.	luxerās							
15.	nābam							
16.	captāverint							
17.	remōvimus							
18.	vastāveram							
19.	rīdēre							
20.	domāvistī							

Identify all possible gender, number, and case combinations for the following phrases and translate them. An example is given below.

	PHRASE	GENDER, NUMBER, CASE	TRANSLATION
	bonīs patribus	Masc. Pl. Dat. Masc. Pl. Abl.	to/for the good fathers by/with/from the good fathers
21.	rēge carō		
22.	amorī aeternō		
23.	gigantēs horrendōs		
24.	pāx beāta		
25.	tua vulnera		

26.	centaurī ferī		
27.	senex avārus		
28.	dracōnem caldum		
29.	flūmen īrātum		
30.	pulchra nōmina		
31.	corpore foedō		
32.	magnā laude		
33.	meīs amīcīs		
34.	bellī iūstī		
35.	ōrīs antīquīs		
36.	capitum vestrōrum		

37.	itineribus stultīs		
38.	castrōrum malōrum		
39.	matris doctae		
40.	cōpiae nostrae		

3 UNIT THREE

UNIT 3 GOALS

Lessons 17–24

By the end of Unit 3, students should be able to . . .

- Decline first, second, and third person personal pronouns
- Decline and identify third declension i-stem nouns
- Decline third declension adjectives
- Know basic Latin numerals, both cardinal and ordinal
- Conjugate a first or second conjugation verb in the present, imperfect, future, perfect, pluperfect, and future perfect passive indicative
- Translate sentences using all of the concepts learned in Units 1–3
- Know all vocabulary from Lessons 17-24
- Write out from memory the *Symbolum Nicaenum* (Nicene Creed)

LESSON 17

Personal Pronouns

Word List

PRONOUNS

1. ego: *I*

2. nōs: *we*

3. is, ea, id: *he, she, it, they; this, that*

4. tū: *you (sg.)*

5. vōs: *you (pl.)*

ADJECTIVES

6. albus, -a, -um: *(dead) white*

7. argenteus, -a, -um: *silver*

8. āter, -tra, -trum: *(dead) black, dark*

9. aureus, -a, -um: *golden, gold*

10. caeruleus, -a, -um: *blue*

11. candidus, -a, -um: *(glittering) white*

12. hyacinthinus, -a, -um: *blue, purplish-blue, violet*

13. niger, -gra, grum: (shining) *black, dark-colored*

14. purpureus, -a, -um: *purple; dark-red, dark-violet, dark-brown*

15. ruber, -bra, -brum: *red, ruddy*

16. viridis, -e: *green; fresh, young, vigorous*

VERBS

17. flōreō, -ēre, -uī, ——: *I flourish*

18. torreō, -ēre, torruī, tostum: *I burn, parch, dry up*

CONJUNCTIONS

19. enim (postpositive conj.): *indeed, truly, certainly; for*

PREPOSITIONS

20. ante (+ acc.): *before*

21. post (+ acc.): *after, behind*

INTERJECTIONS

22. ecce: *behold!*

Memorization

Crēdō in ūnum Deum, Patrem omnipotentem, Factōrem caelī et terrae,

vīsibilium omnium et invīsibilium.

I believe in God the Father Almighty, Maker of heaven and earth, of all things visible and invisible.

Et in ūnum Dominum Iēsum Christum, Fīlium Deī Ūnigenitum,

And in one Lord Jesus Christ, the Only-Begotten Son of God.

Grammar

Personal Pronouns

During the first half of this year, you have perhaps felt hampered by the lack of pronouns (as did I). It gets awkward saying, "The king is good. The people love the king and the people give honor to the king"—where the pronoun "him" would make this flow so much better. Pronouns (which take the place of a noun) are extremely handy. In this chapter you will learn the personal pronouns—that is, pronouns for first, second, and third person. I have already sprinkled a few of these into your translations, and you have encountered some of them in your memorizations.

Pronouns function the same way as nouns—they have gender, number, and case. The gender of course is dependent upon the pronoun's antecedent (which is the word the pronoun takes the place of). If someone were talking about a girl, they would say, *Ea discipula est*; if they were talking about a boy, they would say, *Is discipulus est*. In the first example *ea* is feminine, while in the second *is* is masculine.

Let's begin with the first and second person pronouns.

First Person Personal Pronouns

	LATIN SINGULAR	ENGLISH SINGULAR	LATIN PLURAL	ENGLISH PLURAL
NOMINATIVE	ego	I [subject]	nōs	we [subject]
GENITIVE	meī	of me	nostrum	of us
DATIVE	mihi	to/for me	nōbīs	to/for us
ACCUSATIVE	mē	me [object]	nōs	us [object]
ABLATIVE	mē	by/with/from me	nōbīs	by/with/from us

Second Person Personal Pronouns

	LATIN SINGULAR	ENGLISH SINGULAR	LATIN PLURAL	ENGLISH PLURAL
NOMINATIVE	tū	you [subject]	vōs	you (pl.) [subject]
GENITIVE	tuī	of you	vestrum	of you (pl.)
DATIVE	tibī	to/for you	vōbīs	to/for you (pl.)
ACCUSATIVE	tē	you [object]	vōs	you (pl.) [object]
ABLATIVE	tē	by/with/from you	vōbīs	by/with/from you (pl.)

You might be tempted to confuse *nōs* and *vōs*, so make sure you keep these two straight. Remember our memory devices for *noster* and *vester*: *Pater Noster* means "Our Father" not "Your Father," and the phrase, "Where's your *vestrum*?"

When you chant these pronouns out loud, it is more rhythmical to chant through the singulars first and then the plurals, rather than sticking with first person singular and plural, then second person singular and plural: *ego, meī, mihi, mē, mē! tū, tuī, tibī, tē, tē! nōs, nostrum, nōbīs, nōs, nōbīs! vōs, vestrum, vōbīs, vōs, vōbīs!* (If you don't believe me, try doing it *ego-nōs, tū-vōs,* and you will find that I am right.)

One very important thing to note about the first and second personal pronouns is that their genitives (*meī, tuī, nostrum,* and *vestrum*) are not used to show possession. If I wanted to say "my king" or "your daughter," I would use the possessive adjectives that we have already learned (*meus, tuus, noster, vester*): *meus rex* or *tua fīlia.* So what are these genitives used for? We have not really discussed uses of the genitive other than possession, but there are other usages which will be mentioned later on as they come up. For now don't use the genitive of these pronouns to show possession, because they are used to show other things, such as the partitive and objective genitives.

You may wonder why we need the nominatives of these pronouns, since Latin verb endings already contain a subject pronoun. We have been able to say "I love" or "you do not love" for months now without having to use *ego* or *tū*. These nominative pronouns were often added to express emphasis. If we want to make some sort of contrast, we can throw them in: *Ego amō, sed tū nōn amās.* "I love, but you do not love." Of course very often this emphasis cannot be translated into English without using italics or underlining the words or with intonation.

And now to the third person pronouns. This chart may look a bit intimidating because it has lots of tiny little words. Thankfully, you actually know most of these endings already. Except for the forms in bold below, all you have to do is put a First or Second Declension ending onto an *e*, and you have your pronoun.

Third Person Personal Pronouns—Singular

| | MASCULINE | FEMININE | NEUTER | |
	HE/HIS/HIM	SHE/HERS/HER	IT/ITS (THIS/THAT)	ENGLISH
NOM.	**is**	ea	**id**	he/she/it
GEN.	**eius**	**eius**	**eius**	of him/his, of her/hers, of it/its
DAT.	**eī**	**eī**	**eī**	to/for him, to/for her, to/for it
ACC.	eum	eam	**id**	him/her/it
ABL.	eō	eā	eō	by/with/from him/her/it

Third Person Personal Pronouns—Plural

| | MASCULINE | FEMININE | NEUTER | |
	THEY	THEY	THEY	ENGLISH
NOM.	eī	eae	ea	they
GEN.	eōrum	eārum	eōrum	of them, their
DAT.	eīs	eīs	eīs	to/for them
ACC.	eōs	eās	ea	them
ABL.	eīs	eīs	eīs	by/with/from them

When you chant this one out loud, it flows better if you go horizontally first rather than vertically: *is, ea, id! eius, eius, eius! eī, eī, eī! eum, eam, id!* etc. You may want to practice this chart regularly and practice guessing the different forms from memory.

The third person pronoun is quite handy, because not only does it function as a personal pronoun, but it can also be used as an adjective where it means "this, that" (making it what is called a demonstrative adjective).

Here are a few examples to illustrate: *Ego eam amō*, "I love her." *Ego eam fēminam amō*, "I love this woman."

And what about the genitive of this pronoun? Rest easy—it is a normal old genitive of possession. Thus we would say, *Ego fīliam eius amō*, "I love his daughter" (or "her daughter," depending on the context).

Demonstrative adjectives simply do not have a vocative, so when you are declining a noun/adjective phrase, you can leave out the vocative of *is, ea,* and *id.*

A lot of this lesson consists of memorizing words. However, once you have memorized them, you will discover you are able to use pronouns and also to start saying "this" and "that," powerfully increasing your Latin abilities. This will also lay the groundwork for demonstratives in the future, so learn this lesson well.

Review

Be sure to review third declension endings, and any perfect, pluperfect, and future perfect endings that you might still be a bit weak on.

Lesson 17 Worksheet

A. Vocabulary

Translate the following words from Latin to English or English to Latin as appropriate. For the verbs, also fill in the missing principal parts. For each preposition, include which case(s) it takes.

1. golden: _____

2. vōs: _____

3. āter: _____

4. you (sg.): _____

5. ecce: _____

6. caeruleus: _____

7. flōreō, flōrēre, _____, _____: _____

8. (glittering) white: _____

9. is: _____

10. violet: _____

11. enim: _____

12. before: _____

13. niger: _____

14. post: _____

15. purple: _____

16. I: _____

17. ruber: _____

18. argenteus: _____

19. albus: _____

20. green: _____

21. I parch: _____, _____, _____, _____

22. nōs: _____

23. Get the colored pencils out. Choose five of your new color adjectives and draw an object in each color in the space below. Write the Latin color word in the space below each drawing.

B. Grammar

Fill in the charts (from memory, if possible).

1. First Person Personal Pronouns

	LATIN SINGULAR	LATIN PLURAL
NOMINATIVE		
GENITIVE		
DATIVE		
ACCUSATIVE		
ABLATIVE		

2. Second Person Personal Pronouns

	LATIN SINGULAR	LATIN PLURAL
NOMINATIVE		
GENITIVE		
DATIVE		
ACCUSATIVE		
ABLATIVE		

3. Third Person Personal Pronouns

	SINGULAR			PLURAL		
	MASC.	FEM.	NEUT.	MASC.	FEM.	NEUT.
NOM.						
GEN.						
DAT.						
ACC.						
ABL.						

Identify and translate all possible options for the following pronouns. An example is given below.

	PRONOUN	GENDER, NUMBER, CASE	TRANSLATION
	eōrum	Masc. Pl. Gen. Neut. Pl. Gen.	their(s), of them their(s), of them
4.	vōbīs		
5.	eī		
6.	eā		
7.	nōs		
8	id		
9.	eae		
10.	mihi		

11.	nostrum		
12.	eōs		
13.	mē		

14. Give a synopsis of *torreō* in the second person plural.

	LATIN	ENGLISH
PRESENT ACT.		
IMPERFECT ACT.		
FUTURE ACT.		
PERFECT ACT.		
PLUPERFECT ACT.		
FUTURE PERF. ACT.		

C. Memorization

Fill in the blanks for the first two lines of the *Symbolum Nicaenum*.

Crēdō _____ _____ Deum, _____ omnipotentem, _____ caelī _____
_____, vīsibilium _____ et _____.

_____ in ūnum _____ _____ _____, _____
Deī _____,

D. English to Latin Translation

Translate each sentence from English to Latin. Include subject pronouns wherever possible.

1. Behold, God gave the Son to us and we love and praise Him because He is good.

_____

_____

2. The fierce centaur had attacked us and seized our gold and now he will give you our wealth.

_____

_____

3. The sky was blue and the sun was shining but then the purple dragon flew from his dark cave.

_____

_____

4. The king gave the queen a silver crown but his crown was gold.

_____

_____

5. Then the angry pirate says to us, "Give me your money or your lives!"

_____

_____

6. Indeed, black horses have carried us from the town but this white horse will carry you to the castle.

_____

_____

_____

7. After the peace with their enemy, their fields and grasses flourished.

_____

_____

8. Our mother gives us good cookies and we give her our love.

_____

_____

9. The little girls were holding violet flowers and gave them to you and your queen.

_____

_____

10. Their brothers were boys before that war, but now they are men and soldiers.

_____

_____

E. Latin to English Translation

1 Frāter meus es, sed tē nōn amō. Pater noster agricola erat, et ego fīlius bonus eius sum quod et ego agricola sum. Tū fīlius malus eius est quod tū poēta es. Tū labōrem sōlemque nōn amās, sed lūnam candidam amās et eī noctīque[1] ātrae cantās. Dē stellīs purpureīs et pulchrā lūce candidā eārum cantās. Tū multās fēminās amāvistī, et cum eīs in agrīs errāvistī. Tū eīs flōrēs rubrōs et hyacinthinōs et albōs

5 dedistī, sed eīs aurea aut argentea numquam dare potuistī quod ea nōn tenēs. Ōlim eī pīrātae patriam nostram oppugnābant; itaque tū in spēluncam ātram festīnāvit et exspectāvit. Post proelium tū in oppidum dēnique intrāvit. Tū mīles nōn es, sed ego mīles et vir sum. Pater noster tibī gladium magnum dederat, sed eum gladium nōn amās et itaque ego eum occupāvī. Ego gladiō eius pugnābō. Ego labōrem amābō et multum aurum argentumque tenēbō, et bonam fēminam amābō. Nōs laetī erimus. Tū in tuā

10 spēluncā diū habitābis et carmina creābis, sed laetus eris?

Glossary
1. *noctī*: dative singular of *nox, noctis* (f): night

LESSON 18

Third Declension i-stems

Word List

NOUNS

1. animal, -ālis (n): *animal*

2. avis, avis (f): *bird*

3. canis, canis (m/f): *dog*

4. hostis, hostis (m): *enemy (of the state)*

5. ignis, ignis (m): *fire*

6. mare, maris (n): *sea*

7. moenia, -ium (n, pl.): *fortifications, city walls*

8. mōns, montis (m): *mountain*

9. mors, mortis (f): *death*

10. nāvis, nāvis (f): *ship*

11. nox, noctis (f): *night*

12. nūbēs, nūbis (f): *cloud, gloom*

13. turris, turris (f): *tower, turret*

14. urbs, urbis (f): *city*

15. vallēs, vallis (f): *valley, vale*

16. vestis, vestis (f): *clothing, garment*

ADVERBS

17. ergō: *therefore, then, consequently, accordingly*

CONJUNCTIONS

18. quia (conj.): *because, since*

19. sī (conj.): *if*

PREPOSITIONS

20. prō (+ abl.): *before, in front of; for (the sake of), instead of*

Memorization

Crēdō in ūnum Deum, Patrem omnipotentem, Factōrem caelī et terrae,

vīsibilium omnium et invīsibilium.

Et in ūnum Dominum Iēsum Christum, Fīlium Deī Ūnigenitum,

Et ex Patre nātum ante omnia saecula.

Begotten also of the Father before all worlds.

Deum dē Deō, Lūmen dē Lūmine, Deum vērum dē Deō vērō,

God of God, Light of Light, very God of very God,

Grammar

Third Declension i-Stems

Happily, Third Declension i-stem nouns aren't all that much different from regular old Third Declension nouns. They just have an extra *i* sprinkled here and there.

Third Declension Masculine/Feminine i-Stem

	LATIN SG.	ENGLISH SINGULAR	LATIN PL.	ENGLISH PLURAL
NOMINATIVE	X	a/the *noun* [subject]	-ēs	the *nouns* [subject]
GENITIVE	-is	of the *noun*, the *noun's*	**-ium**	of the *nouns*, the *nouns'*
DATIVE	-ī	to/for the *noun*	-ibus	to/for the *nouns*
ACCUSATIVE	-em	a/the *noun* [direct object]	-ēs	the *nouns* [direct object]
ABLATIVE	**-e/-ī**	by/with/from the *noun*	-ibus	by/with/from the *nouns*
VOCATIVE	X	[O] *noun!*	-ēs	[O] *nouns!*

Third Declension Neuter i-Stem

	LATIN SG.	ENGLISH SINGULAR	LATIN PL.	ENGLISH PLURAL
NOMINATIVE	X	a/the *noun* [subject]	**-ia**	the *nouns* [subject]
GENITIVE	-is	of the *noun*, the *noun's*	**-ium**	of the *nouns*, the *nouns'*
DATIVE	-ī	to/for the *noun*	-ibus	to/for the *nouns*
ACCUSATIVE	X	a/the *noun* [object]	**-ia**	the *nouns* [object]
ABLATIVE	**-ī**	by/with/from the *noun*	-ibus	by/with/from the *nouns*
VOCATIVE	X	[O] *noun!*	**-ia**	[O] *nouns!*

Notice that masculine and feminine i-stem nouns have an *i* in the genitive plural, making the ending *-ium* rather than *-um*, while neuter nouns have an *-ī* instead of an *-e* in the ablative singular, and *-ia* instead of *-a* in the nominative and accusative (and vocative) plural, and the *-ium* in the genitive plural. (Once in a while, masculine/feminine i-stems will also have *-ī* in the ablative singular.) Notice that you do not have to learn a whole new declension: this is simply a variation of the regular ol' Third Declension.

How do you know if a Third Declension noun is an i-stem or not? Believe it or not, there actually are guidelines for determining this. Consider the following chart:

IF THE NOUN IS	IT'S AN I-STEM IF	EXAMPLES
Masculine or Feminine	1. The nominative ends in *-is* or *-es* *and* the nominative and genitive have the same number of syllables (called "parisyllabic").	canis, canis (m/f) *dog* nūbēs, nūbis (f) *cloud, gloom*
	2. The nominative ends in *-s* or *-x* *and* the noun stem ends in two consonants. (The nominatives of most of these nouns are one syllable.)	mors, mortis (m) *death* nox, noctis (f) *night*
Neuter	3. The nominative ends in *-al, -ar,* or *-e*.	animal, -ālis (n) *animal* mare, maris (n) *sea*

The first two rules may look a bit complicated, but they actually are pretty straightforward. From now on, analyze each Third Declension noun in your vocab lists to see if it is an i-stem or not. When you are figuring out the declension of a noun, you have to look at both the nominative and the genitive singular, because of course the genitive not only gets you started on the correct chant, but it also gives you the stem. Similarly, look first at the nominative of the Third Declension noun. If it ends with *-es* or *-is*, such as *canis*, then you should look at the genitive. If the genitive "rhymes" with the nominative (i.e., has two syllables if the nominative has two syllables), then it's an i-stem.

With the second rule, you again need to look at both the nominative and the genitive. Say the nominative ends in *-s* or *-x*, as with *nox*. Look at the genitive singular, and take off the *-is* to find the stem: *noct-*. If the stem ends in two consonants (which *noct-* does), then it's an i-stem. Compare *nox* to *rex*. Yes, the nominative does end in *-x*, but if you look at the genitive *rēgis*, the stem *rēg-* does not end in two consonants, and therefore *rex* is not an i-stem.

The rule for neuter i-stems is much easier, because you don't even need to look at the genitive. If the nominative ends in *-al*, *-ar*, or *-e*, then it's an i-stem. Simple!

Now go over the new nouns and use the above guidelines to explain how you know each one is an i-stem.

Review

Be sure to review the perfect, pluperfect, and future perfect endings, as well as the pronouns that we learned so recently.

Lesson 18 Worksheet

A. Vocabulary

Translate the following words from Latin to English or English to Latin as appropriate. For the verbs, also fill in the missing principal parts. For each preposition, include which case(s) it takes.

1. death: _____

2. urbs: _____

3. torreō, -ēre, _____, _____: _____

4. sea: _____

5. vestis: _____

6. avis: _____

7. mōns: _____

8. animal: _____

9. red: _____

10. nāvis: _____

11. sī: _____

12. fortifications: _____

13. nūbēs: _____

14. dog: _____

15. enim: _____

16. turris: _____

17. ergō: _____

18. fire: _____

19. prō: (+ _____) _____

20. nox: _____

21. valley: _____

22. quia: _____

23. purpureus: _____

24. hostis: _____

25. green: _____

B. Grammar

1. Decline "that dark night," *ea nox ātra*.

	LATIN SINGULAR	LATIN PLURAL
NOM.		
GEN.		
DAT.		
ACC.		
ABL.		
VOC.		

2. Decline "this blue sea," *id mare caeruleum*.

	LATIN SINGULAR	LATIN PLURAL
NOM.		
GEN.		
DAT.		
ACC.		
ABL.		
VOC.		

3. Give a synopsis of *vastō* in the third person plural.

	LATIN	ENGLISH
PRESENT ACT.		
IMPERFECT ACT.		
FUTURE ACT.		
PERFECT ACT.		
PLUPERFECT ACT.		
FUTURE PERF. ACT.		

C. Memorization

Fill in the blanks.

_____ _____ _____ Deum, _____ _____,

Factōrem _____ _____ _____, vīsibilium _____ _____ _____.

_____ _____ ūnum _____ _____ Christum, _____ _____

    Ūnigenitum,

_____ ex _____ nātum _____ _____ saecula.

_____ dē Deō, Lūmen _____ _____, Deum _____ _____ _____ vērō,

D. English to Latin Translation

Translate each sentence from English to Latin. Use subject pronouns wherever possible.

1. I have always loved the blue seas and the wild songs of the birds there.

    _____

2. Oswald had killed the fiery dragon of fire before the king and therefore had saved his daughter in the turret.

    _____

    _____

3. Our clothing was black and silver but theirs was purple and gold.

    _____

    _____

    _____

4. His dogs are faithful and he gives them good food, and so they hunt many deer well.

    _____

5. If wild animals and birds hasten from the dark forest, then the dragon is flying from the purple mountains to the forest.

    _____

    _____

6. Before the great battle of the twin seas, the enemies' black ships had sailed to our land and attacked our shores.

    _____

    _____

7. We declared the word of God to them and to their children, but they were foolish and laughed at us.

_____

_____

8. Grasses were flourishing in the valleys but then the dragon flew over them and burned them.

_____

_____

9. The silvery castle with the fortifications and turrets was beautiful in front of the purplish-blue mountains.

_____

_____

10. After the death of my faithful old dog, I sat in the dark night and wept under the silvery moon.

_____

_____

E. Latin to English Translation

1 **Dē Fātō Pīrātae Īrātī**

Ōlim erat pīrāta īrātus. Is īrātus semper fuerat. Magnam nāvem ātram habēbat et cor eius ātrum erat. Vestēs eius ātrae rubraeque erant, et cibus eius bellum erat. Is oppida vestra et moenia urbium nostrārum oppugnābat. Is pīrāta cum bonīs malīsque pugnābat. Multa animālia ab eīs terrīs occupābat et pīrātīs

5 ea prō cibō dābat. Fēminās autem et puellās occupābat et eās ad nāvem ātram portābat. Ūnā[1] nocte, is multum vīnum pōtābat et pīrātīs dēclārāvit: "Ego magnus vir et bonus pīrāta sum! Aurum argentumque teneō; fēminās et vīnum et carmen habeō. Ego deus sum!" Sed tum dormīvit[2] et somniāvit:[3] Camēlus Magnus et Horrendus Mortis ab Montibus Purpureīs Tenēbrārum festīnāverat, et in diaetam[4] eius in nāve intrāvit. "Stulte!" āit. "Tū deus nōn es. Ego Mors sum, et ad tē festīnō. Tē ad meōs Montēs

10 Purpureōs Tenēbrārum portābō." Ergō Camēlus Mortis pīrātam superbum[5] et īrātum occupāvit, et eum in tenēbrās montium portāvit. Nōs eum iterum[6] numquam vīdimus, et terra pācem habuit.

Glossary
1. _ūnus, -a, -um:_ one; here it is in the ablative matching _nocte,_ which is showing "time when"
2. _dormiō, -īre, -īvī, -ītum:_ I sleep
3. _somniō (1):_ I dream
4. _diaeta, -ae (f):_ cabin (of a ship)
5. _superbus, -a, -um:_ proud, haughty
6. _iterum:_ again

_____

_____

_____

_____

LESSON 19
Third Declension Adjectives

Word List

NOUNS

1. asinus, -ī (m): *donkey*
2. bōs, bovis (m/f): *cow, bull, ox; (pl.) cattle*
3. elephantus, -ī (m): *elephant*
4. piscis, -is (m): *fish*

ADJECTIVES

5. altus, -a, -um: *high, lofty, deep*
6. brevis, -e: *short, small, brief*
7. celer, celeris, celere: *swift, quick*
8. dulcis, -e: *sweet*
9. fēlix, (gen.) -līcis: *lucky, fortunate, happy*
10. fortis, -e: *strong, brave*
11. infēlix, (gen.) -līcis: *unlucky, unfortunate, miserable*

12. ingēns, (gen.) -entis: *huge, vast, enormous*
13. mediōcris, -e: *ordinary*
14. omnis, -e: *every, all*
15. potēns, (gen.) -entis: *powerful*

VERBS

16. augeō -ēre, auxī, auctum: *I increase*
17. vexō (1): *I vex, ravage, annoy*

ADVERBS/PREPOSITIONS

18. inter (+acc.): *between, among*
19. paene (adv.): *almost*
20. prope (adv./prep. + acc.): *near, next to*

Memorization

Crēdō in ūnum Deum, Patrem omnipotentem, Factōrem caelī et terrae,

> vīsibilium omnium et invīsibilium.

Et in ūnum Dominum Iēsum Christum, Fīlium Deī Ūnigenitum,

Et ex Patre nātum ante omnia saecula.

Deum dē Deō, Lūmen dē Lūmine, Deum vērum dē Deō vērō,

Genitum, nōn factum, consubstantiālem Patrī: per quem omnia facta sunt;

> *Begotten, not made, [being] of one substance with the Father: by whom all things were made;*

Quī propter nōs hominēs et propter nostram salūtem dēscendit dē caelīs,

> *Who for us men and for our salvation descended from heaven,*

Grammar

Third Declension Adjectives

We will continue to reinforce and expand the use of the Third Declension by learning Third Declension Adjectives in this lesson. Thus far all adjectives have been First/Second Declension Adjectives, such as *bonus, -a, -um* or *ruber, -bra, -brum*. Third Declension adjectives can be a little intimidating because their nominatives vary, but once you get into the chant, they are pretty normal. They decline like Third Declension i-stems, except that the masculine/feminine ablative singular has an *-ī* like the neuter (in bold):

| | SINGULAR | | PLURAL | |
	MASC./FEM.	NEUTER	MASC./FEM.	NEUTER
NOM.	X	X	-ēs	-ia
GEN.	-is	-is	-ium	-ium
DAT.	-ī	-ī	-ibus	-ibus
ACC.	-em	X	-ēs	-ia
ABL.	**-ī**	-ī	-ibus	-ibus
VOC.	X	X	-ēs	-ia

As I mentioned, the only tricky thing with these adjectives is getting past the nominatives. They are sorted into three categories: three termination, two termination, and single termination. "Termination" is simply a fancy grammatical term for "ending." All the First/Second Declension adjectives you have learned were three termination—because the dictionary listing gave three nominative endings, one each for masculine, feminine, and neuter: *-us, -a, -um*. Three termination Third Declension adjectives generally end in *-r, -is, -e*. The adjective *celer, celeris, celere* ("swift") is from this lesson's vocabulary list and is declined as follows:

| | SINGULAR | | | PLURAL | | |
	MASCULINE	FEMININE	NEUTER	MASCULINE	FEMININE	NEUTER
NOM.	celer	celeris	celere	celerēs	celerēs	celeria
GEN.	celeris	celeris	celeris	celerium	celerium	celerium
DAT.	celerī	celerī	celerī	celeribus	celeribus	celeribus
ACC.	celerem	celerem	celere	celerēs	celerēs	celeria
ABL.	celerī	celerī	celerī	celeribus	celeribus	celeribus
VOC.	celer	celeris	celere	celerēs	celerēs	celeria

Notice how besides the nominative, the masculine and feminine columns are exactly the same. Thus, they don't need to be written out separately unless you are dying to do so.

Two termination Third Declension Adjectives generally end in *-is, -e*. This means that the masculine and feminine adjectives share the same form in the nominative, ending in *-is*, and the neuter nominative ends in *-e*. You have already learned a two termination adjective: *viridis, -e*, "green." It would be declined as follows:

	SINGULAR		PLURAL	
	MASC./FEM.	NEUTER	MASC./FEM.	NEUTER
NOM.	viridis	viride	viridēs	viridia
GEN.	viridis	viridis	viridium	viridium
DAT.	viridī	viridī	viridibus	viridibus
ACC.	viridem	viride	viridēs	viridia
ABL.	viridī	viridī	viridibus	viridibus
VOC.	viridis	viride	viridēs	viridia

Single termination Third Declension Adjectives will vary in their nominative. Because masculine, feminine, and neuter all share the same nominative, the dictionary will usually list the genitive so that you can find the stem. *Ingēns, -entis* means "huge" and is declined as follows:

	SINGULAR		PLURAL	
	MASC./FEM.	NEUTER	MASC./FEM.	NEUTER
NOM.	ingēns	ingēns	ingentēs	ingentia
GEN.	ingentis	ingentis	ingentium	ingentium
DAT.	ingentī	ingentī	ingentibus	ingentibus
ACC.	ingentem	ingēns	ingentēs	ingentia
ABL.	ingentī	ingentī	ingentibus	ingentibus
VOC.	ingēns	ingēns	ingentēs	ingentia

The masculine/feminine and neuter do share many of the same forms, but they are given separately in the chart above because of those few important differences. Notice how the Third Declension neuter adjectives follow our two neuter rules:

1. The nominative, accusative, and vocative endings are the same.

2. The nominative and accusative plurals end in *-a*.

All of these adjectives, no matter what their termination, can modify nouns of any declension. Remember that **an adjective must match the noun it modifies in gender, number, and case, but not necessarily in declension**.

We have already seen this with First/Second Declension nouns modifying nouns of First, Second, or Third Declension: *agricola malus, vir malus, draco malus*. Similarly, a Third

Declension Adjective can modify a First Declension noun: *nauta celer*, "swift sailor"; a Second Declension noun: *equus celer*, "swift horse"; or a Third Declension noun: *draco celer*, "swift dragon." The adjective simply must match the noun in gender, number, and case.

Here are a few example noun-adjective phrases fully declined. Jot down a few of your own adjective and noun pairs that match but are in different declensions.

draco celer, "swift dragon" (masculine)

	LATIN SINGULAR	LATIN PLURAL
NOM.	draco celer	dracōnēs celerēs
GEN.	dracōnis celeris	dracōnum celerium
DAT.	dracōnī celerī	dracōnibus celeribus
ACC.	dracōnem celerem	dracōnēs celerēs
ABL.	dracōne celerī	dracōnibus celeribus
VOC.	Ō draco celer	Ō dracōnēs celerēs

id crustulum ingēns, "that huge cookie" (neuter)

	LATIN SINGULAR	LATIN PLURAL
NOM.	id crustulum ingēns	ea crustula ingentia
GEN.	eius crustulī ingentis	eōrum crustulōrum ingentium
DAT.	eī crustulō ingentī	eīs crustulīs ingentibus
ACC.	id crustulum ingēns	ea crustula ingentia
ABL.	eō crustulō ingentī	eīs crustulīs ingentibus
VOC.	Ō crustulum ingēns	Ō crustula ingentia

fēmina fēlix, "lucky woman" (feminine)

	LATIN SINGULAR	LATIN PLURAL
NOM.	fēmina fēlix	fēminae fēlīcēs
GEN.	fēminae fēlīcis	fēminārum fēlīcium
DAT.	fēminae fēlīcī	fēminīs fēlīcibus
ACC.	fēminam fēlīcem	fēminās fēlīcēs
ABL.	fēminā fēlīcī	fēminīs fēlīcibus
VOC.	Ō fēmina fēlix	Ō fēminae fēlīcēs

Finally, keep in mind that Third Declension Adjectives are capable of all the things adjectives are capable of—they can act as substantives and predicates.

Substantive examples: *Omnēs Oswaldum dracōnemque vidērunt*, "All [people] saw Oswald and the dragon."

Here *omnēs* is masculine or feminine, nominative plural, and is acting as a noun (substantive). Another example would be *Omnia dēclārāvit*, "He declared all [things]"—*omnia* is neuter plural accusative.

This lesson may seem to be an overwhelming test of your ability to be logical and careful, but just keep the nouns or adjectives in the declensions they were born in and pay attention to their endings. If you need to, go back and review Lesson 7 on First/Second Declension adjectives.

Review

Be sure to review the perfect, pluperfect, and future perfect if you don't have those down cold. Also, keep working on the pronouns during this lesson.

Lesson 19 Worksheet

A. Vocabulary

Translate the following words from Latin to English or English to Latin as appropriate. For the verbs, also fill in the missing principal parts. For each preposition, include which case(s) it takes.

1. almost: _____

2. bōs: _____

3. augeō, _____, _____, _____: _____

4. ecce: _____

5. fish: _____

6. fēlix: _____

7. brevis: _____

8. donkey: _____

9. swift: _____

10. sea: _____

11. ingēns: _____

12. prope: (+ _____) _____

13. ergō: _____

14. unlucky: _____

15. dulcis: _____

16. enim: _____

17. altus: _____

18. strong: _____

19. between: _____

20. mediōcris: _____

21. I annoy: _____, _____, _____, _____

22. quia: _____

23. all: _____

24. potēns: _____

25. elephantus: _____

B. Grammar

1. Give a synopsis of *vexō* in the second person plural.

	LATIN	ENGLISH
PRESENT ACT.		
IMPERFECT ACT.		
FUTURE ACT.		
PERFECT ACT.		
PLUPERFECT ACT.		
FUTURE PERF. ACT.		

2. Decline *this brave king.*

	LATIN SINGULAR	LATIN PLURAL
NOM.		
GEN.		
DAT.		
ACC.		
ABL.		
VOC.		

3. Decline *green grass.*

	LATIN SINGULAR	LATIN PLURAL
NOM.		
GEN.		
DAT.		
ACC.		
ABL.		
VOC.		

4. Decline *powerful pirate.*

	LATIN SINGULAR	LATIN PLURAL
NOM.		
GEN.		
DAT.		
ACC.		
ABL.		
VOC.		

Identify and translate all possible options for the following pronouns. An example is given below.

	PHRASE	GENDER, NUMBER, CASE	TRANSLATION
	vallī mediōcrī	Fem. Sg. Dat. Fem. Sg. Abl.	to/for the ordinary valley by/with/from the ordinary valley
5.	fortēs asinōs		
6.	amōre fēlīcī		
7.	omnium urbium		
8.	crustula dulcia		
9	bōs celeris		
10.	populum potentem		
11.	proeliō brevī		

12.	ōrīs infēlīcibus		
13.	turrēs altās		
14.	piscis celeris		
15.	mare ingēns		
16.	gigās fēlix		
17.	fēminae dulcis		
18.	flōrī rubrō		
19.	avis nigra		

C. Memorization

Fill in the blanks.

_____

_____

_____

_____ _____ _____ nātum _____ omnia _____.

Deum _____ _____, _____ dē Lūmine, _____ vērum dē Deō _____,

_____, _____ factum, _____ _____: per _____ omnia

_____ sunt;

Quī _____ _____ hominēs _____ _____ nostram _____ _____

___ dē caelīs,

D. English to Latin Translation

Translate each sentence from English to Latin.

1. All the animals of the green forest loved the lucky man and sat at his feet.

   _____

   _____

2. Indeed, his donkeys kept ravaging our fields and therefore we seized his grain and swift horses.

   _____

   _____

3. The deep blue sea is huge and powerful, and you (pl.) fear it.

   _____

   _____

4. I watched the sweet daughter of the farmer when she was watching all his cattle, and I loved her.

   _____

   _____

5. The turrets of the castle were high and beautiful, and from them the king could see all his kingdom.

   _____

   _____

6. The brave man had hunted tigers and elephants in the black forest because he loved the powerful king's daughter.

   _____

   _____

7. We saw many swift fish where they were swimming in the waves of the sea.

   _____

8. The king's and queen's garments were purple and gold and glittering white, and their crowns shone.

   _____

   _____

9. I am the fierce enemy of your kingdom; fear me, everyone!

   _____

10. Grasses are green, the sky is blue; cookies are sweet, and I love you.

    _____

    _____

E. Latin to English Translation

1 **Pons[1] Asinōrum**

Ōlim erant trēs[2] frātres: Iūlius, Fabius, et Oswaldus.[3] Iulius postnatus[4] et mīles fortis erat. Is cum mīlitibus rēgis in terrā longinquā diū pugnāverat. Fabius medius[5] frāter erat, et is poēta infēlix erat. Nec pugnāvit nec labōrāvit, sed semper sedēbat et pōtābat et carmina misera dulciaque cantābat. Oswaldus

5 iuvenissimus[6] fīlius erat, et is cum matre eōrum viduātā[7] in agrō semper laborābat. Tempora mala in terrā erant, et eī nec cibum neque pecūniam nōn habuērunt. Ergō māter eōrum eīs āit: "Festīnāte ab agrō et trāns Pons Asinōrum. Ibī gigās brevis sed foedus sub ponte habitat, et omnibus enigma[8] rogat. Sī eī bene respondent, eīs multum aurum dat. Sī eī male respondent, eōs necat et mandūcat. Bene eī respondēte, meī fīliī, et tum pecūniam cibumque habēbimus!" Sed Fabius in villā sēdit et pōtāvit; itaque Oswaldus

10 ad pontem festīnāvit. Ibī stetit gigās brevis sed foedus, et rogāvit: "Quid[9] quattuor[10] crūrēs[11] mane,[12] duō[13] crurēs meridīe,[14] et trēs crūrēs vespere[14] habet?" Oswaldus cōgitāvit, et tum respondit: "Homō." Gigās īrātus erat, sed eī aurum dedit quod bene responderat. Itaque Oswaldus et māter frūmentum et cibum habēre potuērunt, sed Fabius pōtābat.

Glossary
1. *pons, pontis* (m): bridge (so, is it an i-stem?)
2. *trēs*: three
3. *Iūlius, Fabius,* and *Oswaldus* are all second declension names
4. *postnatus, -i* (m): oldest [son]
5. *medius, -a, -um*: middle (of)
6. *iuvenissimus, -a, -um*: youngest
7. *viduātā*: widowed, from the verb *viduō*

8. *enigma, -matis* (n): riddle
9. *quid*: what?
10. *quattuor*: four
11. *crūs, crūris* (m): leg
12. *mane*: in the morning
13. *duo*: two
14. *meridīe*: at noon
15. *vespere*: ablative of time when

_____

_____

_____

_____

_____

_____

_____

_____

_____

_____

_____

_____

F. For Fun: *Litterae Mixtae Comparātaeque*

Unscramble the letters in the left column to form a Latin adjective, then pair it with a noun from the list on the right to make a sensible phrase. You must use logic to match them all correctly since each adjective and noun can only be used once!

	SCRAMBLED LETTERS	UNSCRAMBLED LATIN ADJECTIVE	MATCHING NOUN
1.	bauls		
2.	mārutār		
3.	urōpperu		
4.	ilercse		
5	diviīr		
6.	caddian		
7.	aeīur		
8.	ēsculd		
9.	lsrceeīua		
10.	ōuumbrrr		

nox
moenia
hostium
navium
avibus
piscī
vallēs
elephantus
piscis
igne

LESSON 20

Verbs: Present, Imperfect & Future Passive Indicative

Word List

NOUNS

1. arbor, arboris (f): *tree*
2. cēna, -ae (f): *dinner, meal*
3. epulae, -ārum (f, pl.): *feast*
4. eques, -quitis (m): *knight, horseman, cavalryman*
5. matrimōnium, -ī (n): *marriage*
6. pastor, pastōris (m): *shepherd*

ADJECTIVES

7. ācer, ācris, ācre: *sharp, eager; fierce*
8. difficilis, -e: *difficult*
9. facilis, -e: *easy*
10. fessus, -a, -um: *tired, weary*
11. lātus, -a, -um: *wide, broad*
12. longus, -a, -um: *long*
13. tristis, -e: *sad, gloomy, dismal*
14. vīvus, -a, -um: *living*

VERBS

15. ardeō, ardēre, arsī, ——: *I burn, blaze*
16. mūtō (1): *I change*
17. properō (1): *I hurry, rush*

ADVERBS/CONJUNCTIONS

18. certātim: *eagerly*
19. minūtātim: *gradually, bit by bit*
20. sīcut: *as, just as, like*

Memorization

Crēdō in ūnum Deum, Patrem omnipotentem, Factōrem caelī et terrae,
   vīsibilium omnium et invīsibilium.

Et in ūnum Dominum Iēsum Christum, Fīlium Deī Ūnigenitum,

Et ex Patre nātum ante omnia saecula.

Deum dē Deō, Lūmen dē Lūmine, Deum vērum dē Deō vērō,

Genitum, nōn factum, consubstantiālem Patrī: per quem omnia facta sunt;

Quī propter nōs hominēs et propter nostram salūtem dēscendit dē caelīs,

Et incarnātus est dē Spīritū Sanctō ex Marīā virgine, et homō factus est.

   And was incarnate by the Holy Ghost of the virgin Mary, and was made man.

Crucīfīxus etiam prō nōbīs sub Pontiō Pīlātō; passus, et sepultus est,

   He was crucified also for us under Pontius Pilate; suffered, and was buried,

Grammar

Present, Imperfect, and Future Passive Indicative

This is rather an important lesson since we are going to introduce you to the passive voice in three of the six tenses! Recall that a verb has five attributes: person, number, tense, voice, and mood. So you have learned all persons (first, second, and third), both numbers (singular and plural), and six tenses (present, imperfect, future, perfect, pluperfect, future perfect), and several moods (indicative, imperative, and infinitive). However all of this has been in the active voice; now it's time to learn about the passive voice.

Consider the statement "Oswald killed the dragon." Can you turn that sentence into a passive, conveying similar meaning?

The correct answer would be "The dragon was killed by Oswald" or "The dragon has been killed by Oswald." If you guessed, "Oswald was killed by the dragon," this is actually the opposite of "Oswald killed the dragon." When a verb is in the active voice, the subject *performs* the action. When a verb is passive, the subject *receives* the action.

Now turn a verb of each tense from active into the passive:

Oswald loves the princess.

> *The princess is loved [is being loved] by Oswald.*

The pirates were singing many songs.

> *Many songs were being sung by the pirates.*

The enemy will attack our town.

> *Our town will be attacked by the enemy.*

The king gave the princess to Oswald in marriage.

> *The princess was given [has been given] by the king to Oswald in marriage.*

The angry goddess had changed him into a dog.

> *He had been changed into a dog by the angry goddess.*

The donkey will have carried great burdens to town.

> *Great burdens will have been carried to town by the donkey.*

In this lesson we will focus on the present passive system: present, imperfect, and future passive. Here are the chants:

Present Passive Indicative

	LATIN SINGULAR	ENGLISH SINGULAR	LATIN PLURAL	ENGLISH PLURAL
1ST	-r	I am (being) *verbed*	-mur	we are (being) *verbed*
2ND	-ris	you are (being) *verbed*	-minī	you (pl.) are (being) *verbed*
3RD	-tur	he/she/it is (being) *verbed*	-ntur	they are being *verbed*

Imperfect Passive Indicative

	LATIN SINGULAR	ENGLISH SINGULAR		LATIN PLURAL	ENGLISH PLURAL
1ST	**-bar**	I was (being) *verbed*		**-bāmur**	we were (being) *verbed*
2ND	**-bāris**	you were (being) *verbed*		**-bāminī**	you (pl.) were (being) *verbed*
3RD	**-bātur**	he/she/it was (being) *verbed*		**-bantur**	they were (being) *verbed*

Future Passive Indicative

	LATIN SINGULAR	ENGLISH SINGULAR		LATIN PLURAL	ENGLISH PLURAL
1ST	**-bor**	I will be *verbed*		**-bimur**	we will be *verbed*
2ND	**-beris**	you will be *verbed*		**-biminī**	you (pl.) will be *verbed*
3RD	**-bitur**	he/she/it will be *verbed*		**-buntur**	they will be *verbed*

Though this may seem like a lot, look carefully at the charts. Once you learn the present passive chant, you are well on your way to knowing the other two because the *-r, -ris, -tur,* etc. is also found at the end of the imperfect and future passive endings. Also, the passive endings are similar to the active endings: *-mus* becomes *-mur*, *-s* becomes *-ris*, *-t* becomes *-tur*, and *-nt* becomes *-ntur*. Finally, the tenses are the same: *-ba-* is the sign of the imperfect, whether active or passive, and *-bo-, -bi-,* and *-bu-* appear in the future in the same places (with the exception of *-beris* versus *-bis* in the second person singular).

To form the present, imperfect, or future passive, simply follow the method for forming their active equivalents. Go to the second principal part (the present active infinitive), remove the *-re*, and you have the present stem. Then you can add any of the endings above. *Necāre* and *vidēre* are conjugated below as examples from the First and Second Conjugations. As with the present active in the First Conjugation, the *ā* contracts with the *ō* and remains simply *ō*: *amō* (not *amaō*), "I love" and *amor* (not *amāor*), "I am loved." The stem vowel *ē* of the Second Conjugation, however, does not contract: *videō* becomes *videor*, etc.

Necō—First Conjugation Verb
Present Passive Indicative

	LATIN SINGULAR	ENGLISH SINGULAR		LATIN PLURAL	ENGLISH PLURAL
1ST	necor	I am (being) killed		necāmur	we are (being) killed
2ND	necāris	you are (being) killed		necāminī	you (pl.) are (being) killed
3RD	necātur	he/she/it is (being) killed		necantur	they are (being) killed

Imperfect Passive Indicative

	LATIN SINGULAR	ENGLISH SINGULAR		LATIN PLURAL	ENGLISH PLURAL
1ST	necābar	I was (being) killed		necābāmur	we were (being) killed
2ND	necābāris	you were (being) killed		necābāminī	you (pl.) were (being) killed
3RD	necābātur	he/she/it was (being) killed		necābantur	they were (being) killed

Future Passive Indicative

	LATIN SINGULAR	ENGLISH SINGULAR		LATIN PLURAL	ENGLISH PLURAL
1ST	necābor	I will be killed		necābimur	we will be killed
2ND	necāberis	you will be killed		necābiminī	you (pl.) will be killed
3RD	necābitur	he/she/it will be killed		necābuntur	they will be killed

Videō—Second Conjugation Verb*
Present Passive Indicative

	LATIN SINGULAR	ENGLISH SINGULAR		LATIN PLURAL	ENGLISH PLURAL
1ST	videor	I am (being) seen, I seem		vidēmur	we are (being) seen, we seem
2ND	vidēris	you are (being) seen, you seem		vidēminī	you (pl.) are (being) seen, you (pl.) seem
3RD	vidētur	he/she/it is (being) seen, he/she/it seems		videntur	they are being seen, they seem

Imperfect Passive Indicative

	LATIN SINGULAR	ENGLISH SINGULAR		LATIN PLURAL	ENGLISH PLURAL
1ST	vidēbar	I was (being) seen, I was seeming		vidēbāmur	we were (being) seen, we were seeming
2ND	vidēbāris	you were (being) seen, you were seeming		vidēbāminī	you (pl.) were (being) seen, you (pl.) were seeming
3RD	vidēbātur	he/she/it was (being) seen, he/she/it was seeming		vidēbantur	they were (being) seen, they were seeming

Future Passive Indicative

	LATIN SINGULAR	ENGLISH SINGULAR		LATIN PLURAL	ENGLISH PLURAL
1ST	vidēbor	I will be seen, I will seem		vidēbimur	we will be seen, we will seem
2ND	vidēberis	you will be seen, you will seem		vidēbiminī	you (pl.) will be seen, you (pl.) will seem
3RD	vidēbitur	he/she/it will be seen, he/she/it will seem		vidēbuntur	they will be seen, they will seem

One more concept that goes hand-in-hand with the passive: ablative of agent (with *ab*). All of the English examples above had an agent: Something was done by someone. To express that someone (the agent), use *ā* or *ab* plus the ablative (use *ab* if the word following begins with a vowel; either *ā* or *ab* if a consonant): *Draco ab Oswaldō necābātur*, "The dragon was being killed by Oswald." Remember that if it is a thing—not a person—performing the passive action, we can use our good old ablative of means/instrument: *Draco gladiō necābātur*, "The dragon was being killed by the sword."

* Note the special passive meaning of *videō*. It makes sense with an example such as: "He is seen to be happy" which is basically the same as "He seems to be happy."

Our favorite verb exercise, the synopsis, will now look a bit different:

ACTIVE			PASSIVE		
	LATIN	ENGLISH		LATIN	ENGLISH
PRES.	necāmus	we kill		necāmur	we are (being) killed
IMPF.	necābāmus	we were killing		necābāmur	we were (being) killed
FUT.	necābimus	we will kill		necābimur	we will be killed
PERF.	necāvimus	we (have) killed			
PLUPF.	necāverāmus	we had killed			
FT. PF.	necāverimus	we will have killed			

The perfect, pluperfect, and future perfect passives are in gray because they will not be taught until Lesson 6. When a portion of the synopsis is blacked out (i.e., in black, not gray), it means that that particular form does not exist in Latin.

Review

Be sure to review the third declension i-stem nouns and the adjective endings. Also, keep reviewing your pronouns.

Lesson 20 Worksheet

A. Vocabulary

Translate the following words from Latin to English or English to Latin as appropriate. For the verbs, also fill in the missing principal parts.

1. mūtō, _____, _____,

   _____: _____

2. ācer: _____

3. feast: _____

4. ardeō, _____, _____, _____:

   _____

5. fessus: _____

6. paene: _____

7. tree: _____

8. longus: _____

9. (dead) black: _____

10. marriage: _____

11. minūtātim: _____

12. facilis: _____

13. shepherd: _____

14. sī: _____

15. difficult: _____

16. cēna: _____

17. lātus: _____

18. properō, _____, properāvī,

    _____: _____

19. sīcut: _____

20. night: _____

21. vīvus: _____

22. omnis: _____

23. knight: _____

24. certātim: _____

25. tristis: _____

B. Grammar

Identify whether the main verbs of the following sentences are active or passive.

1. You had been eating ice cream for two hours. _____

2. His mother was sending many messengers to the faraway land. _____

3. I will not be seen by anyone. _____

4. After that we were told the truth. _____

5. The queen will listen to the bard's song. _____

6. By then I will have received the reward for capturing the pirate. _____

7. You were taken to the castle dungeon by the soldiers. _____

8. The grass is being trampled by the neighbor's goats. _____

9. He has been wounded horribly in the battle. _____

10. We have been poor but happy. _____

11. Give a synopsis of *mūtō* in the second person plural.

	ACTIVE		PASSIVE	
	LATIN	ENGLISH	LATIN	ENGLISH
PRES.				
IMPF.				
FUT.				
PERF.				
PLUPF.				
FT. PF.				

12. Give a synopsis of *vastō* in the first person singular.

	ACTIVE		PASSIVE	
	LATIN	ENGLISH	LATIN	ENGLISH
PRES.				
IMPF.				
FUT.				
PERF.				
PLUPF.				
FT. PF.				

13. Give a synopsis of *moveō* in the third person plural.

	ACTIVE		PASSIVE	
	LATIN	ENGLISH	LATIN	ENGLISH
PRES.				
IMPF.				
FUT.				
PERF.				
PLUPF.				
FT. PF.				

C. Memorization

Fill in the blanks.

_____

_____

_____

Deum _____ _____, _____ dē Lūmine, _____ vērum dē _____ _____,

_____, nōn _____, _____ Patrī: _____ _____

_____ facta _____;

Quī _____ _____ hominēs ____ _____ nostram _____

   dēscendit _____ _____,

_____ incarnātus _____ dē Spīritū _____ ex Marīā _____, et _____

   factus est.

_____ etiam prō _____ sub _____ Pīlātō; _____, et sep-

   ultus _____,

D. English to Latin Translation

Translate each sentence from English to Latin.

1. Our land was being burned by the dragon; the trees were blazing and the fields dried up.

   _____

   _____

2. The river is wide, the road is long, and the journey will seem difficult.

   _____

3. I love the handsome pirate, but I am not loved by him.

   _____

4. Bit by bit all of the huge dinner is being eaten by the short and small boy.

   _____

   _____

5. When will glory and praise be given to the true king

   _____

6. The bad sailor was drinking much wine and then purple elephants were seen by him.

   _____

   _____

7. There will be a marriage between you and the king's daughter, and a great feast will be eaten.

   _____

   _____

   _____

8. The great battle was being fought and now all the knights and soldiers are weary.

   _____

   _____

9. Great and horrible things were predicted by the strange woman in the dark cave.

   _____

   _____

10. On the high mountain we were being hunted by the giant, and therefore we hastened eagerly to the castle.

    _____

    _____

E. Latin to English Translation

1 **Apollō et Daphne**

Ōlim erat nympha[1] pulchra, fīlia deī flūminis. Daphne[2] appellābātur. Ea virōs nōn amābat, quod
Cupīdō,[3] deus amōris, eam in corde sagittā plumbeā[4] petīverat.[5] Ea autem ab Apolline[6] certātim
amābātur, quod is ab Cupīdine sagittā aureā petēbātur. Sīcut Diāna,[7] soror Apollinis, Daphne silvās
5 amāvit et in eīs semper erat. Apollō ad eam ibī festīnāvit et eī verba amōris cantāvit: "Ō Daphne
pulchra, ego nec agricola nec miser sum—deus sum! Ego tibī amōre ardeō! Erit mātrimōnium inter
nōs?" Daphne eī nōn respondit, sed ab eō festīnāvit. Et Apollō properāvit, et eam captāvit sīcut
leō cervum captat. Ea fessa erat, et victōria Apollinī ab Cupīdine dabātur, sed Daphne patrī deō
flūminis clamāvit: "O pater! Mē nunc servā!" Clāmor[8] eius audiēbātur,[9] et ea in arborem pulchram
10 minutatim mutabātur. Apollō, "Tū esse uxor[10] mea nōn potes," āit, "sed tū arbor meus eris! Folia[11]
tua sīcut corōna multīs dabuntur, et tū laudem glōriamque daberis." Itaque laurus[12] arbor Apollinis
semper erit.

Glossary

1. *nympha, -ae* (f): nymph
2. *Daphne, -ēs* (f): Daphne
3. *Cupīdō, -dinis* (m): Cupid (son of Venus and god of love)
4. *plumbeus, -a, -um*: leaden, of lead
5. *petō, -ere, -īvī, -ītum*: I shoot
6. *Apollō, -inis* (m): Apollo (god of prophesy, music, archery, the sun, etc.)
7. *Diāna, -ae* (f): Diana, virgin goddess of the moon and hunting
8. *clāmor, -ōris* (m): shout, cry
9. *audiō, -īre, -īvī, -itum*: I hear
10. *uxor, -ōris* (f): wife
11. *folium, -ī* (n): leaf
12. *laurus, -ī* (f): laurel-tree

LESSON 21
Numerals / Review of Present Passive System

Word List

ROMAN	CARDINAL	ENGLISH
I	ūnus, -a, -um	one
II	duo, duae, duo	two
III	trēs, tria	three
IV (IIII)	quattuor	four
V	quīnque	five
VI	sex	six
VII	septem	seven
VIII	octō	eight
IX	novem	nine
X	decem	ten
XI	ūndecim	eleven
XII	duodecim	twelve

XIII	tredecim	thirteen
XIV (XIIII)	quattuordecim	fourteen
XV	quīndecim	fifteen
XVI	sēdecim	sixteen
XVII	septendecim	seventeen
XVIII	duodēvīgintī	eighteen
XIX (XVIIII)	ūndēvīgintī	nineteen
XX	vīgintī	twenty
XXI	vīgintī ūnus (ūnus et vīgintī)	twenty-one
L	quīnquāgintā	fifty
C	centum	one hundred
D	quīngentī	five hundred
M	mīlle	one thousand

Memorization

Crēdō in ūnum Deum, Patrem omnipotentem, Factōrem caelī et terrae, vīsibilium omnium et invīsibilium.

Et in ūnum Dominum Iēsum Christum, Fīlium Deī Ūnigenitum,

Et ex Patre nātum ante omnia saecula.

Deum dē Deō, Lūmen dē Lūmine, Deum vērum dē Deō vērō,

Genitum, nōn factum, consubstantiālem Patrī: per quem omnia facta sunt;

Quī propter nōs hominēs et propter nostram salūtem dēscendit dē caelīs,

Et incarnātus est dē Spīritū Sanctō ex Marīā virgine, et homō factus est.

Crucīfixus etiam prō nōbīs sub Pontiō Pīlātō; passus, et sepultus est,

Et resurrēxit tertiā die, secundum Scriptūrās, et ascendit in caelum, sedet ad dexteram Patris.

> *And He rose again on the third day, according to the Scriptures, and ascended into heaven, [and] sits at the right hand of the Father.*

Et iterum ventūrus est cum glōriā, iūdicāre vīvōs et mortuōs, cuius regnī nōn erit fīnis.

> *And He will come again with glory, to judge the living and the dead, whose kingdom shall have no end.*

Grammar

Numerals

In this lesson we will be learning about cardinal numerals, that is, the normal numbers like one, two, three, etc. Happily, most cardinal numerals are indeclinable. This means that you only need to learn the chants for *ūnus, duo, trēs*, and the plural of *mīlle*, and that's it!

Numbers are adjectives, and only the first four numbers actually decline. As adjectives, numbers will match the nouns they modify in gender, number, and case.

Here are the declensions of these numbers, with the odd forms in bold:

	SINGULAR				PLURAL		
	MASCULINE	FEMININE	NEUTER		MASCULINE	FEMININE	NEUTER
NOM.	ūnus	ūna	ūnum		**duo**	duae	**duo**
GEN.	**ūnīus**	**ūnīus**	**ūnīus**		duōrum	duārum	duōrum
DAT.	**ūnī**	**ūnī**	**ūnī**		duōbus	duābus	duōbus
ACC.	ūnum	ūnam	ūnum		duōs	duās	**duo**
ABL.	ūnō	ūnā	ūnō		duōbus	duābus	duōbus

Notice that *ūnus* has a genitive and dative that look similar to the third person pronoun *is, ea, id* endings. The other forms are fairly regular. Also—although this probably should go with saying—*ūnus* only has a singular because it means "one" (which cannot be plural), and *duo* and the rest only have plurals because, well, they are plural by nature.

	PLURAL			SINGULAR	PLURAL
	M/F	N		M/F/N	N
NOM.	trēs	tria		mīlle	mīlia
GEN.	trium	trium		mīlle	mīlium
DAT.	tribus	tribus		mīlle	mīlibus
ACC.	trēs	tria		mīlle	mīlia
ABL.	tribus	tribus		mīlle	mīlibus

Note that although in the singular *mīlle* is indeclinable, in the plural it is not (and it loses one *l*). Also, the singular *mīlle* functions as an adjective while the plural *mīlia* is a Third Declension neuter i-stem noun. Just as in English, we say "thousands of his soldiers," in Latin you can use a genitive (called the partitive genitive or genitive of the whole)—*mīlia mīlitum eius*. With other cardinals you will generally use a preposition such as *ex* or *dē—ūnus ex mīlitibus eius*, "one of his soldiers."

Review

Be sure to review the present, imperfect, and future passive endings that you learned in the last lesson, and be sure to review the Third Declension i-stem nouns and adjective endings. Don't lose what you've learned!

Lesson 21 Worksheet

A. Vocabulary

Read each problem *carefully* and answer with the correct number in the correct format.

1. Count to twenty in Latin using only *even cardinal* numbers:

   _____

   _____

2. Count to twenty-one in Latin using only *odd Roman* numerals:

   _____

   _____

3. My neighbor Iulius was born in MCMLIX, and his wife Livia in MCMLXIII. Who is older? By how much?

   _____

   _____

4. In what year were you born? (Give Roman and Arabic numerals.)

   _____

5. How old are you? (Answer with a Latin cardinal number.)

   _____

6. If your favorite book were written in 1818, in Roman numerals that year would be

   _____

7. *Duodēvīgintī* plus *quīngentī* plus *septem* minus *quattuor* equals (give Latin cardinal):

   _____

8. God gave _____ Commandments to Moses for the _____ tribes to observe (give both Latin cardinals and Roman numerals).

9. L minus XXXVII plus CIX minus VI equals (give Roman numeral):

   _____

10. There are _____ pennies to a nickel,

    _____ nickels to a dime,

    _____ quarters to a dollar, and

    _____ minutes in a quarter of an hour (give Latin cardinals only).

B. Grammar

1. Decline *one turret.*

	LATIN SINGULAR
NOM.	
GEN.	
DAT.	
ACC.	
ABL.	
VOC.	

2. Decline *two shepherds.*

	LATIN PLURAL
NOM.	
GEN.	
DAT.	
ACC.	
ABL.	
VOC.	

3. Decline *three wounds.*

	LATIN PLURAL
NOM.	
GEN.	
DAT.	
ACC.	
ABL.	
VOC.	

4. Give a synopsis of *oppugnō* in the second person plural.

	ACTIVE		PASSIVE	
	LATIN	ENGLISH	LATIN	ENGLISH
PRES.				
IMPF.				
FUT.				
PERF.				
PLUPF.				
FT. PF.				

C. Memorization

Fill in the blanks.

_____

_____

_____

_____

_____

_____

_____

_____ propter _____ hominēs _____ _____ nostram _____

_____ dē _____,

_____ _____ est _____ _____ Sanctō _____ _____ _____,

et homō _____ _____.

_____ etiam _____ _____ sub _____ Pīlātō; _____, _____

sepultus _____,

Et _____ tertiā _____, secundum _____, et _____

in _____, _____ _____ dexteram _____.

_____ iterum _____ est cum _____ iūdicāre _____

et _____, cuius r_____nōn erit _____.

E. Translation

Translate each sentence from English to Latin.

1. You will give five beautiful black horses to the king, and they will be praised by him.

   _____

   _____

2. All the king's horses and all the king's men could not save this one wretched man.

   _____

   _____

3. Two of his daughters were seen in the forest by three soldiers.

   _____

   _____

4. Our Lord gave food to thousands and then good words were spoken by Him.

   _____

   _____

5. The blessed farmer lived at the foot of the purple mountains and had one beautiful wife, six happy children, and eight large dogs.

   _____

   _____

6. Five hundred cookies were eaten by the greedy children in your town yesterday.

   _____

   _____

7. The king and queen will give a great feast to fifty of the knights because three ugly giants were killed by them.

   _____

   _____

8. There are twenty tall turrets in my castle, but five of them are gloomy.

_____

_____

9. We were hunting twelve deer in the dark forest but were seen by one of them and they all hastened away from us.

_____

_____

10. I am a beautiful woman and am loved by two farmers; however, my one heart will be given to the handsome pirate.

_____

_____

D. Latin to English Translation

Fābula Īōnis

1   Ōlim erat deus flūminis, nōmine Īnachus.[1] Multōs līberōs tenēbat—fortasse[2] quīnque, fortasse septem. Ūna ex fīliābus eius erat Īō[3] pulchra. Ea ab Iove[4] amābātur et certātim captābātur, sed ab eō festīnāvit. Nōn autem occultāre[5] potuit et ab eō occupābātur. Iuppiter Iūnōnem timuit, et Īō ergō in candidam

5   bovem pulchram mūtābātur. Iūno[6] bovem vīdit et suspīciōsa[7] erat—itaque dēclārāvit: "Dā mihi eam bovem!" Quod Iuppiter eam timuit, eī Īōnem bovem dedit. Īō ab Argō,[8] gigante antīquō centum cum oculīs, tum spectābātur. Duo ad montem longinquum horrendumque ambulāvērunt ubi Argus eam semper spectābat. Īō misera erat, et miser Iuppiter. Ergō Mercuriō[9] rogāvit: "Tū Īōnem servābis? Argum necā!" Mercurius ad montem volāvit, et in pastōrem mūtābātur. Is Argō avēnīs[10] cantāvit. Ūnus ex centum

10   oculīs dormīvit,[11] tum alius.[12] Dēnique omnēs centum oculī dormīvērunt. Tum Mercurius Argum gladiō necāvit et Īō liberābātur. Iūno tristis erat, et oculōs Argī in caudā[13] avis cārae, pāvōnis,[14] collocāvit.[15] Et īrāta erat, et Īōnem miseram per mundum captābat. Dēnique Iuppiter Iūnōnem clēmentiam[16] rogāvit. Et quattuor crūra[17] bovis in duo crūra hominis mūtābātur—et Īō fēmina nunc erat.

Glossary

1. *Īnachus, -ī* (m): Inachus, god of the Inachus River in Argos
2. *fortasse:* perhaps
3. *Īō, -ōnis* (f): Io, a beautiful nymph and daughter of Inachus
4. *Iuppiter, Iovis* (m): Jupiter/Jove, king of the gods; called Zeus by the Greeks
5. *occultō* (1): I hide
6. *Iūno, -ōnis* (f): Juno, queen of the gods and wife of Jupiter; called Hera by the Greeks
7. *suspīciōsus, -a, -um:* suspicious
8. *Argus, -ī* (m): Argus, a hundred-eyed giant (*oculus, -ī* (m): eye)
9. *Mercurius, -ī* (m): Mercury, the messenger god
10. *avēna, -ae* (f): pan pipe, shepherd's pipe
11. *dormiō, -īre, -īvī, ītum:* I sleep
12. *alius, alia, aliud:* another, other
13. *cauda, -ae* (f): tail
14. *pāvō, -ōnis* (m): peacock
15. *collocō* (1): I place, set, arrange
16. *clēmentia, -ae* (f): mercy, clemency
17. *crūs, crūris* (n): leg

F. Lūdus Numerōrum

To play:

1. The numbers I–IX must appear once in each column.

2. I–IX must also appear once in each row.

3. I–IX can only appear once in each 3x3 box in the grid.

	I		VI			VII	II	IV
VI			IX		II		VIII	
II	IV	VIII	I		V		VI	
	II	VII		V		VI		III
VIII		I		IX		II		VII
	IX		IV	II	VII	VIII		
VII	III					I	V	VIII
I		IX	V	VIII	III			
		II		I	IV		III	VI

Thanks to www.sudokukingdom.com for the arabic numeral version of this puzzle.

Lesson 22

Perfect, Pluperfect & Future Perfect Passive Indicative

Word List

NOUNS

1. amita, -ae (f): *aunt*

2. avia, -ae (f): *grandmother*

3. avunculus, -ī (m): *uncle (mother's brother)*

4. avus, -ī (m): *grandfather, ancestor*

5. coniūnx, -iugis (m/f): *husband, wife*

6. consōbrīnus, -ī (m) *or* consōbrīna, -ae (f): *cousin (mother's side)*

7. familia, -ae (f): *household, family*

8. mulier, mulieris (f): *woman*

9. orbus, -ī (m) *or* orba, -ae (f): *orphan*

10. patruēlis, -is (m/f): *cousin (father's side)*

11. patruus, -ī (m): *uncle (father's brother)*

12. vidua, -ae (f): *widow*

ADJECTIVES

13. orbus, -a, -um: *deprived of parents or children, bereft*

14. vērus, -a, -um: *true*

VERBS

15. iuvō, -āre, iūvī, iūtum: *I help*

16. gaudeō, -ēre, gāvīsus sum: *I rejoice*

17. labōrō (1): *I work*

18. occultō (1): *I hide, conceal*

ADVERBS/CONJUNCTIONS

19. deinde: *from that place, then, thereupon, next*

20. etiam: *even, also, besides, still*

INTERJECTIONS

21. heu (eheu): *alas! oh! (expressing grief or pain)*

Memorization

Crēdō in ūnum Deum, Patrem omnipotentem, Factōrem caelī et terrae, vīsibilium omnium et invīsibilium.

Et in ūnum Dominum Iēsum Christum, Fīlium Deī Ūnigenitum,

Et ex Patre nātum ante omnia saecula.

Deum dē Deō, Lūmen dē Lūmine, Deum vērum dē Deō vērō,

Genitum, nōn factum, consubstantiālem Patrī: per quem omnia facta sunt;

Quī propter nōs hominēs et propter nostram salūtem dēscendit dē caelīs,

Et incarnātus est dē Spīritū Sanctō ex Marīā virgine, et homō factus est.

Crucifīxus etiam prō nōbīs sub Pontiō Pīlātō; passus, et sepultus est,

Et resurrēxit tertiā die, secundum Scriptūrās, et ascendit in caelum, sedet ad dexteram Patris.

Et iterum ventūrus est cum glōriā, iūdicāre vīvōs et mortuōs, cuius regnī nōn erit fīnis.

Et in Spīritum Sanctum, Dominum et vīvificantem: Quī ex Patre Fīliōque prōcēdit.

And [I believe] in the Holy Ghost, the Lord and Giver of Life: Who proceeds from the Father and the Son.

Quī cum Patre et Fīliō simul adōrātur et conglōrificātur: Quī locūtus est per prophētās.

Who with the Father and the Son together is worshipped and glorified: Who spoke by the prophets.

Grammar

Perfect, Pluperfect, and Future Perfect Passive Indicative

By now you should be fairly solid on the present passive system—present, imperfect, and future tense. All of these are formed using the second principal part. In this lesson we add the perfect passive system—perfect, pluperfect, and future perfect. All of these are formed using the fourth principal part.

Consider *necō necāre necāvī necātum*. The fourth principal part is the perfect passive participle, and it is used to form the perfect passive verb system. A participle is a verbal adjective, and thus can modify a noun or pronoun in gender, number, and case. For instance, in English if we take the verb "I kill" and make it an adjective, it becomes "killing" in the present or "killed" in the past. Rather than functioning as a verb, it functions as an adjective. For example, "That kraken is a killing machine" or "the killed men were buried." In both cases the participle modifies the noun, which shows that it's not really a verb, but is actually an adjective.

The full form of the perfect passive participle is actually *necātus, -a, -um* (masculine, feminine, and neuter—looks like an adjective, doesn't it?). For convenience, in this book I have listed the neuter form by way of abbreviation; some dictionaries will simply give the masculine form.

Take a moment to consider some English passive indicatives: *The dragon was killed, the dragon had been killed, the dragon will have been killed.* Notice that English requires the use of helping verbs to form the passive: *was* for the perfect, *had* and *been* for the pluperfect, and the whopping *will have been* for the future perfect. Similarly, Latin perfect passives will use the "helping verb" *sum* along with the fourth principal part.

For the perfect tense, simply take the fourth principal part of the verb, and conjugate it with the present chant of *sum*:

Perfect Passive Indicative of *necō*

	LATIN SINGULAR	ENGLISH SINGULAR		LATIN PLURAL	ENGLISH PLURAL
1ST	necātus/a/um sum	I was/have been killed		necātī/ae/a sumus	we were/have been killed
2ND	necātus/a/um es	you were/have been killed		necātī/ae/a estis	you (pl.) were/have been killed
3RD	necātus/a/um est	he/she/it was/has been killed		necātī/ae/a sunt	they were/have been killed

Notice that we will only use the nominative forms of the participle, because these adjectives are functioning as predicate adjectives with *sum*—they must agree with the case of the subject (which will always be nominative). They must also agree with the subject in number; thus the plurals have the plural nominative form of the adjective—*necātī, -ae, -a*. And finally, these verbs show us the gender of their subjects (which can be very helpful). A few examples:

Draco necātus est.	*The dragon has been killed.*
Avis necāta est.	*The bird has been killed.*
Animal necātum est.	*The animal has been killed.*
Dracōnēs necātī sunt.	*The dragons have been killed.*
Avēs necātae sunt.	*The birds have been killed.*
Animālia necāta sunt.	*The animals have been killed.*

Once you have understood how the perfect passives work, the next two tenses should follow easily and logically. The pluperfect passive will be conjugated with the imperfect of *sum*, and the future perfect passive with the future of *sum*.

Pluperfect Passive Indicative of *necō*

	LATIN SINGULAR	ENGLISH SINGULAR		LATIN PLURAL	ENGLISH PLURAL
1ST	necātus/a/um eram	I had been killed		necātī/ae/a erāmus	we had been killed
2ND	necātus/a/um erās	you had been killed		necātī/ae/a erātis	you (pl.) had been killed
3RD	necātus/a/um erat	he/she/it had been killed		necātī/ae/a erant	they had been killed

Future Perfect Passive Indicative of *necō*

	LATIN SINGULAR	ENGLISH SINGULAR		LATIN PLURAL	ENGLISH PLURAL
1ST	necātus/a/um erō	I will have been killed		necātī/ae/a erimus	we will have been killed
2ND	necātus/a/um eris	you will have been killed		necātī/ae/a eritis	you (pl.) will have been killed
3RD	necātus/a/um erit	he/she/it will have been killed		necātī/ae/a erunt	they will have been killed

And now our example sentences using these tenses:

Draco necātus erat.	*The dragon had been killed.*
Avis necāta erat.	*The bird had been killed.*
Animal necātum erat.	*The animal had been killed.*
Dracōnēs necātī erant.	*The dragons had been killed.*
Avēs necātae erant.	*The birds had been killed.*
Animālia necāta erant.	*The animals had been killed.*

Draco necātus erit.	*The dragon will have been killed.*
Avis necāta erit.	*The bird will have been killed.*
Animal necātum erit.	*The animal will have been killed.*
Dracōnēs necātī erunt.	*The dragons will have been killed.*
Avēs necātae erunt.	*The birds will have been killed.*
Animālia necāta erunt.	*The animals will have been killed.*

A reminder on the future perfect passive, third person plural: remember that when *erō* is a word, the third person plural is *erunt*; when it's an ending, it's -*erint*. Because *sum* is the helping word for participles, it will be *erunt*.

Our verb synopsis in the indicative is now complete, and will look like this:

	ACTIVE			PASSIVE	
	LATIN	ENGLISH		LATIN	ENGLISH
PRES.	necō	I kill		necor	I am (being) killed
IMPF.	necābam	I was killing		necābar	I was (being) killed
FUT.	necābō	I will kill		necābor	I will be killed
PERF.	necāvī	I (have) killed		necātus/a/um sum	I was/have been killed
PLUPF.	necāveram	I had killed		necātus/a/um eram	I had been killed
FT. PF.	necāverō	I will have killed		necātus/a/um erō	I will have been killed

Review

Make sure you review the numbers you learned last time, perhaps counting actual items in your house. Also, make sure you review those pesky perfect, pluperfect, and future perfect active endings, as well as the present, imperfect, and future perfect passives. We're going to add more to our synopses soon!

Lesson 22 Worksheet

A. Vocabulary

Translate the following words from Latin to English or English to Latin as appropriate.

1. aunt: _____

2. sixteen: _____

3. gaudeō: _____

4. I hide: _____

5. mother's brother: _____

6. father's brother: _____

7. vestis: _____

8. avus: _____

9. I help: _____

10. sweet: _____

11. female cousin (mother's side): _____

12. labōrō: _____

13. mulier: _____

14. etiam: _____

15. grandmother: _____

16. male cousin (father's side): _____

17. orphan: _____

18. sīcut: _____

19. alas: _____

20. vidua: _____

21. true: _____

22. coniūnx: _____

23. deinde: _____

24. hyacinthinus: _____

25. household: _____

B. Grammar

1. Give a synopsis of *iuvō* in the third person plural.

	ACTIVE		PASSIVE	
	LATIN	ENGLISH	LATIN	ENGLISH
PRES.				
IMPF.				
FUT.				
PERF.				
PLUPF.				
FT. PF.				

2. Give a synopsis of *removeō* in the second person singular.

	ACTIVE			PASSIVE	
	LATIN	ENGLISH		LATIN	ENGLISH
PRES.					
IMPF.					
FUT.					
PERF.					
PLUPF.					
FT. PF.					

3. Draw your family tree below. Label your mother, father, grandparents, aunts, uncles, and cousins using your Latin family vocabulary. **Answers will vary.**

4. Count to twenty twice—first with Roman numerals, then with Latin cardinals.

Roman numerals: _____

_____

Latin cardinals: _____

_____

_____

_____

C. Memorization

Fill in the blanks.

_____

_____

_____

_____

_____

_____

_____

_____

_____

_____

_____

_____

_____

_____ _____ tertiā _____, _____ Scriptūrās, _____

_____ in _____, sedet ad _____ _____.

_____ iterum _____ est cum _____, _____ _____et mortuōs,

_____ regnī nōn _____ _____.

Et ____ Spīritum _____, _____ et vīvificantem: _____   ex   Patre

_____ _____.

_____ cum _____ et Fīliō _____ adōrātur _____ _____:

Quī _____ est per _____.

D. English to Latin Translation

Translate each sentence from English to Latin.

1. Three krakens had been seen in the dark and purple waves, but we still sailed to the unlucky island.

   _____

   _____

2. Tomorrow, if the dragon will have been killed, the king's daughter will be given to the knight in marriage.

   _____

   _____

3. The five wretched orphans were carried to the farmhouse and we helped them there.

   _____

   _____

4. My aunt once watched the centaurs' feast because she had hidden among the tall trees of the forest.

   _____

   _____

5. Soon all the cookies will have been eaten and all the milk will have been drunk by the nine cousins.

   _____

   _____

6. Thousands of eager soldiers rushed to the castle because the enemy's ships had been seen on the shore.

   _____

   _____

7. My father has four brothers; these men are my uncles and they all work in our fields.

   _____

   _____

8. The poor widow's horses had been seized by the evil pirates, and all her gold besides was carried to their cave.

   _____

   _____

9. The weary farmers were rejoicing because the crops had been carried from the fields.

   _____

   _____

10. You had been seen with the wild sailors by our grandfather, and he was not happy.

_____

_____

E. Latin to English Translation

1 **Porcus Mediōcris**

Mediōcris sum. Mea familia magna est, et in eā multī fortēs potentēsque sunt. Avus meus ūnus ex equitibus rēgis erat, et contrā dracōnēs, gigantēs, et hostēs bene pugnābat. Venēnō cētī dēnique necātus est. Trēs avunculī meī nautae sunt, et in septem maribus nāvigāvērunt. Pater meus mīles magnus est,
5 et māter mea docta mulier et consōbrīna rēgīnae est. Etiam sorōrēs meae duae pulchrae sunt et bene cantant; duōbus dominīs magnīs in patriā in mātrimōniō datae sunt. Sed ego mediōcris sum. Nōmen meum est Eduardus.[1] Spectō porcōs familiae, et eīs cibum dat. Herī autem ūnus ex porcīs mihi ōrāvit: "Tū, puer, mē līberā et tibī multum aurum dabō!" Respondī, "Porcus es. Quōmodo[2] aurum tenēre potes?" Porcus autem ōrāvit, "Mē līberā! Tē ad spēluncam dīvitiārum portābō." Ergō, ab porcō per agrōs et ab
10 villā familiae meae portātus sum. Omnēs rīsērunt; etiam equī bōvēsque rīsērunt. Ego cōgitābam, "Sī is porcus vēra nōn ōrat, eum necābō et mandūcābō." Porcus in Silvam Tristem properāvit et mē ad ōs spēluncae portāvit. Intrāvī, et ecce! Mīlia nummōrum[3] aureōrum in spēluncā occultāta erant! "Decem nummī tuī erunt," porcus āit, "sed sī mē pugnābis et necābis, omnēs habēbis." "Tē nec pugnābō nec necābō," respondī. "Laetus cum decem nummīs sum." Porcus in virginem pulchram repentē mutātus
15 est. "Ego," ea āit, "ūnica[4] fīlia rēgis sum. In porcum ab malā novercā[5] meā mutāta sum. Quod avārus nōn erās, carmen[6] dēlētum est!" Nunc ego, Eduardus mediōcris, coniugem pulchram et milia nummōrum aureōrum et regnum teneō.

Glossary
1. _Eduardus:_ a 2nd declension name
2. _quōmodo:_ how? in what way?
3. _nummus, -ī_ (m): coin
4. _ūnicus, -a, -um:_ one, only, sole
5. _noverca, -ae_ (f): step-mother
6. _carmen_ can also mean "spell, enchantment"

_____

_____

_____

_____

_____

_____

_____

LESSON 23
More Numerals: Ordinals

Word List

ROMAN NUMERALS	CARDINALS	ENGLISH	ORDINALS	ENGLISH
I	ūnus, -a, -um	one	prīmus, -a, -um	first
II	duo, duae, duo	two	secundus	second
III	trēs, tria	three	tertius	third
IV (IIII)	quattuor	four	quārtus	fourth
V	quīnque	five	quīntus	fifth
VI	sex	six	sextus	sixth
VII	septem	seven	septimus	seventh
VIII	octō	eight	octāvus	eighth
IX	novem	nine	nōnus	ninth
X	decem	ten	decimus	tenth
XI	ūndecim	eleven	ūndecimus	eleventh
XII	duodecim	twelve	duodecimus	twelfth
XIII	tredecim	thirteen	tertius decimus	thirteenth
XIV (XIIII)	quattuordecim	fourteen	quārtus decimus	fourteenth
XV	quīndecim	fifteen	quīntus decimus	fifteenth
XVI	sēdecim	sixteen	sextus decimus	sixteenth
XVII	septendecim	seventeen	septimus decimus	seventeenth
XVIII	duodēvīgintī	eighteen	duodēvīcēsimus	eighteenth
XIX (XVIIII)	ūndēvīgintī	nineteen	ūndēvīcēsimus	nineteenth
XX	vīgintī	twenty	vīcēsimus	twentieth
XXI	vīgintī ūnus (ūnus et vīgintī)	twenty-one	vīcēsimus prīmus	twenty-first
L	quīnquāgintā	fifty	quīnquāgēsimus	fiftieth
C	centum	one hundred	centēsimus	one hundredth
D	quīngentī	five hundred	quīngentēsimus	five hundredth
M	mīlle	one thousand	mīllēsimus	one thousandth

Memorization

Crēdō in ūnum Deum, Patrem omnipotentem, Factōrem caelī et terrae, vīsibilium omnium et invīsibilium.

Et in ūnum Dominum Iēsum Christum, Fīlium Deī Ūnigenitum,

Et ex Patre nātum ante omnia saecula.

Deum dē Deō, Lūmen dē Lūmine, Deum vērum dē Deō vērō,

Genitum, nōn factum, consubstantiālem Patrī: per quem omnia facta sunt;

Quī propter nōs hominēs et propter nostram salūtem dēscendit dē caelīs,

Et incarnātus est dē Spīritū Sanctō ex Mariā virgine, et homō factus est.

Crucifīxus etiam prō nōbīs sub Pontiō Pīlātō; passus, et sepultus est,

Et resurrēxit tertiā die, secundum Scriptūrās, et ascendit in caelum, sedet ad dexteram Patris.

Et iterum ventūrus est cum glōriā, iūdicāre vīvōs et mortuōs, cuius regnī nōn erit fīnis.

Et in Spiritum Sanctum, Dominum et vivificantem: Quī ex Patre Fīlioque prōcēdit.

Quī cum Patre et Fīliō simul adōrātur et conglōrificātur: Quī locūtus est per prophētās.

Et ūnam, sanctam, catholicam et apostolicam ecclēsiam.

And in one, holy, catholic, and apostolic church.

Confiteor ūnum baptisma in remissiōnem peccātōrum.

I confess one baptism for the remission of sins.

Et expectō resurrectiōnem mortuōrum, et vītam ventūrī saeculī. Āmēn.

And I look for the resurrection of the dead, and the life of the world to come. Amen.

Grammar

Ordinal Numbers

In order to let the passive voice settle in, this lesson is a cinch. Your have already learned cardinal numbers for counting (*ūnus, duo, trēs*, etc.); now we will add the ordinal numbers, which are for putting things in their proper order: first, second, third, and so on. Even though I only listed *primus* as having -*us*, -*a*, -*um* endings, all of them decline as -*us*, -*a*, -*um* adjectives, so nothing too worrisome there.

Don't get confused: these are adjectives, not adverbs. Thus, if you wanted to say "First I did this, and second I did that," you would need to use adverbs (*primum* or *primō* for "first," *secundō* or *deinde* for "second"). Neither are ordinal numbers fractions! *Tertius* means "third" as in "third place," not as in "one-third cup of flour."

Finally, I want to briefly explain Roman numerals, in case you've never encountered them before or if you need a little review. The Romans liked to count toward a certain number (5, 10, 15, 20, etc.), and then phrase the number just before it in terms of subtraction. Thus we have the capital I's building up for 1 (I), 2 (II), and 3 (III), but then the number 4 is written as IV, "one before 5", since 5 is represented by the letter V. (Just to keep you on your toes, sometimes they'd write the number 4 with 4 IIII's.) Now we'll count toward ten (X), but using our V so we don't have to write so many capital I's: 6 (VI), 7 (VII), 8 (VIII), and then 9 is written as "one before ten" (IX).

Now that we have the numeral for 10 (X), we will build off of that for 11 (XI), 12 (XII), 13 (XIII), and 14, which can be written either as XIV, "ten and one before five," or XIIII. Now let's work up to twenty: 15 will be XV, 16 (XVI), 17 (XVII), 18 (XVIII), and 19 either as XIX "ten and one before ten" or XVIIII. Twenty is XX, "two tens." The numbers 21-30, 31-40, and 41-50 are formed on the same principles. 30 is written XXX, and 40 is written as "ten before 50," so since 50 is represented by L, 40 is XL. 60 will be LX, 61 (LXI), and so on. 70 is LXX, 80 LXXX, and then 90 is of course "ten before 100," so XC.

When you get to 500, the Romans would use the letter D, and 1,000 is a little easier because it's represented by an M, which stands for mīlle. Movies used to use Roman numerals to show the date they were made, so that was always a fun challenge to figure out that MCMLXXIV means 1974, because the first M means "1,000" plus the CM that means "one hundred before 1,000"; in other words, 900. So now we're at 1900. Then we add the LXX, meaning 70, plus IV, 4. Thus MCMLXXIV is 1974. Once we got into the 2000s, this game wasn't as fun because everything is just MM-something. This edition of the book was written in 2019, also known as MMXIX. Easy, right?

Review

Be sure to review your numbers, as well as your passive forms. Also go over Third Declension i-stem nouns and adjective endings if you're rusty. Rehashing these old forms will help you prepare for your test.

Lesson 23 Worksheet

A. Vocabulary

Translate the following words from Latin to English or English to Latin as appropriate.

1. twentieth: _____
2. fish: _____
3. septimus: _____
4. third: _____
5. octāvus: _____
6. thirteenth: _____
7. quārtus: _____
8. decimus: _____
9. moenia: _____
10. quīntus: _____
11. eleventh: _____
12. prīmus: _____
13. amita: _____
14. duodecimus: _____
15. sixth: _____

16. vīcēsimus prīmus: _____
17. fourteenth: _____
18. quīngentēsimus: _____
19. quīntus decimus: _____
20. ninth: _____
21. ūndēvigintī: _____
22. sextus decimus: _____
23. seventeenth: _____
24. mīllēsimus: _____
25. ūndēvīcēsimus: _____
26. fiftieth: _____
27. duodēvīcēsimus: _____
28. centēsimus: _____
29. bit by bit: _____
30. secundus: _____

B. Grammar

1. Give a synopsis of *dēleō* in the third person plural.

	ACTIVE			PASSIVE	
	LATIN	ENGLISH		LATIN	ENGLISH
PRES.					
IMPF.					
FUT.					
PERF.					
PLUPF.					
FT. PF.					

2. Match each Roman numeral with both of the appropriate cardinal and ordinal numbers from the lists on the right.

ROMAN NUMERAL	LETTERS OF CORRECT MATCHES
I	
II	
III	
IV (IIII)	
V	
VI	
VII	
VIII	
IX	
X	
XI	
XII	
XIII	
XIV (XIIII)	
XV	
XVI	
XVII	
XVIII	
XIX (XVIIII)	
XX	
XXI	
L	
C	
D	
M	

A. duodecim
B. quattuordecim
C. centum
D. vīgintī
E. septendecim
F. ūnus
G. duodēvīgintī
H. sēdecim
I. quīnquāgintā
J. decem
K. quīnque
L. sex
M. ūndēvīgintī
N. duo
O. novem
P. mīlle
Q. quattuor
R. septem
S. tredecim
T. ūndecim
U. quīngentī
V. quīndecim
W. trēs
X. vīgintī ūnus
Y. octō

a. septimus decimus
b. quīnquāgēsimus
c. duodecimus
d. mīllēsimus
e. prīmus
f. sextus
g. septimus
h. quīntus decimus
i. nōnus
j. ūndēvīcēsimus
k. quārtus
l. secundus
m. tertius decimus
n. quīngentēsimus
o. tertius
p. sextus decimus
q. centēsimus
r. duodēvīcēsimus
s. vīcēsimus prīmus
t. vīcēsimus
u. decimus
v. ūndecimus
w. octāvus
x. quārtus decimus
y. quīntus

C. Memorization

Fill in the blanks.

_____

_____

_____

_____

_____

_____

_____

_____

_____

_____

_____

_____

_____

_____

_____

_____

_____ _____ Spīritum _____, Dominum _____ _____: _____

    ex _____ _____ prōcēdit.

Quī _____ _____ _____ _____ simul _____ et _____:

    _____ _____ est per _____.

Et _____, sanctam, _____ et _____ ecclēsiam.

_____ ūnum _____ in remissiōnem _____.

Et expectō _____ _____, et vītam _____ _____.

    _____.

D. English to Latin Translation

Translate each sentence from English to Latin.

1. The happy farmer has three cows—the first is white, the second black, and the third golden.

_____

_____

2. Our castle will have been besieged for a long time by the hundred black ships on the shore.

   _____

   _____

3. Farewell, my son! Farewell, my daughters! Behold, I hasten to a distant land where beasts and giants will be hunted and great wealth will be seized.

   _____

   _____

   _____

4. The five hundredth fiery dragon flew to our city with wings of death, and was also slain by the brave knight.

   _____

   _____

5. We have been summoned to the king's feast and therefore our beautiful purple and blue garments are being prepared for us.

   _____

   _____

6. You had once been loved by two pirates, but you have been given by your father in marriage to the trustworthy sailor.

   _____

   _____

7. Our fourth son was terrified by the old widow's goat and fought it with a little dagger.

   _____

   _____

8. The large woman sang songs badly, and all the dogs howled and crept away from the palace.

   _____

   _____

9. The sad moon and thousands of glittering white stars were shining, and so we stood on the high tower and watched them through the night.

   _____

   _____

10. The unlucky sailor was swimming in the deep sea and was seized by a kraken; you (pl.) were unable to save him.

    _____

    _____

E. Latin to English Translation

1 **Scorpus[1] Maximus**

Ōlim erat certāmen[2] magnum in Circō Maximō[3] in Rōmā.[4] Mīlia et mīlia hominum spectābant. Duodecim quadrīgae[5] post carcerēs[6] stetērunt. Ūnus ex duodecim aurīgīs[7] erat Scorpus, vir fortis et doctus. In duo mille certāminibus superāverat, et nihil timet. Trēs, duo, ūnus—ecce! mappa[8] deiecta est[9]

5 et quadrīgae ex carceribus properāvērunt! Omnēs aurīgae bene gubernant.[10] Scorpus decimus est, nunc octāvus, nunc quīntus! Ad metam[11] appropinquant.[12] Eheu! Quadrīgae secundae in prīmās quadrīgās gubernātae sunt, et naufragium[13] magnum est! Nunc Scorpus tertius aurīga est, et curriculum[14] prīmum bene perficit.[15] Erunt septem curricula. Post curriculum secundum et tertium et quārtum, Scorpus tertius etiam est. Superāre poterit? In curriculō quintō, in spinam[16] ab aurīgā quārtō paene gubernātur, sed ab

10 equīs eius fortibus līberātur. In curriculō sextō, aurīgam secundum appropinquat, et eum ad mētam superat! Nunc est Gaius, aurīga prīmus. Scorpus ab Gaiō[17] rīdētur et vexātur, sed fortis est et certātim gubernat. Dēnique mēta curriculī septimī! Scorpus equīs bona verba clāmat, et deōs ōrat. Gaius retrō[18] spectat, et spīnam nōn videt. In spīnam gubernat, et naufragium paene habet. Scorpus prīmus nunc est, et omnēs superat! Turbae clāmant ululantque. Nunc multās dīvitiās et fāmam[19] magnam habēbit.

Glossary

1. *Scorpus* is a second declension name.
2. *certāmen, -minis* (n): contest, race
3. *Circus Maximus, Circī Maximī* (m): the Circus Maximus, a famous racetrack at the foot of the Palatine Hill in Rome
4 *Roma, -ae* (f): Rome
5. *quadrīgae, -ārum* (f): four-horse chariot
6. *carcer, -eris* (m): prison; generally in pl., starting gates (of a horse race)
7. *aurīga, -ae* (m/f): charioteer, driver
8. *mappa, -ae* (f): starting flag (lit., "a napkin")
9. *dēiciō, -icere, -iēci, -iectum:* I throw down, cast down, hurl down

10. *gubernō* (1): I steer, direct, govern
11. *mēta, -ae* (f): turning-post, goal
12. *appropinquō* (1): I approach, draw near
13. *naufragium, -ī* (n): wreck, crash (lit., "shipwreck")
14. *curriculum, -ī* (n): lap (of a race), course
15. *perficiō, -ere, -fēci, -fectum:* I complete, finish
16. *spīna, -ae* (f): barrier (lit., "spine," the wall dividing the race course in half lengthwise)
17. *Gaius* is a second declension noun.
18. *retrō:* back(ward), behind
18. *fāma, -ae* (f): report, reputation, fame

LESSON 24

Review & Test

Word List

No new word list this lesson. Review all the vocabulary from Lessons 17–23.

Memorization

No new memorization this lesson. Review the entirety of the *Symbolum Nicaenum*.

Grammar

There is no new chant this lesson. Students should review all of their chants because of the cumulative nature of the Latin language! Be sure to review:

first, second, third, and third i-stem declension nouns

first/second and third declension adjectives

personal pronouns

cardinal and ordinal numerals

the entire active indicative verb system

the entire passive indicative verb system

Lesson 24 Worksheet

A. Vocabulary

Translate the following words from Latin to English or English to Latin as appropriate. Include case(s) for prepositions.

1. facilis: _____

2. eighteen: _____

3. argenteus: _____

4. prope: _____

5. fourteenth: _____

6. urbs: _____

7. minūtātim: _____

8. eight: _____

9. ante: _____

10. mūtō: _____

11. fifth: _____

12. brevis: _____

13. eighteenth: _____

14. green: _____

15. marriage: _____

16. dulcis: _____

17. thirteen: _____

18. shiny white: _____

19. eighth: _____

20. nāvis: _____

21. twenty-first: _____

22. ergō: _____

23. twenty-one: _____

24. elephant: _____

25. all, every: _____

26. 500: _____

27. ecce: _____

28. third: _____

29. augeō: _____

30. tree: _____

31. sixteen: _____

32. golden: _____

33. fortis: _____

34. family: _____

35. sharp: _____

36. dog: _____

37. thirteenth: _____

38. wide: _____

39. albus: _____

40. iuvō: _____

41. vīvus: _____

42. in front of: _____

43. avus: _____

44. huge: _____

45. seventh: _____

46. hostis: _____

47. widow: _____

48. four: _____

49. quia: _____

50. is: _____

51. (dead) black: _____

52. twelve: _____

53. post: (+ ___) _____

54. six: _____

55. 100th: _____

56. epulae: _____

57. high: _____

58. ninth _____

59. sīcut: _____

60. purpureus: _____

61. difficult: _____

62. fourth: _____

63. death: _____

64. fifty: _____

65. properō: _____

66. tenth: _____

67. vallēs: _____

68. fifteenth: _____

69. ardeō: _____

70. nineteen: _____

71. violet: _____

72. between: _____

73. seventeenth: _____

74. one: _____

75. nūbēs: _____

76. 1,000: _____

77. cow: _____

78. fourteen: _____

79. ego: _____

80. avia: _____

81. cēna: _____

82. 500th: _____

83. turris: _____

84. nineteenth: _____

85. tristis: _____

86. second: _____

87. flōreō: _____

88. consōbrīna: _____

89. ten: _____

90. infēlix: _____

91. etiam: _____

92. fire: _____

93. patruus: _____

94. eagerly: _____

95. alas!: _____

96. vōs: _____

97. long: _____

98. aunt: _____

99. moenia: _____

100. twelfth: _____

101. celer: _____

102. potēns: _____

103. fifteen: _____

104. fessus: _____

105. I parch: _____

106. twenty: _____

107. night: _____

108. labōrō: _____

109. seven: _____

110. caeruleus: _____

111. fiftieth: _____

112. fēlix: _____

113. first: _____

114. vestis: _____

115. avunculus: _____

116. ordinary: _____

117. twentieth: _____

118. mare: _____

119. knight: _____

120. sixteenth: _____

121. asinus: _____

122. nine: _____

123. I rejoice: _____

124. paene: _____

125. indeed: _____

126. occultō: _____

127. two: _____

128. avis: _____

129. five: _____

130. patruēlis: _____

131. niger: _____

132. sixth: _____

133. piscis: _____

134. seventeen: _____

135. mulier: _____

136. red: _____

137. one hundred: _____

138. pastor: _____

139. eleventh: _____

140. mōns: _____

141. orbus: _____

142. three: _____

143. if: _____

144. coniūnx: _____

145. eleven: _____

146. true: _____

147. animal: _____

148. 1,000th: _____

149. vexō: _____

150. next: _____

B. Grammar

1. Give the principal parts for *iuvō*:

_____

Now fully conjugate *iuvō*.

Present Active Indicative

	LATIN SINGULAR	ENGLISH SINGULAR		LATIN PLURAL	ENGLISH PLURAL
1ST					
2ND					
3RD					

Present Passive Indicative

	LATIN SINGULAR	ENGLISH SINGULAR		LATIN PLURAL	ENGLISH PLURAL
1ST					
2ND					
3RD					

Imperfect Active Indicative

	LATIN SINGULAR	ENGLISH SINGULAR		LATIN PLURAL	ENGLISH PLURAL
1ST					
2ND					
3RD					

Imperfect Passive Indicative

	LATIN SINGULAR	ENGLISH SINGULAR		LATIN PLURAL	ENGLISH PLURAL
1ST					
2ND					
3RD					

Future Active Indicative

	LATIN SINGULAR	ENGLISH SINGULAR		LATIN PLURAL	ENGLISH PLURAL
1ST					
2ND					
3RD					

Future Passive Indicative

	LATIN SINGULAR	ENGLISH SINGULAR		LATIN PLURAL	ENGLISH PLURAL
1ST					
2ND					
3RD					

Perfect Active Indicative

	LATIN SINGULAR	ENGLISH SINGULAR		LATIN PLURAL	ENGLISH PLURAL
1ST					
2ND					
3RD					

Perfect Passive Indicative

	LATIN SINGULAR	ENGLISH SINGULAR		LATIN PLURAL	ENGLISH PLURAL
1ST					
2ND					
3RD					

Pluperfect Active Indicative

	LATIN SINGULAR	ENGLISH SINGULAR		LATIN PLURAL	ENGLISH PLURAL
1ST					
2ND					
3RD					

Pluperfect Passive Indicative

	LATIN SINGULAR	ENGLISH SINGULAR		LATIN PLURAL	ENGLISH PLURAL
1ST					
2ND					
3RD					

Future Perfect Active Indicative

	LATIN SINGULAR	ENGLISH SINGULAR		LATIN PLURAL	ENGLISH PLURAL
1ST					
2ND					
3RD					

Future Perfect Passive Indicative

	LATIN SINGULAR	ENGLISH SINGULAR		LATIN PLURAL	ENGLISH PLURAL
1ST					
2ND					
3RD					

2. Decline *green field*.

	LATIN SINGULAR	LATIN PLURAL
NOM.		
GEN.		
DAT.		
ACC.		
ABL.		
VOC.		

3. Decline *ugly ship (use alnus)*.

	LATIN SINGULAR	LATIN PLURAL
NOM.		
GEN.		
DAT.		
ACC.		
ABL.		
VOC.		

4. Decline *swift animal.*

	LATIN SINGULAR	LATIN PLURAL
NOM.		
GEN.		
DAT.		
ACC.		
ABL.		
VOC.		

5. Decline the first person personal pronoun.

	LATIN SINGULAR	LATIN PLURAL
NOM.		
GEN.		
DAT.		
ACC.		
ABL.		

6. Decline the second person personal pronoun.

	LATIN SINGULAR	LATIN PLURAL
NOM.		
GEN.		
DAT.		
ACC.		
ABL.		

3. Decline the third person personal pronoun.

	SINGULAR			PLURAL		
	MASC.	FEM.	NEUT.	MASC.	FEM.	NEUT.
NOM.						
GEN.						
DAT.						
ACC.						
ABL.						

C. Memorization

Write out the entire *Symbolum Nicaenum* from memory.

_____

_____

_____

_____

_____

_____

_____

D. English to Latin Translation

Translate each sentence and then parse the selected verbs. For indicative and imperative, give person, number, tense, voice, and mood; for infinitive, tense, voice and mood. Also identify the first principal part.

Example:

Draco ab Oswaldō necātus est.

a. Translation: **The dragon was [_or_ has been] killed by Oswald.**

b. Parse _necātus est:_ **third person singular perfect passive indicative of _necō_**

1. Avia nostra līberīs crustula vīgintī dedit et ea omnia ab eīs certātim mandūcāta sunt.

a. Translation: _____

_____

b. Parse _dedērunt:_ _____

c. Parse _mandūcāta sunt:_ _____

2. Mundus lūnaque sōlque stellaeque ā Deō omnēs creātī sunt, et eōs cūrat.

a. Translation: _____

_____

b. Parse _creātī sunt:_ _____

c. Parse _cūrat:_ _____

3. Nōs diū nāvigāverāmus, et dominum pīrātārum dēnique rogāvimus, "Ubi sumus?"

a. Translation: _____

_____

b. Parse _nāvigāverāmus:_ _____

c. Parse _sumus:_ _____

4. Fābulae horrendae dē dracōne caldō narrātae erant, et in caelō suprā montibus ātrīs nunc vidētur.

a. Translation: _____

_____

b. Parse *narrātae erant*: _____

c. Parse *vidētur*: _____

5. Amita mea ab tuīs caprīs tribus vexāta est quod eōs domāre nōn potuistī.

a. Translation: _____

_____

_____

b. Parse *domāre*: _____

c. Parse *potuistī*: _____

6. Equus eius nōnus et asinus duodecimus in agrīs iacēbant quia multa magna ab eīs herī portāta erant.

a. Translation: _____

_____

b. Parse *iacēbant*: _____

c. Parse *portāta erant*: _____

7. In Silvā Ātrā ā centaurō malō oppugnātus sum, sed eum meō Gladiō Ingentī Fātī dēlēvī.

a. Translation: I_____

_____

b. Parse *oppugnātus sum*: _____

c. Parse *dēlēvī*: _____

8. Sī omnēs servī miserī līberātī erunt, eī gaudēbunt et dominum bonum iūstumque laudābunt.

a. Translation: _____

_____

b. Parse *līberātī erunt*: _____

c. Parse *gaudēbunt*: _____

9. Patruus avārus meus aurum argentumque auxit et diū flōruit, sed omnēs dīvitiae eius igne magnō herī cremātae sunt.

    a. Translation: _____

    _____

    _____

    b. Parse *auxit:* _____

    c. Parse *cremātae sunt:* _____

10. Puerī stultī nōn bene doctī erant, itaque in ōs Spēluncae Noctis Mortisque errāvērunt.

    a. Translation: _____

    _____

    b. Parse *doctī erant:* _____

    c. Parse *errāvērunt:* _____

11. "Leō," semper āiō, "rex bēstiārum est et numquam superābitur."

    a. Translation: _____

    _____

    b. Parse *āiō:* _____

    c. Parse *est:* _____

12. Mīlitēs hostium bene exercitī erant, et mīlia ex eīs nostram urbem infēlīcem vastāvērunt.

    a. Translation: _____

    _____

    b. Parse *exercitī erant:* _____

    c. Parse *vastāvērunt:* _____

13. Frāter malus rēgis corōnam nōn meret; ergō ab eō ea ab rēge verō servīsque eius fīdīs removēbitur.

    a. Translation: _____

    _____

    b. Parse *meret:* _____

    c. Parse *removēbitur:* _____

14. Avus meus mē monuit: "Cavē, cavē pīrātam pulchrum quōd malus est, dē malō cōgitat, et multum vīnum pōtat!"

   a. Translation: _____

   _____

   _____

   b. Parse *monuit:* _____

   c. Parse *cavē:* _____

15. Fīlia tertia rēgis in turre altā habitāvit ubi deōs fātumque ōrābat et amōrem vērum exspectābat.

   a. Translation: _____

   _____

   b. Parse *habitāvit:* _____

   c. Parse *ōrābat:* _____

4 UNIT FOUR

Unit 4 Goals

Lessons 25–32

By the end of Unit 4, students should be able to . . .

- Decline fourth declension nouns
- Decline fifth declension nouns
- Decline the demonstrative pronouns *hic*, *ille*, and *iste*
- Conjugate a third, fourth, or third *-iō* conjugation verb in the present, imperfect, future, perfect, pluperfect, and future perfect active and passive indicative
- Translate sentences using all of the concepts learned in Units 1–4
- Know all vocabulary from Lessons 25–32
- Write out from memory Psalm 23 from the Vulgate

LESSON 25

Fourth Declension Nouns

Word List

NOUNS

1. cantus, -ūs (m): *song, singing*

2. cornū, -ūs (n): *horn*

3. domus, -ūs (f): *house, home*

4. exercitus, -ūs (m): *army*

5. frūctus, -ūs (m): *fruit, profit*

6. genū, -ūs (n): *knee*

7. Iēsus, -ūs (m): *Jesus*

8. manus, -ūs (f): *hand*

9. portus, -ūs (m): *harbor, port*

10. spīritus, -ūs (m): *spirit, breath*

11. tonitrus, -ūs (m): *thunder*

12. vultus, -ūs (m): *face, expression*

ADJECTIVES

13. salvus, -a, -um: *safe, saved, well, sound*

14. sanctus, -a, -um: *holy, sacred, consecrated*

VERBS

15. appropinquō (1): *I approach, draw near*

16. foveō, -ēre, fōvī, fōtum: *I cherish, love, esteem*

17. gubernō (1): *I steer, direct, govern*

ADVERBS/PREPOSITIONS

18. iterum: *again, a second time*

19. propter (+ acc.): *because of, on account of, near*

20. quōmodo: *how, in what way*

Memorization

¹Psalmus Dāvīd.

> *A Psalm of David.*

Dominus reget mē et nihil mihi dēerit

> *The Lord will guide me and I will lack nothing (lit., "nothing will be lacking to me")*

Grammar

Fourth Declension Noun Endings

We are now ready to learn the fourth of the five Latin declensions! It's fairly straightforward, and the neuter variant is especially fun to chant.

The Fourth Declension functions exactly like the others, so all that you need to do is add these endings to your repertoire. As with the Third Declension, Fourth Declension masculine and feminine nouns share the same set of endings. Most Fourth Declension nouns are masculine, with several feminines and a mere handful of neuters (though important ones).

And whether masculine, feminine, or neuter, Fourth Declension nouns are the same in the Vocative and the Nominative. The chants for both are as follows:

Fourth Declension Masculine/Feminine Endings

	LATIN SINGULAR	ENGLISH SINGULAR		LATIN PLURAL	ENGLISH PLURAL
NOMINATIVE	-us	a/the *noun* [subject]		-ūs	the *nouns* [subject]
GENITIVE	-ūs	of the *noun*, the *noun's*		-uum	of the *nouns*, the *nouns'*
DATIVE	-uī	to/for the *noun*		-ibus	to/for the *nouns*
ACCUSATIVE	-um	a/the *noun* [object]		-ūs	the *nouns* [object]
ABLATIVE	-ū	by/with/from the *noun*		-ibus	by/with/from the *nouns*
VOCATIVE	-us	O *noun*		-ūs	O *nouns*

Fourth Declension Neuter Endings

	LATIN SINGULAR	ENGLISH SINGULAR		LATIN PLURAL	ENGLISH PLURAL
NOMINATIVE	-ū	a/the *noun* [subject]		-ua	the *nouns* [subject]
GENITIVE	-ūs	of the *noun*, the *noun's*		-uum	of the *nouns*, the *nouns'*
DATIVE	-ū	to/for the *noun*		-ibus	to/for the *nouns*
ACCUSATIVE	-ū	a/the *noun* [object]		-ua	the *nouns* [object]
ABLATIVE	-ū	by/with/from the *noun*		-ibus	by/with/from the *nouns*
VOCATIVE	-ū	O *noun*		-ua	O *nouns*

As with nouns in all other declensions, we find the stem of Fourth Declension from the genitive by taking off the *-ūs.*

In the masculine/feminine chant, notice that the nominative and vocative singular are a short *-us*, while long *ūs* is found in the genitive singular and nominative, accusative, and vocative plurals. This is one of those spots where learning a few macrons can pay off by helping you distinguish between these cases.

Also notice that Fourth Declension neuters still follow our neuter noun guidelines:

1. The nominative, accusative, and vocative singulars and plurals are all the same.

2. The plural nominative, accusative, and vocative end in *-a.*

Here are two nouns declined as examples and for edification:

manus, -ūs (f) *hand*

	LATIN SINGULAR	ENGLISH SINGULAR		LATIN PLURAL	ENGLISH PLURAL
NOMINATIVE	manus	a/the hand [subject]		manūs	the hands [subject]
GENITIVE	manūs	of the hand, the hand's		manuum	of the hands, the hands'
DATIVE	manuī	to/for the hand		manibus	to/for the hands
ACCUSATIVE	manum	a/the hand [object]		manūs	the hands [object]
ABLATIVE	manū	by/with/from the hand		manibus	by/with/from the hands
VOCATIVE	Ō manus	O hand!		-ūs	O hands!

genū, -ūs (n) *knee*

	LATIN SINGULAR	ENGLISH SINGULAR		LATIN PLURAL	ENGLISH PLURAL
NOMINATIVE	genū	a/the knee [subject]		genua	the knees [subject]
GENITIVE	genūs	of the knee, the knee's		genuum	of the knees, the knees'
DATIVE	genū	to/for the knee		genibus	to/for the knees
ACCUSATIVE	genū	a/the knee [object]		genua	the knees [object]
ABLATIVE	genū	by/with/from the knee		genibus	by/with/from the knees
VOCATIVE	Ō genū	O knee!		Ō genua	O knees!

	LATIN SINGULAR	LATIN PLURAL
NOM.	domus	domūs
GEN.	domūs [or domī]	domuum [or domōrum]
DAT.	domuī [or domō]	domibus
ACC.	domum	domūs [or domōs]
ABL.	domū [or domō]	domibus
VOC.	domus	domūs

A note on *domus*: It will sometimes appear with Second Declension endings in a few of its cases.

The declension of *Iēsus* is also slightly irregular (as happens with many names in the Vulgate, actually—some do not decline at all!).

	LATIN SINGULAR
NOM.	Iēsus
GEN.	Iēsu
DAT.	Iēsu
ACC.	Iēsum
ABL.	Iēsu
VOC.	Ō Iēsu

Review

Review those passive forms from last term (Lessons 20 and 22), especially the perfects, pluperfects, and future perfects. Also, review pronouns again (Lessonn 17), since they're so important.

Lesson 25 Worksheet

A. Vocabulary

Translate the following words from Latin to English or English to Latin as appropriate. For the verbs, also fill in the missing principal parts. For each preposition, include which case(s) it takes.

1. holy: _____

2. cantus: _____

3. hand: _____

4. domus: _____

5. I approach: _____

_____

6. exercitus: _____

7. vultus: _____

8. gubernō, _____:

_____

9. iterum: _____

10. Jesus: _____

11. salvus: _____

12. how: _____

13. harbor: _____

14. propter: (+ ___) _____

_____

15. foveō, _____:

_____

16. spirit: _____

17. frūctus: _____

18. cornū: _____

19. thunder: _____

20. genū: _____

B. Grammar

1. Decline *my gloomy house.*

	LATIN SINGULAR	LATIN PLURAL
NOM.		
GEN.		
DAT.		
ACC.		
ABL.		
VOC.		

2. Decline *that evil army.*

	LATIN SINGULAR	LATIN PLURAL
NOM.		
GEN.		
DAT.		
ACC.		
ABL.		
VOC.		

3. Decline *one ordinary knee.* For the plural, use *two ordinary knees.*

	LATIN SINGULAR	LATIN PLURAL
NOM.		
GEN.		
DAT.		
ACC.		
ABL.		
VOC.		

4. Give a synopsis of *foveō* in the first person plural.

	ACTIVE		PASSIVE	
	LATIN	ENGLISH	LATIN	ENGLISH
PRES.				
IMPF.				
FUT.				
PERF.				
PLUPF.				
FT. PF.				

C. Memorization

Fill in the blanks.

[1]Psalmus _____.

_____ reget ___ et _____ mihi _____

D. English to Latin Translation

Translate each sentence from English to Latin.

1. Those two disciples of Jesus had been called "Sons of Thunder."

   _____

2. The leader of the pirates steered their ship into our harbor and then seven homes were burned by their army.

   _____

   _____

3. The brave knight approached the castle of the wicked queen and asked again concerning the princess [lit., "king's daughter"] in the high tower.

   _____

   _____

   _____

4. Silver and gold had been cherished by the greedy old man for a long time, and now he loves riches, not people.

   _____

   _____

5. The giant had two big hands, two huge knees, and one ugly face.

   _____

   _____

6. Because of the Holy Spirit, many in the church will help widows and orphans.

   _____

   _____

7. The poet was singing songs of love to the woman for a long time but he was never loved by her.

   _____

   _____

8. How did the deer swim to the distant island in the deep sea?

_____

_____

9. Because of the great danger of the bull's horns, we hastened out of the field into the farmhouse.

_____

_____

10. The bad children seized much fruit from your grandmother's tree and carried it into town.

_____

_____

E. Latin to English Translation

1 **Fābula dē Porcīs Pinguibus**[1]

Cūr, tū rogās, sunt multī porcī magnī pinguēsque in oppidō nostrō? Tibī narrābō. Ōlim exercitus magnus ad patriam nostram appropinquāverat. Rex exercitūs in omnia oppida patriae nostrae intrāvit et clāmāvit: "Vōs omnēs meī servī eritis! Frūmentum vestrum et fructūs et vīnum mihi dabuntur, et

5 multōs ad regnum meum portābō!" Vultūs nostrī miserī erant et genua nostra tremēbant.[2] Manūs nostrās sustulimus[3] et deam nostrī oppidī ōrāvimus. Rex hostium ad castellum in monte prope oppidum nostrum deinde festīnāvit et id obsēdit. Mīlitēs in castellō bene pugnābant, sed castellum dēnique captum est.[4] Rex malus per moenia ad templum[5] properāvit. Simulacrum[6] aureum deae occupāvit et id ē templō portāvit. Omnia sacra aurea ab exercitū eius ex templō tum portāta sunt. Nōs flēvimus

10 ululāvimusque, sed dea īrāta erat. Erant fulgura[7] et tonitrūs dē nūbibus ātrīs in caelīs. Rex malus malī exercitūs dēnique timuit. Ad caelum vīdit, et vōx deae audīta[8] est: "Vōs avārī estis sīcut porcī pinguēs harae;[9] porcī vōs nunc semper eritis!" Et is exercitusque in porcōs statim mūtātī sunt, et eī servī nostrī nunc sunt.

Glossary
1. *pinguis, -e:* fat
2. *tremō, -ere, -uī, ——:* I tremble, quake
3. *tollō, -ere, sustulī, sublātum:* I lift up, raise
4. *capiō, -ere, cēpī, captum:* I capture
5. *templum, -ī* (n): temple, shrine
6. *simulācrum, -ī* (n): statue
7. *fulgur, -uris* (n): lightning
8. *audiō, -īre, -īvī, -ītum:* I hear
9. *hara, -ae* (f): pig-sty

_____

_____

_____

_____

LESSON 26

Verbs: Third Conjugation Active & Imperative

Word List

NOUNS

1. lingua, -ae (f): *language, tongue*
2. littera, -ae (f) : *letter of the alphabet; (pl.) letter, epistle*
3. metus, -ūs (m): *fear, dread*
4. tempestās, -tātis (f): *weather, storm*

ADJECTIVES

5. medius, -a, -um: *middle (of), midst (of)*
6. novus, -a, -um: *new*

VERBS

7. agō, -ere, ēgī, actum: *I do, act, drive*
8. crēdō, -ere, -didī, -ditum: *I believe*
9. currō, -ere, cūcurrī, cursum: *I run*
10. dīcō, -ere, dīxī, dictum: *I say, speak*
11. dūcō, -ere, dūxī, ductum: *I lead, guide*
12. lūdō, lūdere, lūsī, lūsum: *I play, tease, trick*
13. mittō, -ere, mīsī, missum: *I send, let go*
14. pōnō, -ere, posuī, positum: *I put, place*
15. regō, -ere, rexī, rectum: *I rule*
16. scrībō, -ere, scripsī, scriptum: *I write*
17. vincō, -ere, vīcī, victum: *I defeat, conquer*

ADVERBS/PREPOSITIONS

18. fortasse: *perhaps*
19. quoniam: *because, since*
20. super (+ acc./+ abl.): *over, above, beyond*

Memorization

[1]Psalmus Dāvīd.

Dominus reget mē et nihil mihi dēerit.

[2]In locō pascuae ibī mē conlocāvit;

> *In a place of pasture, there He will establish me;*

super aquam refectiōnis ēducāvit mē.

> *beside the water of restoration He will lead me.*

Grammar

Third Conjugation Verbs, Active:

Until now, you have been chugging along using just two of the five Latin conjugations, and it is high time you learned another. The Third Conjugation is a bit trickier than the first and second, but only in the present system. In the perfect system it conjugates just like all the other verbs you have dealt with thus far.

Let's review the First and Second Conjugation stem vowels. Let's take the words *necō, necāre, necāvī, necātum* and *videō, vidēre, vīdī, vīsum*. To find the present stem we take the second principal parts and remove the *-re*, getting *necā-* and *vidē-*. For a First Conjugation verb like *necō*, the stem vowel is *ā*, and for a Second Conjugation verb such as *videō*, it is *ē*. Once we have the stem, conjugating is easy: all one has to do is slap the endings *-ō, -s, -t* or *-bam, -bās, -bat* or *-bō, -bis, -bit* onto that stem.

However, since the stem vowel of the Third Conjugation is a short *e*, a few interesting things happen. We find this stem in the same way as the other two conjugations—second principal part, take off the *-re*: *mittō, mittere, mīsī, missum*, "I send." Our present stem for *mittō* is *mitte-*. That short *e* morphs quite a bit when various endings are added. Here are the present vowels:

	SINGULAR	PLURAL
1ST	-ō-	-i-
2ND	-i-	-i-
3RD	-i-	-u-

When conjugated in the present active tense then, *mittō* looks like this:

Present Active Indicative of *mittō*

	LATIN SINGULAR	ENGLISH SINGULAR		LATIN PLURAL	ENGLISH PLURAL
1ST	mittō	I send		mittimus	we send
2ND	mittis	you send		mittitis	you (pl.) send
3RD	mittit	he/she/it sends		mittunt	they send

Why does the stem vowel change like this? Say "eh" and "ih" and note how your tongue stays in the same position, though of course the "eh" is made a little bit more back in the mouth than the "ih." These two are actually closely related. The other weird thing is *-unt*, but remember that the third person plural ending *-int* sounds very nasally. Doesn't a round, rolling vowel like *-unt* sound better? Of course, you can always chant *ō, i, i, i, i, u!* over and over until it is entrenched.

The imperfect is not as strange; our short *-e* stem vowel becomes a long *ē* for the whole chant:

Imperfect Active Indicative of *mittō*

	LATIN SINGULAR	ENGLISH SINGULAR		LATIN PLURAL	ENGLISH PLURAL
1ST	mittēbam	I was sending		mittēbāmus	we were sending
2ND	mittēbās	you were sending		mittēbātis	you (pl.) were sending
3RD	mittēbat	he/she/it was sending		mittēbant	they were sending

The future of the Third Conjugation is where it really gets interesting. Instead of using *-bō, -bis, -bit* for the future, Third Conjugation verbs undergo a vowel change and add regular endings! Here are the vowels of the future:

	SINGULAR	PLURAL
1ST	-a-	-ē-
2ND	-ē-	-ē-
3RD	-e-	-e-

To these vowels, *-m, -s, -t, -mus, -tis, -nt* are added. Why is the first person singular is an *-m* rather than an *-ō*? Remember that some of their first person singular verbs end in *-m* not *-ō*: *-bam* and *sum*, for example. Think of it as an alternative first person singular ending. Here is our example verb conjugated in the future:

Future Active Indicative of *mittō*

	LATIN SINGULAR	ENGLISH SINGULAR		LATIN PLURAL	ENGLISH PLURAL
1ST	mittam	I will send		mittēmus	we will send
2ND	mittēs	you will send		mittētis	you (pl.) will send
3RD	mittet	he/she/it will send		mittent	they will send

As you learn this, chant *-am, -ēs, -et, -ēmus, -ētis, -ent!* as an alternate future active chant, rather than *a, ē, e, ē, ē, e*.

Happily, Third Conjugation verbs are perfectly normal in the perfect system. Simply remove the *-ī* from the third principal part, and add the usual perfect, pluperfect, and future perfect endings:

Perfect Active Indicative of *mittō*

	LATIN SINGULAR	ENGLISH SINGULAR		LATIN PLURAL	ENGLISH PLURAL
1ST	mīsī	I (have) sent		mīsimus	we (have) sent
2ND	mīsistī	you (have) sent		mīsistis	you (pl.) (have) sent
3RD	mīsit	he/she/it (has) sent		mīsērunt	they (have) sent

Pluperfect Active Indicative of *mittō*

	LATIN SINGULAR	ENGLISH SINGULAR		LATIN PLURAL	ENGLISH PLURAL
1ST	mīseram	I had sent		mīserāmus	we had sent
2ND	mīserās	you had sent		mīserātis	you (pl.) had sent
3RD	mīserat	he/she/it had sent		mīserant	they had sent

Future Perfect Active Indicative of *mittō*

	LATIN SINGULAR	ENGLISH SINGULAR		LATIN PLURAL	ENGLISH PLURAL
1ST	mīserō	I will have sent		mīserimus	we will have sent
2ND	mīseris	you will have sent		mīseritis	you (pl.) will have sent
3RD	mīserit	he/she/it will have sent		mīserint	they will have sent

While First and Second Conjugation verbs are very regular in their stems (usually *-ō, -āre, -āvī, -ātum,* and *-eō, -ēre, -uī, -itum*), Third Conjugation verbs often have more irregular principal parts, and thus you should be especially careful to learn them.

Third Conjugation Imperatives

To form a Third Conjugation singular imperative, follow the known procedure for imperatives of other conjugations: Go to the second principal part. Chop off the *-re*, and there it is. Thus, *mittere* becomes *mitte!* "send!" However, in the plural, the weight of the *-te* ending squishes that short *e* so that it slims up into an *i*: *mittite* (not *mittete*)! "send!"

A couple of Third Conjugation verbs have irregular singular imperatives: *dūcō* becomes *dūc* (not *dūce*); the imperative of *dīcō* is *dīc* (not *dīce*).

The stems may seem really complicated at first, but it's actually not that difficult and doesn't change that much. All regular Third Conjugation nouns can be recognized by having the second principal part end in *-ere*, without a macron over the *-e*. All present tense verbs end in *-ō, -is, -it, -imus, -itis, -unt*. All imperfects are *-ēbam, -ēbās, -ēbat, -ēbāmus, -ēbātis, -ēbant*. All futures end in *-am, -ēs, -et, -ēmus, -ētis, -ent*.

Work extra on memorizing the vowel endings, especially for the present and future, and you'll be fine. Don't move on until you understand these endings. They make up perhaps the majority of verbs.

Review

Make sure you review your fourth declension endings, and that you review your passives of all six tenses. That will help you prepare for your next lesson.

Lesson 26 Worksheet

A. Vocabulary

Translate the following words from Latin to English or English to Latin as appropriate. For the verbs, also fill in the missing principal parts. For each preposition, include which case(s) it takes.

1. dicō, _____, _____, _____: _____

2. I rule: _____, _____, _____, _____

3. fortasse: _____

4. middle (of): _____

5. tempestās: _____

6. lūdō, _____, _____, _____: _____

7. agō, _____, _____, _____: _____

8. I send: _____, _____, _____, _____

9. currō, _____, _____, _____: _____

10. quoniam: _____

11. pōnō, _____, _____, _____: _____

12. super _____

13. language: _____

14. I believe: _____, _____, _____, _____

15. littera: _____ _____

16. I write: _____, _____, _____, _____

17. metus: _____

18. dūcō, _____, _____, _____: _____

19. new: _____

20. vincō, _____, _____, _____: _____

B. Grammar

1. Conjugate *dūcō* in full in the active indicative.

Present Active Indicative

	LATIN SINGULAR	ENGLISH SINGULAR		LATIN PLURAL	ENGLISH PLURAL
1ST					
2ND					
3RD					

Imperfect Active Indicative

	LATIN SINGULAR	ENGLISH SINGULAR		LATIN PLURAL	ENGLISH PLURAL
1ST					
2ND					
3RD					

Future Active Indicative

	LATIN SINGULAR	ENGLISH SINGULAR		LATIN PLURAL	ENGLISH PLURAL
1ST					
2ND					
3RD					

Perfect Active Indicative

	LATIN SINGULAR	ENGLISH SINGULAR		LATIN PLURAL	ENGLISH PLURAL
1ST					
2ND					
3RD					

Pluperfect Active Indicative

	LATIN SINGULAR	ENGLISH SINGULAR		LATIN PLURAL	ENGLISH PLURAL
1ST					
2ND					
3RD					

Future Active Indicative

	LATIN SINGULAR	ENGLISH SINGULAR		LATIN PLURAL	ENGLISH PLURAL
1ST					
2ND					
3RD					

2. Decline *new fear.*

	LATIN SINGULAR	LATIN PLURAL
NOM.		
GEN.		
DAT.		
ACC.		
ABL.		
VOC.		

3. Give a synopsis of *pōnō* in the second person plural.

	ACTIVE		PASSIVE	
	LATIN	ENGLISH	LATIN	ENGLISH
PRES.				
IMPF.				
FUT.			*Third conjugation passive still to come!*	
PERF.				
PLUPF.				
FT. PF.				

C. Memorization

Fill in the blanks.

²In _____ pascuae _____ mē _____

_____ aquam _____ ēducāvit _____

D. English to Latin Translation

Translate each sentence from English to Latin.

1. That pirate will do many evil things, and then perhaps he will be killed by a brave sailor in a battle on the sea.

   _____

   _____

2. We are running out of the middle of the dark forest because we were teasing a wild pig and now it is hunting us.

   _____

   _____

3. You (sg.) believe in God the Father, Son, and Holy Spirit, and you will believe in these true things always.

   _____

   _____

4. I will write a beautiful letter to the poet because I love him and perhaps I will be loved by him.

   _____

   _____

5. The old knight could not conquer the dragon because his sword was not new.

   _____

   _____

6. The king will send five hundred knights into the middle of the battle with the giants, but will they defeat them?

   _____

   _____

7. There was great fear among the children because of the huge storm and angry thunder.

   _____

   _____

8. You (pl.) disciples were all speaking in seventeen new languages because you were moved by the Holy Spirit.

   _____

   _____

9. Jesus will put [His] hands over her and she will be well.

_____

10. Our leaders are leading us again to the port of the king of the pirates, but we are weary and wretched.

_____

E. Latin to English Translation

Mark 3:1–7 (Paraphrase)

1   Et Iēsus intrāvit iterum synagogam[1] et erat ibī homō. Is manum āridam[2] habet, et Pharisaeī Iēsum spectābant. Etiam invicem[3] rogābant, "Cūrābit Iēsus hominem sabbatīs?"[4]—quod eum accusāre cupiēbant.[5] Et Iēsus āit hominī manū cum āridā: "Surge[6] in medium." Et dīcit eīs, "Licet[7] sabbatīs bene facere[8] aut male? Animam salvam facere aut perdere?"[9] Eī autem tacēbant.[10] Iēsus īrātus est quoniam

5   corda eōrum caeca[11] erant, et dīcit hominī: "Extende[12] manum tuam." Et eam extendit et manus eius salva est. Pharisaeī autem invicem rogābant, "Quōmodo Iēsum perdēmus?"

Glossary

1. *synagoga, -ae* (f): synagogue
2. *āridus, -a, -um*: dry, withered
3. *invicem*: reciprocally (i.e., "[to] one another")
4. *sabbata, -ōrum* (n, pl.): Sabbath; *sabbatīs* is an ablative of time when, "on the Sabbath"
5. *cupiō, -ere, -īvī, -ītum*: I desire, wish (for)
6. *surgo, -ere, surrexī, surrectum*: I rise, arise
7. *licet*: it is permitted/allowed
8. *facio, -ere, fēci, factum*: I make, do
9. *perdō, -ere, -didī, -ditum*: I destroy, kill
10. *taceō, -ēre, -uī, -itum*: I am silent
11. *caecus, -a, -um*: blind
12. *extendō, -ere, -tendī, -tensum*: I stretch out, extend

_____
_____
_____
_____
_____
_____
_____
_____
_____
_____
_____
_____
_____
_____

Lesson 27

Verbs: Third Conjugation Passive

Word List

NOUNS

1. arcus, -ūs (m): *bow, arch, rainbow*

2. grātia, -ae (f): *grace, favor, kindness, thanks*

3. lacus, -ūs (m): *lake, tub, hollow*

4. poena, -ae (f): *penalty, punishment*

5. vēritas, -tātis (f): *truth*

6. versus, -ūs (m): *row, line (of poetry), furrow*

ADJECTIVES

7. āridus, -a, -um: *dry*

8. caecus, -a, -um: *blind*

9. grātus, -a, -um: *grateful, pleasing*

VERBS

10. cadō, -ere, cecidī, casum: *I fall, sink, drop*

11. frangō, -ere, frēgī, fractum: *I break, smash, shatter*

12. grātiās agō (+ dat.): *I give thanks, I thank*

13. iungō, -ere, iūnxī, iunctum: *I join, unite, yoke*

14. perdō, -ere, perdidī, perditum: *I destroy, ruin, lose*

15. poenās dō: *I pay the penalty*

16. tangō, -ere, tetigī, tactum: *I touch, strike*

17. vehō, -ere, vexī, vectum: : *I carry, convey*

18. vīvō, -ere, vixī, victum: *I live*

ADVERBS, CONJUNCTIONS, AND PREPOSITIONS

19. atque (acc.): *and, and also*

20. cito: *quickly, fast, speedily*

21. cōram (+ abl.): *in the presence of, before;* (adv.): *personally, openly*

22. modo: *only, just, merely, but*

Memorization

[1]Psalmus Dāvīd.

Dominus reget mē et nihil mihi dēerit.

[2]In locō pascuae ibī mē conlocāvit;

super aquam refectiōnis ēducāvit mē.

[3]Animam meam convertit.

> *He directs my soul.*

Dēdūxit mē super sēmitās iūstitiae

> *He has led me along paths of righteousness*

propter nōmen suum.

> *because of His name.*

Grammar

Third Conjugation Verbs, Passive:

Like its active counterpart, the Third Conjugation passive is a bit tricky in the present system (due to those vowels) but perfectly normal in the perfect system. Review the vowel chant from the present active: *ō, i, i, i, i, u!*

These will be your vowels for the present passive—with one exception (second person singular):

	SINGULAR	PLURAL
1ST	-ō	-i-
2ND	-e-	-i-
3RD	-i-	-u-

The present passive tense of *mittō* will conjugate like this:

Present Passive Indicative

	LATIN SINGULAR	ENGLISH SINGULAR	LATIN PLURAL	ENGLISH PLURAL
1ST	mittor	I am (being) sent	mittimur	we are sent
2ND	mitteris	you are sent	mittiminī	you (pl.) are sent
3RD	mittitur	he/she/it is sent	mittuntur	they are sent

To remember this weird second person singular exception, again think about how nasally this word would sound if it were *-iris*.

The imperfect passive is simple like the active, with that long *-ē-* for the whole chant:

Imperfect Passive Indicative

	LATIN SINGULAR	ENGLISH SINGULAR	LATIN PLURAL	ENGLISH PLURAL
1ST	mittēbar	I was being sent	mittēbāmur	we were being sent
2ND	mittēbāris	you were being sent	mittēbāminī	you (pl.) were being sent
3RD	mittēbātur	he/she/it was being sent	mittēbantur	they were being sent

The future passive of the Third Conjugation also employs a vowel change rather than using our customary *-bor, -beris, -bitur*. We use the same *a, e, e, e, e, e* pattern, but in the passive the third person singular *-ē-* will be long rather than short as in the active:

	SINGULAR	PLURAL
1ST	-a-	-ē-
2ND	-ē-	-ē-
3RD	-ē-	-e-

To this set of vowels we add our regular, basic passive endings: *-r, -ris, -tur, -mur, -minī, -ntur*:

Future Passive Indicative

	LATIN SINGULAR	ENGLISH SINGULAR		LATIN PLURAL	ENGLISH PLURAL
1ST	mittar	I will be sent		mittēmur	we will be sent
2ND	mittēris	you will be sent		mittēminī	you (pl.) will be sent
3RD	mittētur	he/she/it will be sent		mittentur	they will be sent

If it is helpful, you can chant *-ar, -ēris, -ētur, -ēmur, -ēminī, -entur!* as an alternate future passive chant. Note that the difference between the second person singular present passive and the second singular future passive is that short versus long vowel: *mitteris*, you are being sent; *mittēris*, you will be sent.

We come now to the perfect passive system of the Third Conjugation, where you may rejoice—they are formed just like the perfect passives we have been practicing. Use the 4th principal part plus the appropriate form of *sum*, and you're set!

Perfect Passive Indicative

	LATIN SINGULAR	ENGLISH SINGULAR		LATIN PLURAL	ENGLISH PLURAL
1ST	missus/a/um sum	I was/have been sent		missī/ae/a sumus	we were/have been sent
2ND	missus/a/um es	you were/have been sent		missī/ae/a estis	you (pl.) were/have been sent
3RD	missus/a/um est	he/she/it was/has been sent		missī/ae/a sunt	they were/have been sent

Pluperfect Passive Indicative

	LATIN SINGULAR	ENGLISH SINGULAR		LATIN PLURAL	ENGLISH PLURAL
1ST	missus/a/um eram	I had been sent		missī/ae/a erāmus	we had been sent
2ND	missus/a/um erās	you had been sent		misī/ae/a erātis	you (pl.) had been sent
3RD	missus/a/um erat	he/she/it had been sent		missī/ae/a erant	they had been sent

Future Perfect Passive Indicative

	LATIN SINGULAR	ENGLISH SINGULAR		LATIN PLURAL	ENGLISH PLURAL
1ST	missus/a/um erō	I will have been sent		missī/ae/a erimus	we will have been sent
2ND	missus/a/um eris	you will have been sent		missī/ae/a eritis	you (pl.) will have been sent
3RD	missus/a/um erit	he/she/it will have been sent		missī/ae/a erunt	they will have been sent

Once again, the vowels are not as difficult as they appear at first. Know the vowel endings, especially for the present and future, and you'll be fine.

This is a spot to make sure you've been learning each verb's conjugation as you've studied its meaning. A Second Conjugation verb ending in *–et* is present tense (*videt*, "he sees"), but a Third Conjugation verb ending in *–et* is future tense (*vertet*, "he will turn")!

Review

Review your fourth declension nouns and your pronouns during this lesson.

Lesson 27 Worksheet

A. Vocabulary

Translate the following words from Latin to English or English to Latin as appropriate. For the verbs, also fill in the missing principal parts. For each preposition, include which case(s) it takes.

1. lacus: _____

2. perdō, _____, _____, _____: _____

3. I fall: _____, _____, _____, _____

4. ac: _____

5. I touch, strike: _____, _____, _____, _____

6. arcus: _____

7. poena: _____

8. fortasse: _____

9. grātus: _____

10. blind: _____

11. cito: _____

12. truth: _____

13. frangō, _____, _____, _____: _____

14. I ride: _____, _____, _____, _____

15. versus: _____

16. āridus: _____

17. tonitrus: _____

18. middle: _____

19. grātia: _____

20. again: _____

21. cōram: _____

22. I join: _____, _____, _____, _____

23. currō, _____, _____, _____: _____

24. modo: _____

25. because of: _____

B. Grammar

1. Conjugate *dūcō* in the passive indicative only.

Present Passive Indicative

	LATIN SINGULAR	ENGLISH SINGULAR		LATIN PLURAL	ENGLISH PLURAL
1ST					
2ND					
3RD					

Imperfect Passive Indicative

	LATIN SINGULAR	ENGLISH SINGULAR		LATIN PLURAL	ENGLISH PLURAL
1ST					
2ND					
3RD					

Future Passive Indicative

	LATIN SINGULAR	ENGLISH SINGULAR		LATIN PLURAL	ENGLISH PLURAL
1ST					
2ND					
3RD					

Perfect Passive Indicative

	LATIN SINGULAR	ENGLISH SINGULAR		LATIN PLURAL	ENGLISH PLURAL
1ST					
2ND					
3RD					

Pluperfect Passive Indicative

	LATIN SINGULAR	ENGLISH SINGULAR		LATIN PLURAL	ENGLISH PLURAL
1ST					
2ND					
3RD					

Future Perfect Passive Indicative

	LATIN SINGULAR	ENGLISH SINGULAR		LATIN PLURAL	ENGLISH PLURAL
1ST					
2ND					
3RD					

2. Give a synopsis of *perdō* in the third person plural.

	ACTIVE		PASSIVE	
	LATIN	ENGLISH	LATIN	ENGLISH
PRES.				
IMPF.				
FUT.				
PERF.				
PLUPF.				
FT. PF.				

C. Memorization

Fill in the blanks.

_____

_____

_____

_____

_____ meam _____

Dēdūxit _____ super _____ iūstitiae

_____ nōmen _____

D. English to Latin Translation

Translate each sentence from English to Latin.

1. We all were afraid in the presence of the evil king, and fell to our faces on the ground.

   _____

   _____

2. Your land will be destroyed if the fiery dragon will fly to it on wings of death.

   _____

   _____

3. The bad little boy did not speak the truth, and therefore he paid the penalty.

   _____

   _____

4. After the storm a rainbow was seen in the heavens, and beautiful lines of poetry will be written about it.

   _____

   _____

5. We had yoked the two cows and then they carried us into the town with our grain.

   _____

   _____

6. The beautiful woman smiled at the wretched poet and now songs are being written quickly to her by the grateful man.

   _____

   _____

7. "You are being destroyed by much wine," the pirate's grandmother was telling him, but he only laughed.

8. The dry tree is being broken by the storm, but will it also fall over our house?

9. My aunt and uncle live near a great lake and all their food is carried there in boats.

10. A man's withered hand is now whole and many blind can see because of Jesus' grace.

E. Latin to English Translation

1 **Fābula Midae[1] I: Cāsus[2] Infēlix in Alchemiā[3]**

Ōlim Sīlēnus,[4] magister amīcusque Bacchī,[5] multum vīnum pōtāverat et ab Bacchō errāverat. Ab servīs Midae, rex Phrygiae,[6] inventus est.[7] Midās eī epulās multās et magnās dedit, ac eum ad deum vīnī deinde dūxit. Bacchus gaudēbat quoniam Sīlēnus salvus erat et dīxit: "Ō Midās, rogā ūllum[8] prō praemiō[9]
5 tuō et tibī dabō." Midās stultus avārusque erat, et respondit: "Id mihi dā: Quandō ūllum tangam, in aurum mūtābitur." Bacchus tristis erat propter stultitiam[10] Midae, sed dīxit: "Id dātur." Midās ad rēgiam ambulāvit, et lapidem[11] tetigit—in aurum mūtātus est! Deinde arborem tetigit, deinde frūctum—duo nunc aurum erant! Laetus erat. "Dīvitiās," āit, "magnās habēbō." In rēgiā servīs dīxit: "Mihi epulās magnās et multum vīnum portāte!" Cibum in ōs pōnere temptāvit,[12] sed in aurum iam mūtātus erat.
10 Atque vīnum eius in aurum mūtātum est, et id nōn pōtāre potuit. Nunc Midās tristis erat—"Quōmodo vivam sī nec mandūcāre nec pōtāre poterō?" dīxit. "Bacche, mē iuvā!" Itaque Bacchus dīxit, "In flūmine Pactōlō[13] lavā,[14] et salvus eris." Midās ergō ad flūmen cito properāvit et in eō lāvit. Deinde omnia tangere potuit, et in aurum nōn mūtāta sunt. Postea[15] erat autem semper multum aurum in eō flūmine et prope terram. Midās vītām dīvitiārum tum relīquit[16] et in agrīs montibusque habitāvit.

Glossary
1. *Midās, -ae* (m): Midas, king of Phrygia
2. *casus, -ūs* (m): incident, event; misfortune, downfall
3. *alchemia, -ae* (f): alchemy, the study of how to turn metals into gold
4. *Sīlēnus, -ī* (m): Silenus, pudgy old fellow (usually drunk), former tutor and longtime companion of Bacchus
5. *Bacchus, -ī* (m): Bacchus, the god of wine
6. *Phrygia, -ae* (f): Phrygia, a land in Asia Minor
7. *inveniō, -īre, -vēnī, -ventum:* I find
8. *ūllus, -a, -um:* anyone, anything
9. *praemium, -ī* (n): reward
10. *stultitia, -ae* (f): foolishness, folly
11. *lapis, -idis* (m): stone
12. *temptō* (1): I attempt
13. *Pactōlus, -ī* (m): Pactolus, a river in Lydia in Asia Minor
14. *lavō, -āre, lāvī, lōtum/lavātum:* I wash
15. *postea:* afterwards
16. *relinquō, -ere, -līquī, -lictum:* I abandon

F. For Fun: Mythology Matching

How well do you know the major Roman gods? For each god or goddess below, correctly match the deity up with its correct Greek name and description from the lists on the right..

GOD/GODDESS	GREEK NAME	DESCRIPTION
Bacchus		
Ceres		
Diana		
Juno		
Jupiter		
Mars		
Mercury		
Minerva		
Neptune		
Phoebus		
Pluto		
Venus		
Vulcan		

A. Aphrodite   1. goddess of wisdom

B. Hera   2. king of the gods

C. Poseidon   3. god of war

D. Zeus   4. goddess of agriculture

E. Hephaestus   5. messenger god

F. Hades   6. goddess of the hunt

G. Dionysius   7. god of prophecy

H. Demeter   8. god of fire

I. Athena   9. queen of the gods

J. Hermes   10. god of wine

K. Artemis   11. goddess of love

L. Apollo   12. god of the underworld

M. Ares   13. god of the sea

LESSON 28
Nouns: Fifth Declension / Time Constructions

Word List

NOUNS

1. cāsus, -ūs (m): *event, incident; misfortune, downfall*

2. diēs, diēī (m/f): *day, period of time*

3. faciēs, -ēī (f): *shape, form; face; character*

4. fidēs, -eī (f): *faith*

5. merīdiēs, -ēī (m): *noon*

6. rēs, reī (f): *thing*

7. spēs, speī (f): *hope*

VERBS

8. cēdō, -ere, cessī, cessum: *I go, move, yield*

9. cōgō, cōgere, coēgī, coactum: *I drive together, force, compel*

10. dēfendō, -ere, -fendī, -fēnsum: *I defend*

11. dēligō, -ere, -lēgī, -lēctum: *I pick, choose*

12. gerō, -ere, gessī, gestum: *I bear, carry on*, bellum gerō: *I wage war*

13. legō, -ere, lēgī, lēctum: *I read, choose*

14. relinquō, -ere, -līquī, -lictum: *I abandon, leave behind*

15. surgō, -ere, surrēxī, surrēctum: *I (a)rise*

16. vertō, -ere, vertī, versum: *I turn, change*

ADVERBS/conjunctions/PREPOSITIONS

17. iūxta (adv./prep. + acc.): *near (to), close to/by*

18. postea: *afterwards*

19. quam: *as, than, how*

20. secundum (adv./prep. + acc.): *after; according to*

Memorization

[1]Psalmus Dāvīd.

Dominus reget mē et nihil mihi dēerit.

[2]In locō pascuae ibī mē conlocāvit;

super aquam refectiōnis ēducāvit mē.

[3]Animam meam convertit.

Dēdūxit mē super sēmitās iūstitiae

propter nōmen suum,

[4]Nam et sī ambulāverō in mediō umbrae mortis,

> *For even if I walk (lit., "will have walked") in the midst of the shadow of death,*

nōn timēbō mala quoniam tū mēcum es;

> *I will not fear evils because you are with me;*

virga tua et baculus tuus ipsa mē consōlāta sunt.

> *Your rod and Your staff themselves have comforted me.*

Grammar

Fifth Declension Noun Endings:

Rejoice! You have now reached the fifth and *final* Latin noun declension. Although it does not contain a boatload of nouns, those it does are quite important (e.g., *diēs*, "day" or *rēs*, "thing"). By now you should be familiar enough with gender, number, and case that learning a new declension will not be difficult—just a few more endings to memorize, that's all!

Most fifth declension nouns are feminine, with the exception of *diēs* and its compound *meridiēs*, which are masculine. There are no neuters. Here are the new endings:

LATIN SINGULAR	ENGLISH SINGULAR	LATIN PLURAL	ENGLISH PLURAL
NOMINATIVE -ēs	a/the *noun* [subject]	-ēs	the *nouns* [subject]
GENITIVE -eī/-ēī	of the *noun*, the *noun's*	-ērum	of the *nouns*, the *nouns'*
DATIVE -eī/-ēī	to/for the *noun*	-ēbus	to/for the *nouns*
ACCUSATIVE -em	a/the *noun* [object]	-ēs	the *nouns* [object]
ABLATIVE -ē	by/with/from the *noun*	-ēbus	by/with/from the *nouns*
VOCATIVE -ēs	O *noun*	-ēs	O *nouns*

As usual, an adjective must match its noun in gender, number, and case (*not* in declension), so a fifth declension noun can of course be modified by a First/Second Declension adjective or a Third Declension adjective. There are no Fourth or Fifth Declension adjectives, in case you were wondering. Here is the Fifth Declension noun *fidēs* ("faith") declined with a couple of adjectives:

	LATIN SINGULAR	LATIN PLURAL
NOMINATIVE	antīqua fidēs fortis	antīquae fidēs fortēs
GENITIVE	antīquae fideī fortis	antīquārum fidērum fortium
DATIVE	antīquae fideī fortī	antīquīs fidēbus fortibus
ACCUSATIVE	antīquam fidem fortem	antīquās fidēs fortēs
ABLATIVE	antīquā fidē fortī	antīquīs fidēbus fortibus
VOCATIVE	Ō antīqua fidēs fortis	Ō antīquae fidēs fortēs

Time Constructions

Now that we've learned words like "day" and "noon," we need to be able to communicate when things happen. There are two ways Latin does this.

1. **Ablative of Time When and Time Within Which:** The first way of expressing time is using the ablative to indicate a point of time when something happens, or the time within which it happened. If you want to say (as in the Creed) that "And He rose again on the third day," you simply put "third day" in the ablative: *Et resurrēxit tertiā diē.* You could also say, "He will rise again within (in) three days": *Tribus diēbus resurget.*

2. **Accusative of Duration of Time:** If you want to express how long it took to do something, you will use the accusative and *not* the ablative: "He remained there for three days" is *Trēs diēs ibī mānsit.* Another example would be "The king waged war for two years." *Rex bellum duōs annōs gessit.*

Review

Be sure to review your Third Conjugation verbs during this lesson, both in active and passive. Don't neglect your First and Second Conjugation passives either!

Lesson 28 Worksheet

A. Vocabulary

Translate the following words from Latin to English or English to Latin as appropriate. For the verbs, also fill in the missing principal parts. For each preposition, include which case(s) it takes.

1. dēligō, _____, _____, _____: _____

2. penalty: _____

3. legō, _____, _____, _____: _____

4. I yield: _____, _____, _____, _____

5. pōnō, _____, _____, _____: _____

6. than: _____

7. iterum: _____

8. gerō, _____, _____, _____: _____

9. surgō, _____, _____, _____: _____

10. day: _____

11. relinquō, _____, _____, _____: _____

12. faciēs: _____

13. secundum: _____

14. cōgō, _____, _____, _____: _____

15. faith: _____

16. iūxta: _____

17. spēs: _____

18. noon: _____

19. cāsus: _____

20. metus: _____

21. rēs: _____

22. afterwards: _____

23. dēfendō, _____, _____, _____: _____

24. āridus: _____

25. cornū: _____

B. Grammar

1. Decline *new thing*.

	LATIN SINGULAR	LATIN PLURAL
NOM.		
GEN.		
DAT.		
ACC.		
ABL.		
VOC.		

2. Decline *unfortunate incident*.

	LATIN SINGULAR	LATIN PLURAL
NOM.		
GEN.		
DAT.		
ACC.		
ABL.		
VOC.		

3. Give a synopsis of *cōgō* in the first person plural.

	ACTIVE		PASSIVE	
	LATIN	ENGLISH	LATIN	ENGLISH
PRES.				
IMPF.				
FUT.				
PERF.				
PLUPF.				
FT. PF.				

C. Memorization

Fill in the blanks.

_____

_____

_____

_____

_____

_____

_____

_____ et _____ ambulāverō in _____ _____ mortis,

nōn _____ mala _____ tū _____ __

_____ tua _____ _____ tuus _____ mē _____ sunt.

D. Verb Parsing

Parse and translate each verb. To parse a verb, list its attributes: person, number, tense, voice, and mood, if it is an indicative verb; if it is an infinitive, give tense, voice, and mood only. Then give the first principal part of the verb it comes from. (Abbreviate but keep your meaning clear.) An example is given below.

	VERB	PERSON	NBR.	TENSE	VOICE	MOOD	1ST PRIN. PART	TRANSLATION
	cūrāverās	2nd	Sg.	Plupf.	Act.	Ind.	cūrō	you had cared for
1.	amātī erunt							
2.	gessit							
3.	legentur							
4.	videntur							
5.	dūceris							
6.	dūcēris							
7.	duxeris							
8.	scrībit							

9.	dēfendit								
10.	victī erātis								
11.	perdor								
12.	regēminī								
13.	audēs								
14.	coactae sumus								
15.	cecidistis								

Identify and translate all possible options for the following noun/adjective combinations.

	PHRASE	GENDER, NUMBER, CASE	TRANSLATION
1.	lacuum mediōcrium		
2.	potēns tempestās		
3.	speī bonae		
4.	caecī patruī		
5.	genū ingentī		
6.	exercituī stultō		
7.	diēs caldī		
8.	mala animālia		

9.	mediās rēs		
10.	hostis celeris		
11.	pulchrīs faciēbus		
12.	manūs albae		
13.	linguae mīrae		
14.	fortī fidē		
15.	agrī viridēs		

E. Latin to English Translation

1 **Fābula Midae II: Aurēs[1] Asīnī**

Post cāsum tactūs[2] aureī, Midās in agrīs montibusque multōs annōs habitābat. Deum Pāna[3] coluit[4] et laetus diū erat. Ōlim autem Apollō[5] ad montēs vēnit.[6] Pān dīxit, "Ego sum mūsicus[7] melior[8] quam Apollō!" sed Apollō dīxit, "Nōn es!" Pān Apollonī nōn cessit; itaque certāmen[9] dēclārātum est. Tmōlus,[10]

5 deus montis, iūdex[11] appellātus est. Pān calamīs[12] cantāvit,[13] et fīdus Midās stupōre[14] victus est. "Quam pulchrum!" clāmāvit. Sed Apollō lyrā[15] deinde cantāvit, et Tmōlus statim dēclārāvit, "Apollō mūsicus melior est!" Midās dīxit, "Nōn est!" et nōn cēssit. Apollō īrātus erat et dīxit: "Aurēs tuae malae stultaeque sunt! Nunc tū aurēs asinī habēbis!" Aurēs Midae in aurēs asinī statim mūtātae sunt! Tristis erat et postea semper mītram[16] purpuream gessit et eās cēlāvit.[17] Tonsor[18] eius autem eās vīdit; itaque Midās dīxit:

10 "Sī dē eīs auribus dīcēs, necāberis!" Sed tonsor sēcrētum[19] nōn occultāre potuit, et ergō in terrā fōdit[20] et sēcrētum in eam susurrāvit.[21] Deinde calamī multī flōruērunt, et in ventō[22] susurrant: "Rēx Midās aurēs asinī habet!"

Glossary

1. *auris, -is* (f): ear
2. *tactus, -ūs* (m): touch
3. *Pān, Pānos* (acc. *Pāna*) (m): Pan, the god of woods, shepherds, and flocks
4. *colō, -ere, coluī, cultum:* I cultivate, inhabit, worship
5. *Apollō, -inis* (m): Apollo, the god of prophesy, music, archery, the sun, etc.
6. *veniō, -īre, vēnī, venturum:* I come
7. *mūsicus, -ī* (m): musician
8. *melior, -ius:* better
9. *certāmen, -minis* (n): contest
10. *Tmōlus, -ī* (m): Tmolus, a god and a mountain in Lydia
11. *iūdex, -dicis* (m): judge
12. *calamus, -ī* (m): reed, reed-pipe
13. *cantō* can also mean "play"; the musical instrument being played takes the ablative
14. *stupor, -ōris* (m): amazement, astonishment
15. *lyra, -ae* (f): lyre
16. *mītra, -ae* (f): turban
17. *celō (1): I hide, conceal*
18. *tonsor, -ōris* (m): barber
19. *sēcrētum, -ī* (n): secret
20. *fodiō, -ere, fōdī, fossum:* I dig
21. *susurrō* (1): I whisper
22. *ventus, -ī* (m): wind

LESSON 29

Verbs: Fourth Conjugation, Active, Passive & Imperative / Irregular Verb *eō*

Word List

NOUNS

1. animus, -ī (m): *mind*

2. pānis, -is (m): *bread*

3. saxum, -ī (n): *rock*

ADJECTIVES

4. ēgregius, -a, -um: *outstanding, excellent*

5. famēlicus, -a, -um: *hungry*

6. improbus, -a, -um: *wicked*

VERBS

7. aperiō, -īre, -uī, apertum: *I open, expose*

8. audiō, -īre, -īvī, -ītum: *I hear, listen to*

9. colō, -ere, coluī, cultum: *I cultivate, inhabit, worship*

10. dormiō, -īre, -īvī, -ītum: *I sleep*

11. eō, īre, iī (īvī), itum: *I go*

12. impediō, -īre, -īvī, -ītum: *I hinder*

13. inveniō, -īre, -vēnī, -ventum: *I come upon, find*

14. resurgō, -ere, -surrēxī, -surrēctum: *I rise again*

15. sciō, -īre, sciī (scīvī), scītum: *I know*

16. veniō, -īre, vēnī, ventum: *I come*

ADVERBS

17. clam: *secretly*

18. magnoperē: *greatly, very much*

19. quoque: *also, too*

20. ūnā: *together, in one*

Memorization

[1]Psalmus Dāvīd.

Dominus reget mē et nihil mihi dēerit.

[2]In locō pascuae ibī mē conlocāvit;

super aquam refectiōnis ēducāvit mē.

[3]Animam meam convertit.

Dēdūxit mē super sēmitās iūstitiae

propter nōmen suum.

[4]Nam et sī ambulāverō in mediō umbrae mortis,

nōn timēbō mala quoniam tū mēcum es;

virga tua et baculus tuus ipsa mē consōlāta sunt.

[5]Parāstī in conspectū meō mensam

You have prepared a table in my sight

adversus eōs quī trībulant mē.

against those who trouble me.

Inpinguāstī in oleō caput meum,

You have anointed my head with (lit., "in") oil,

Grammar

Fourth Conjugation Verbs, Active and Passive:

In the last lesson you learned the last declension. In this one, you get to learn the final conjugation! Like the Third Conjugation, Fourth Conjugation verbs have some tricky vowel changes in the present system, but conjugate normally in the perfect system. The Fourth Conjugation is in some ways easier to learn than the Third, because its philosophy is basically that wherever there can be an -*i*-, there will be an -*i*-. Although many Fourth Conjugation verbs do have irregular principal parts, quite a few of them end like this: -*iō, -īre, -īvī, -ītum.*

The vowel chant for the Fourth Conjugation present tense is identical to that of the Third Conjugation except in the third person plural, where it is -*iu*- rather than simply -*u*-.

	SINGULAR	PLURAL
1ST	-ō	-ī-
2ND	-ī-	-ī-
3RD	-i- (act.) / -ī- (pass.)	-iu-

When conjugated in the Present Active and Passive, a Fourth Conjugation will look something like this: *aperiō, -īre, -uī, apertum*: I open, expose

Present Active Indicative

	LATIN SINGULAR	ENGLISH SINGULAR		LATIN PLURAL	ENGLISH PLURAL
1ST	aperiō	I open		aperīmus	we open
2ND	aperīs	you open		aperītis	you (pl.) open
3RD	aperit	he/she/it opens		aperiunt	they open

Present Passive Indicative

	LATIN SINGULAR	ENGLISH SINGULAR		LATIN PLURAL	ENGLISH PLURAL
1ST	aperior	I am (being) opened		aperīmur	we are (being) opened
2ND	aperīris	you are (being) opened		aperīminī	you (pl.) are (being) opened
3RD	aperītur	he/she/it is (being) opened		aperiuntur	they are (being) opened

Recall that, for Third Conjugation verbs, the second person present passive was *-eris* (rather than *-iris*); thus *dūcō* becomes *dūceris*, "you are led." However, since the Fourth Conjugation has a long ī stem vowel rather than the short i of the Third Conjugation, the long ī remains: *-īris*, as in *aperīris*, "you are opened."

For a Third Conjugation verb, the vowel for the imperfect was simply an *-ē-* for all persons, singular and plural. Since our "rule" for the Fourth Conjugation is that wherever an *-i-* can be found, there it shall be, the imperfect for a Fourth Conjugation has an *-i-* and an *-ē-* all the way down:

	SINGULAR	PLURAL
1ST	-iē-	-iē-
2ND	-iē-	-iē-
3RD	-iē-	-iē-

Our example verb will conjugate in the imperfect like this (pretty simple):

Imperfect Active Indicative

	LATIN SINGULAR	ENGLISH SINGULAR		LATIN PLURAL	ENGLISH PLURAL
1ST	aperiēbam	I was opening		aperiēbāmus	we were opening
2ND	aperiēbās	you were opening		aperiēbātis	you (pl.) were opening
3RD	aperiēbat	he/she/it were opening		aperiēbant	they were opening

Imperfect Passive Indicative

	LATIN SINGULAR	ENGLISH SINGULAR		LATIN PLURAL	ENGLISH PLURAL
1ST	aperiēbar	I was (being) opened		aperiēbāmur	we were (being) opened
2ND	aperiēbāris	you were (being) opened		aperiēbāminī	you (pl.) were (being) opened
3RD	aperiēbātur	he/she/it was (being) opened		aperiēbantur	they were (being) opened

Like the Third Conjugation, the Fourth Conjugation future tense does not use *-bō*, *-bis*, *-bit*, etc. but rather a vowel change. Whereas the future vowels for the third are *a, ē, e, ē, ē, e*, the fourth once more simply sticks an *i* in front of that pattern:

	SINGULAR	PLURAL
1ST	-ia-	-iē-
2ND	-iē-	-iē-
3RD	-ie (act.) / -iē-(pass.)	-ie-

The future active and passive will conjugate like this (and make sure you point out the fine distinction between these forms and the present tense):

Future Active Indicative

	LATIN SINGULAR	ENGLISH SINGULAR		LATIN PLURAL	ENGLISH PLURAL
1ST	aperiam	I will open		aperiēmus	we will open
2ND	aperiēs	you will open		aperiētis	you (pl.) will open
3RD	aperiet	he/she/it will open		aperient	they will open

Future Passive Indicative

	LATIN SINGULAR	ENGLISH SINGULAR		LATIN PLURAL	ENGLISH PLURAL
1ST	aperiar	I will be opened		aperiēmur	we will be opened
2ND	aperiēris	you will be opened		aperiēminī	you (pl.) will be opened
3RD	aperiētur	he/she/it will be opened		aperientur	they will be opened

As you have noticed, it is now more critical than ever to know what conjugation a verb belongs to—and therefore it is important to know those principal parts. A verb could end in *-ētur* and be either present (if Second Conjugation) or future (if Third or Fourth). As you go through the vocabulary list in each new lesson, take a few moments to identify the conjugation of each new verb.

Fourth Conjugation Imperatives

Fourth Conjugation imperatives are formed just like those of the First and Second Conjugations: Go to the second principal part, take off the *-re*, and there you have the singular imperative: *aperīre* becomes *aperī*, open!

Simply add *-te* to make it plural: *aperīte*, open!

LATIN SINGULAR	ENGLISH SINGULAR		LATIN PLURAL	ENGLISH PLURAL
aperī	open!		aperīte	open! (pl.)

Full Conjugation of *eō, īre, iī* or *īvī, itum*, I go

In this lesson we also introduce an irregular, but highly important, Fourth Conjugation verb—*eō*, "I go." It's a bit tricky to learn because it is so short, but basically, most of the forms are an *i-* or an *ī-* slapped on the front of our usual endings. Consider the present:

Present Active* Indicative

	LATIN SINGULAR	ENGLISH SINGULAR		LATIN PLURAL	ENGLISH PLURAL
1ST	eō	I go		īmus	we go
2ND	īs	you go		ītis	you (pl.) go
3RD	it	he goes		eunt	they go

* Although *eō* is intransitive (doesn't take an object) and therefore doesn't have a passive (try making "I go" passive—it simply will not work), some of the compounds of *eō* are transitive and thus have passives. Only the active forms of *eō* are given here, and any passive forms of its compounds found in this book will be duly footnoted!

It doesn't quite match the Third Conjugation because of the e-stem in the first person singular and third person plural, so make sure you simply memorize it. Once you do, it's easy to remember. The imperfect is much easier:

Imperfect Active Indicative

	LATIN SINGULAR	ENGLISH SINGULAR		LATIN PLURAL	ENGLISH PLURAL
1ST	ībam	I was going		ībāmus	we were going
2ND	ībās	you were going		ībātis	you (pl.) were going
3RD	ībat	he was going		ībant	they go

Unlike other Fourth Conjugation verbs, *eō* does use *-bō, -bis, -bit,* etc. in the future tense and not the vowel change, which makes it easy too:

Future Active Indicative

	LATIN SINGULAR	ENGLISH SINGULAR		LATIN PLURAL	ENGLISH PLURAL
1ST	ībō	I will go		ībimus	we will go
2ND	ībis	you will go		ībitis	you (pl.) will go
3RD	ībit	he will go		ībunt	they will go

In the perfect system, *eō* can appear as *i-* or *īv-*. The forms with *īv-* are much less common, and therefore will appear less frequently in this book. This other stem exists, so don't be shocked if you encounter it; however, you don't need to use it. Note that the second person forms begin with the long *ī-*.

Perfect Active Indicative (forms with alternate stem in parentheses)

	LATIN SINGULAR	ENGLISH SINGULAR		LATIN PLURAL	ENGLISH PLURAL
1ST	iī (īvī)	I went/have gone		iimus (īvimus)	we went/have gone
2ND	īstī (īvistī)	you went/have gone		īstis (īvīstis)	you (pl.) went/have gone
3RD	iit (īvit)	he went/has gone		iērunt (īvērunt)	they went/have gone

The pluperfect and future perfect are much easier:

Pluperfect Active Indicative

	LATIN SINGULAR	ENGLISH SINGULAR		LATIN PLURAL	ENGLISH PLURAL
1ST	ieram (īveram)	I had gone		ierāmus (īverāmus)	we had gone
2ND	ierās (īverās)	you had gone		ierātis (īverātis)	you (pl.) had gone
3RD	ierat (īverat)	he had gone		ierant (īverant)	they had gone

Future Perfect Active Indicative

	LATIN SINGULAR	ENGLISH SINGULAR		LATIN PLURAL	ENGLISH PLURAL
1ST	ierō (īverō)	I will have gone		ierimus (īverimus)	we will have gone
2ND	ieris (īveris)	you will have gone		ieritis (īveritis)	you (pl.) will have gone
3RD	ierit (īverit)	he will have gone		ierint (īverint)	they will have gone

Imperative

LATIN SINGULAR	ENGLISH SINGULAR		LATIN PLURAL	ENGLISH PLURAL
ī	go!		īte	go! (pl.)

Review

Be sure to review your Fourth and Fifth Declension nouns, and keep up with your Third Conjugation verbs.

Lesson 29 Worksheet

A. Vocabulary

Translate the following words from Latin to English or English to Latin as appropriate. For the verbs, also fill in the missing principal parts.

1. army: _____

2. famēlicus: _____

3. dormiō, _____, _____, _____: _____

4. aperiō, aperīre, _____, _____: _____

5. I ride: _____, _____, _____, _____

6. quoque: _____

7. I go: _____, _____, _____, _____

8. audiō, _____, _____, _____: _____

9. animus: _____

10. I believe: _____, _____, _____, _____

11. impediō, _____, _____, _____: _____

12. cōgō, _____, _____, _____: _____

13. I know: _____, _____, _____, _____

14. greatly: _____

15. ēgregius: _____

16. clam: _____

17. I come: _____, _____, _____, _____

18. dēligō, _____, _____, _____: _____

19. ūnā: _____

20. bread: _____

21. colō, _____, _____, _____: _____

22. saxum: _____

23. inveniō, _____, _____, _____: _____

24. improbus: _____

25. resurgō, _____, _____, _____: _____

B. Grammar

1. Give a synopsis of *audiō* in the third person singular.

	ACTIVE		PASSIVE	
	LATIN	ENGLISH	LATIN	ENGLISH
PRES.				
IMPF.				
FUT.				
PERF.				
PLUPF.				
FT. PF.				

2. Give a synopsis of *colō* in the second person singular.

	ACTIVE		PASSIVE	
	LATIN	ENGLISH	LATIN	ENGLISH
PRES.				
IMPF.				
FUT.				
PERF.				
PLUPF.				
FT. PF.				

3. Conjugate *eō* in full.

Present Active Indicative

	LATIN SINGULAR	ENGLISH SINGULAR		LATIN PLURAL	ENGLISH PLURAL
1ST					
2ND					
3RD					

Imperfect Active Indicative

	LATIN SINGULAR	ENGLISH SINGULAR		LATIN PLURAL	ENGLISH PLURAL
1ST					
2ND					
3RD					

Future Active Indicative

	LATIN SINGULAR	ENGLISH SINGULAR		LATIN PLURAL	ENGLISH PLURAL
1ST					
2ND					
3RD					

Perfect Active Indicative

	LATIN SINGULAR	ENGLISH SINGULAR		LATIN PLURAL	ENGLISH PLURAL
1ST					
2ND					
3RD					

Pluperfect Active Indicative

	LATIN SINGULAR	ENGLISH SINGULAR		LATIN PLURAL	ENGLISH PLURAL
1ST					
2ND					
3RD					

Future Perfect Active Indicative

	LATIN SINGULAR	ENGLISH SINGULAR		LATIN PLURAL	ENGLISH PLURAL
1ST					
2ND					
3RD					

Imperative

LATIN SINGULAR	ENGLISH SINGULAR		LATIN PLURAL	ENGLISH PLURAL

4. Decline *wicked day.*

	LATIN SINGULAR	LATIN PLURAL
NOM.		
GEN.		
DAT.		
ACC.		
ABL.		
VOC.		

5. Decline *our blessed bread.*

	LATIN SINGULAR	LATIN PLURAL
NOM.		
GEN.		
DAT.		
ACC.		
ABL.		
VOC.		

C. Memorization

Fill in the blanks.

_____

_____

_____

_____

_____

_____

_____

⁴Nam _____ _____ ambulāverō _____ _____ umbrae _____,

nōn _____ _____ quoniam _____ _____ es;

_____ tua _____ _____ tuus _____ mē _____ sunt.

⁵Parāstī in _____ meō _____

_____ eōs _____ _____ mē.

_____ in _____ caput _____,

D. English to Latin Translation

Translate each sentence from English to Latin.

1. The knight's character seemed wicked to us afterwards, and we will never listen to him again.

   _____

   _____

2. On the fifth day the hungry orphans went and found your mother's bread, and they will eat it secretly and speedily.

   _____

   _____

3. The blind man could not sleep for two nights because of the great storm and enormous thunder.

   _____

   _____

4. "The sun rises again, and it is day," said the teacher, "and then the middle of the day is called noon."

   _____

   _____

5. The farmer chooses a wife, the wife chooses a son, and the son will also choose a dog.

_____

_____

6. According to many, his mind is wise but his words are dry; therefore we listen to him but will soon be sleeping.

_____

_____

7. The foolish sailors knew about the great rocks near the shore, but their ship was shattered.

_____

_____

8. The happy mother cherished the singing of the children, but we could not listen to them for a long time.

_____

_____

9. The unlucky army had been exposed in the fields, and so the soldiers went and hid in the rocks and caves of the mountain.

_____

_____

10. I love the king's daughter greatly and because of my burning love I will not be hindered by him!

_____

_____

E. Latin to English Translation

1 **Dē Piscibus**

Ōlim erant duae sorōrēs, Iūlia Iūniaque. Duae pulchrae erant, et faciēs Iūliae ēgregia erat sed Iūniae improba erat. Iūnia omnēs virōs amāvit, et ab improbīs modo amāta est. Bonī autem ab eā cūcurrērunt. Iūlia virōs nōn captāvit, sed labōrāvit et amōrem vērum exspectāvit. Unō diē eques novus ad oppidum

5 eārum īvit. Fortis erat et pulcher, et Iūlia et Iūnia eum fōvērunt. Sī eum in oppidō vīsit, Iūlia urbāna[1] erat sed suum negōtium ēgit.[2] Iūnia autem eum ubīque[3] invēnit et semper eī dīcēbat. Ergō eques Iūniam vitāvit,[4] sed Iūliae saepe dīcēbat. Iūnia invidēbat,[5] et consilium[6] in animō eius dēnique cultum est. Iūliae dīxit: "Ī mēcum[7] in nāve in lacū." Sed Iūlia āit, "Nāvis nostra vetus[8] et pertūsa[9] est." "Nōn est; refecta est,"[10] dīxit Iūnia (sed nāvis nōn refecta erat). "Venī, nōs ūnā in lacū nāvigābimus quod diēs pulcher est."

10 Ergō duae sorōrēs ad lacum iērunt et in nāve nāvigāvērunt. Eques pulcher prope piscābātur.[11] Secundum cōnsilium Iūniae nāvis vetus pertūsaque cadere incēpit.[12] Iūnia equitī ululāvit: "Iuvā! Heu! Nōs iuvā!" Iūlia timuit sed placida[13] mānsit. Ex nāve saluit[14] et Iūniae clāmāvit, "Nāre possumus, scīs!" Ecce! Lacus nōn altus est, et Iūlia stāre potuit. Rīsit. Eques omnia vīderat et quoque rīsit. Iūnia autem īrāta erat. Eques ad Iūliam per aquam ambulāvit. "Cupis[15] mēcum piscārī?" rogāvit. Ergō Iūlia vērum amōrem in

15 lacū invēnit, sed Iūnia vestēs aquōsās[16] et veterem nāvem pertūsam modo habuit.

Glossary

1. *urbānus, -a, -um*: polite
2. *suum negōtium agere*: to mind one's own business (idiom)
3. *ubīque*: everywhere
4. *vitō* (1): I avoid, shun
5. *invideō, -ēre, -vīdī, -vīsum*: I envy
6. *cōnsilium, -ī* (n): plan
7. *mēcum = cum mē: cum* is a coward and likes to hide behind and attach to many personal pronouns.
8. *vetus, (gen.) -teris*: old
9. *pertūsus, -a, -um*: leaky
10. *reficiō, -ere, -fēcī, -fectum*: I repair
11. *piscor, -ārī, -ātus sum*: I fish (Yes, it only has passive forms but it is translated actively—this type of verb is called a deponent and you will learn about it later.) *Piscārī* is the infinitive form, "to fish."
12. *incipiō, -ere, -cēpī, -ceptum*: I begin
13. *placidus, -a, -um*: calm, quiet
14. *saliō, -īre, -uī, saltum*: I jump, leap
15. *cupiō, -ere, cupīvī, cupītum*: I wish (for), desire
16. *aquōsus, -a, -um*: sopping wet

LESSON 30

Demonstratives

Word List

NOUNS

1. adulescens, -entis (m/f): *young man/woman*

2. classis, -is (f): *group, class, fleet (of ships)*

3. cōnsilium, -iī (n): *plan, counsel, advice; wisdom*

4. uxor, -ōris (f): *wife*

PRONOUNS

5. hic, haec, hoc: *this, (pl.) these*

6. ille, illa, illud: *that, (pl.) those; that famous*

7. iste, ista, istud: *that (of yours); such (sometimes used with tone of contempt)*

ADJECTIVES

8. dexter, -tra, -trum (*or* -tera, -terum): *right(-handed); skilled, favorable*

9. sinister, -stra, -strum: *left(-handed); inauspicious*

10. vetus, (gen.) -teris: *old*

VERBS

11. dīmittō, -ere, -mīsī, -missum: *I send away, dismiss, forgive*

12. nesciō, -īre, -īvī, -ītum: *I do not know*

13. occīdō, -ere, -cīdī, -cīsum: *I kill, cut down, slay*

14. trahō, -ere, trāxī, trāctum: *I draw, drag*

15. vinciō, -īre, vīnxī, vīnctum: *I bind, tie*

16. vītō (1): *I avoid, shun*

ADVERBS/CONJUNCTIONS/PREPOSITIONS

17. satis (adv. & indecl. adj./noun): *enough, sufficient(ly)*

18. sīve (sēū): *or;* sīve/sēū...sīve/sēū: *whether...or*

19. tamen: *yet, nevertheless, still*

20. undique: *on/from all sides, from every direction*

Memorization

[1]Psalmus Dāvīd.

Dominus reget mē et nihil mihi dēerit.

[2]In locō pascuae ibī mē conlocāvit;

super aquam refectiōnis ēducāvit mē.

[3]Animam meam convertit.

Dēdūxit mē super sēmitās iūstitiae

propter nōmen suum.

⁴Nam et sī ambulāverō in mediō umbrae mortis,

nōn timēbō mala quoniam tū mēcum es;

virga tua et baculus tuus ipsa mē consōlāta sunt.

⁵Parāstī in conspectū meō mensam

adversus eōs quī trībulant mē.

Inpinguāstī in oleō caput meum,

et calix meus inēbrians quam praeclārus est.

> *and my cup is intoxicating like splendid [wine].*

⁶Et misericordia tua subsequitur mē

> *And Your mercy follows me*

omnibus diēbus vītae meae,

> *all the days of my life,*

Grammar

Demonstratives:

A demonstrative adjective or pronoun points to something (*demonstrō*, I show, point out). You have already been using a demonstrative for some time—*is, ea, id*—which also happens to function as the third person personal pronoun. Now it is time to learn some other extremely common demonstratives.

hic, haec, hoc—this; (pl.) these

Hic, haec, hoc, meaning "this" and "these" in the plural, points to things that are near to the speaker. Imagine a roomful of chairs, and the speaker points to "this chair" right next to him, versus "that chair" way across the room. Although its chant does share similarities to that of *is, ea, id*, the whole thing should be memorized (and, it is easier to chant this one horizontally rather than vertically—*hic, haec, hoc; huius, huius, huius; huic, huic, huic;* etc.) The plural is fairly regular with First and Second Declension adjective endings, except for the neuter plural nominative and accusative. Here is its full declension (odd forms in bold):

	SINGULAR			PLURAL		
	MASCULINE	FEMININE	NEUTER	MASCULINE	FEMININE	NEUTER
NOM.	hic	haec	hoc	hī	hae	**haec**
GEN.	huius	huius	huius	hōrum	hārum	hōrum
DAT.	huic	huic	huic	hīs	hīs	hīs
ACC.	hunc	hanc	hoc	hōs	hās	**haec**
ABL.	hōc	hāc	hōc	hīs	hīs	hīs

ille, illa, illud—that; (pl.) those; that famous

Ille, illa, illud means "that" (or "those" when plural), and as indicated above, points to something farther away from the speaker—"that chair" over there. It can also sometimes imply "that famous," (think *ille eques Oswaldus*) and so of course context would help you out with that one. It is happily a bit more regular than *hic* (unusual forms in bold):

	SINGULAR			PLURAL		
	MASCULINE	FEMININE	NEUTER	MASCULINE	FEMININE	NEUTER
NOM.	**ille**	**illa**	**illud**	illī	illae	illa
GEN.	**illīus**	**illīus**	**illīus**	illōrum	illārum	illōrum
DAT.	**illī**	**illī**	**illī**	illīs	illīs	illīs
ACC.	illum	illam	**illud**	illōs	illās	illa
ABL.	illō	illā	illō	illīs	illīs	illīs

iste, ista, istud—that (of yours); such (sometimes used with tone of contempt)

While *hic* refers to something close to the speaker and *ille* to something distant, *iste, ista, istud* points to something close to the audience: "This is my cookie, that one in your hand is yours." In certain contexts (e.g., Cicero's orations which took place in a courtroom setting), *iste* refers to the speaker's opponent and therefore can have a hostile or contemptuous tone (it is easy to hiss *iste*, but not the other demonstratives). Translating that tone into English can be difficult, so be creative when you translate.

	SINGULAR			PLURAL		
	MASCULINE	FEMININE	NEUTER	MASCULINE	FEMININE	NEUTER
NOM.	**iste**	ista	**istud**	istī	istae	ista
GEN.	**istīus**	**istīus**	**istīus**	istōrum	istārum	istōrum
DAT.	**istī**	**istī**	**istī**	istīs	istīs	istīs
ACC.	istum	istam	**istud**	istōs	istās	ista
ABL.	istō	istā	istō	istīs	istīs	istīs

Note: Demonstratives do not have a vocative. This is possibly because you are already pointing at them by using a demonstrative and you don't need to use a vocative to point to them—plus, I dare you to try to use "this" vocatively—it just doesn't work. Therefore, when you are declining noun-adjective phrases including a demonstrative, you can omit that demonstrative in the vocative.

Usage: Demonstratives can function either as pronouns (standing alone) or as adjectives.

Pronoun: *Ille dracōnem necāvit.*　　That (famous) man killed the dragon.

Adjective: Ille eques dracōnem necāvit. That (famous) knight killed the dragon.

Again, context is king.

Review

Review your Fifth Declension nouns and your Fourth Conjugation verbs. It's important.

Lesson 30 Worksheet

A. Vocabulary

Translate the following words from Latin to English or English to Latin as appropriate. For the verbs, also fill in the missing principal parts.

1. occīdō, _____, _____, _____: _____

2. sīve (sēū): _____

3. vetus: _____

4. I go: _____

5. vītō, _____, _____, _____: _____

6. that famous: _____

7. modo: _____

8. I do not know: _____, _____, _____, _____

9. adulescens: _____

10. hic: _____

11. plan: _____

12. truth: _____

13. vinciō, _____, _____, _____: _____

14. from all sides: _____

15. uxor: _____

16. enough: _____

17. iterum: _____

18. cāsus: _____

19. such: _____

20. classis; _____

21. sinister: _____

22. tamen; _____

23. I draw: _____, _____, _____, _____

24. dīmittō, _____, _____, _____: _____

25. right: _____

B. Grammar

1. Decline *that (famous) left-handed young man.*

	LATIN SINGULAR	LATIN PLURAL
NOM.		
GEN.		
DAT.		
ACC.		
ABL.		
VOC.		

2. Decline *such an old rock* (use *vetus* for "old").

	LATIN SINGULAR	LATIN PLURAL
NOM.		
GEN.		
DAT.		
ACC.		
ABL.		
VOC.		

3. Decline *this ordinary hand.*

	LATIN SINGULAR	LATIN PLURAL
NOM.		
GEN.		
DAT.		
ACC.		
ABL.		
VOC.		

4. Give a synopsis of *vinciō* in the first person singular.

	ACTIVE		PASSIVE	
	LATIN	ENGLISH	LATIN	ENGLISH
PRES.				
IMPF.				
FUT.				
PERF.				
PLUPF.				
FT. PF.				

2. Give a synopsis of *trahō* in the second person singular.

	ACTIVE		PASSIVE	
	LATIN	ENGLISH	LATIN	ENGLISH
PRES.				
IMPF.				
FUT.				
PERF.				
PLUPF.				
FT. PF.				

C. Memorization

Fill in the blanks.

_____

_____

_____

_____

_____

_____

_____

⁴Nam _____ _____ ambulāverō _____ _____ umbrae _____,

nōn _____ _____ quoniam _____ _____ es;

_____ tua _____ _____ tuus _____ mē _____ sunt.

⁵_____ in _____ meō _____

_____ eōs _____ trībulant _____.

_____ in _____ _____ meum,

et _____ meus _____ _____ praeclārus _____.

⁶Et _____ tua _____ mē

_____ diēbus vītae _____,

D. English to Latin Translation

Translate each sentence from English to Latin.

1. If we will believe in Jesus, our evils will be forgiven us and we will rise again in glory.

   _____

   _____

2. That famous man's wife was beautiful and she was greatly desired by many.

   _____

   _____

3. That black fleet has sailed to our shores and the enemy will besiege us for ten years.

   _____

   _____

4. Nevertheless, lead this woman into the fortifications and there she will prepare enough bread and cookies for all the soldiers.

    _____

    _____

5. I was approaching the cave and there I saw a huge dark shape—whether man or beast, I do not know—but I did not go into the cave afterwards.

    _____

    _____

6. This foolish young man did not know about horses, and so he fell down from my tall horse and was dragged by it for a long time.

    _____

    _____

7. Three swift lions attacked this shepherd from all directions and yet he was able to defend the animals and kill all of the lions.

    _____

    _____

8. These men and women cherished that famous woman, because she was their queen and had governed and ruled their land well for many years.

    _____

    _____

    _____

9. The brave soldier put [his] right hand into the fire because he feared neither the king nor the army of the enemy.

    _____

    _____

10. That wicked man's plans were destroyed by this faithful knight, and then that man paid the penalty.

    _____

    _____

E. Latin to English Translation

1 **Thēsēus[1] Mīnōtaurusque[2]**

Ōlim in īnsulā Crētā[3] ille Rex Mīnos[4] habitāvit. Bellum contrā Athēniensēs[5] gesserat et urbem eōrum vīcerat. Ergō dēclārāvit: "Omnī annō nōnō puerōs septem et septem puellās vinciētis, et eōs ad īnsulam meam quam tribūtum[6] mittētis." Cūr prō hīs quattuordecim līberīs rogāvit? In īnsula eius Mīnōtaurus
5 mōnstrum[7] cum capite taurī et corpore virī, quoque habitāvit. Ferus foedusque erat, et carnem[8] hominum modo mandūcābat. Mīnos Daedalō[9] dīxerat: "Mihi fac[10] labyrinthum[11] multīs cum viīs. Mīnōtaurum in labyrinthō pōnam et ex eō deinde īre nōn poterit." Daedalus ergō hunc labyrinthum fēcit et Mīnōtaurus in eō positus est.

Tertiō casū tribūtī, Thēsēus, fīlius Rēgis Aegeī[12] Athēnārum, patrī dīxit: "Ō pater, ad Crētam ībō et
10 ego Mīnōtaurum occīdam." Pater eius tristis erat sed eum īre permīsit.[13] Thēsēus dīxit, "Valē, pater. Sī istam bēstiam occīdam, haec nāvis vēla[14] alba geret; sī nōn, vēla ātra manēbunt!" Ergō, nāvis vēlīs cum ātrīs ab Athēnīs ad Crētam nāvigāvit. Ibī Ariadna[15] fīlia Mīnōis Thēsēum vīdit et amōre prō eō arsit. Eum iūvit et eī pilam[16] ex fīlō[17] dedit. Fīlō viam in medium labyrinthum invēnit, Mīnōtaurum occīdit, et fīlum ex labyrinthō deinde secūtus est.[18] Ab īnsulā cum Ariadnā nāvigāvit, sed eam in parvā īnsulā
15 relīquit. Itaque ea eum maledīxit:[19] "Dē vēlīs albīs nōn cōgitābis!" Thēsēus ad Athēnās nāvigāvit, sed in nāve vēla ātra vīsa sunt. Pater eius in scopulō[20] altō stābat et haec vīdit. Cōgitāvit: "Fīlius meus Thēsēus occīsus est!" et ab scopulō saluit[21] et ergō in mare occīsus est. Itaque hoc mare Mare Aegeum appellātur.

Glossary
1. *Thēsēus, -eī* (m): Theseus, Greek hero and founder of Athens
2. *Mīnōtaurus, -ī* (m): the Minotaur
3. *Crēta, -ae* (f): Crete
4. *Mīnos, Mīnōis (m)*: Minos, a notorious king of Crete
5. *Athēnae, -ārum* (f, pl.): Athens; *Athēniensis, -is* (m/f) an Athenian
6. *tribūtum, -ī* (n): tribute, tax
7. *mōnstrum, -ī* (n): monster
8. *caro, carnis* (f): flesh
9. *Daedalus, -ī* (m): Daedalus, a skilled inventor and craftsman
10. *faciō, -ere, fēcī, factum*: I make, do, build

11. *labyrinthus, -ī* (m): labyrinth, maze
12. *Aegeus, -eī* (m): Aegeus; *Aegeus, -a, -um*: Aegean
13. *permittō, -ere, -mīsī, -missum*: I permit, allow
14. *vēlum, -ī* (n): sail
15. *Ariadna, -ae* (f): Ariadne
16. *pila, -ae* (f): ball
17. *fīlum, -ī* (n): thread, string
18. *sequor, sequī, secūtus sum*: I follow (another deponent—passive in form, active in meaning)
19. *maledīcō, -ere, -dīxī, -dictum*: I speak ill, curse
20. *scopulus, -ī* (m): cliff
21. *saliō, -īre, -uī, saltum*: I jump, leap

F. Crossword Puzzle

Fill in the correct forms of the Latin words, and as appropriate translate the italicized English words into Latin. (Don't use macrons for the Latin words in the puzzle.)

ACROSS

3. *you (pl.) will join*

7. first person plural perfect active indicative of the verb meaning *I believe*

10. *it will be placed*

11. first person singular present active indicative of the verb meaning *I touch*

12. feminine ablative singular of *grātus*

13. nominative singular of the word meaning *wife*

14. the word for *storm* in the accusative singular

16. *she is cherished*

18. *together*

22. first person plural present passive indicative of *trahō*

24. *house*

25. *he was destroying*

26. third person singular present active indicative of the verb meaning *I put*

27. neuter plural dative of *sanctus*

30. *nevertheless*

31. *in what way*

33. first person singular perfect active indicative of *eō*

36. *I will know*

37. third person plural future passive indicative of the verb meaning *I write*

38. *or*

40. *resurgō* in the third person plural future perfect active indicative

42. *you will be ruled*

43. masculine singular accusative of the adjective meaning *left*

46. the word meaning *mind* in the nominative singular

48. neuter singular ablative of *ēgregius*

51. *perhaps*

52. *the wife's*

53. *vehō* in the second person singular future passive indicative

55. *it is choosing*

56. *in the presence of*

57. *you had worshipped*

DOWN

1. *I have broken*

2. first person singular future active indicative of *mittō*

3. *again*

4. *gerō* in the first person singular present passive indicative

5. *he touched*

6. *of the holy ones*

8. *hands* (nominative)

9. ablative singular of *spēs*

14. *tonitrus* in the dative plural

15. *we had approached*

17. *versus* in the nominative plural

19. first person plural imperfect active indicative of the verb meaning *I avoid*

20. *you were hindering*

21. *of the hope*

23. the word meaning *fear* in the ablative singular

28. masculine singular genitive of *novus*

29. second person singular future passive indicative of *iungō*

32. *you (pl.) choose*

34. feminine plural accusative of *iste*

35. *they were being opened*

37. ablative plural of the word meaning *rock*

39. *you will have done*

41. *you have touched*

44. *greatly*

45. *also*

47. the word for *Jesus* in the nominative singular

49. *you will hear*

50. ablative singular of the word meaning *grace*

54. neuter accusative singular of the demonstrative *this*

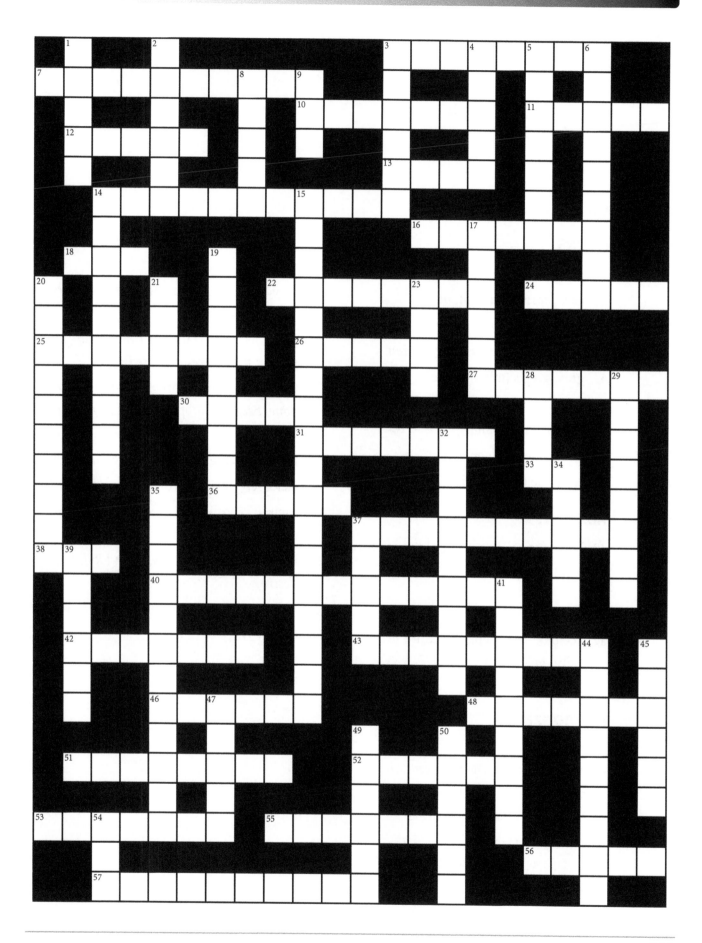

LESSON 31

Verbs: Third -io Conjugation, Active & Passive / Irregular Verbs faciō & fiō

Word List

NOUNS

1. barbarus, -ī (m): *foreigner, barbarian*
2. caro, carnis (f): *flesh, meat*
3. fenestra, -ae (f): *window*
5. gēns, -ntis (f): *clan, tribe, nation*
4. grex, gregis (m): *flock, herd*
6. hōra, -ae (f): *hour*
7. mensa, -ae (f): *table*
8. porta, -ae (f): *door, gate*
9. sella, -ae (f): *seat, chair*

ADJECTIVES

10. barbarus, -a, -um: *foreign, strange, savage*
11. gelidus, -a, -um: *cold, icy*

VERBS

12. accipiō, -ere, -cēpī, ceptum: *I accept, receive, take*
13. capiō, -ere, cēpī, captum: *I take, capture, seize*
14. cupiō, -ere, cupīvī, cupītum: *I wish (for), desire, long (for)*
15. faciō, -ere, fēcī, factum: *I make, do [for present passive system, use* fiō]
16. fiō, fierī, factus sum: *I am made, am done, become, happen [used as passive of* faciō]
17. fugiō, -ere, fūgī, fugitum: *I flee, run away*
18. iaciō, -ere, iēcī, iactum: *I throw, cast, hurl*
19. incipiō, -ere, -cēpī, -ceptum: *I begin, commence*
20. interficiō, -ere, -fēcī, -fectum: *I kill, slay, destroy*
21. rapiō, -ere, rapuī, raptum: *I snatch, seize, carry (off)*

Memorization

¹Psalmus Dāvīd.

Dominus reget mē et nihil mihi dēerit.

²In locō pascuae ibī mē conlocāvit;

super aquam refectiōnis ēducāvit mē.

³Animam meam convertit.

Dēdūxit mē super sēmitās iūstitiae

propter nōmen suum.

⁴Nam et sī ambulāverō in mediō umbrae mortis,

nōn timēbō mala quoniam tū mēcum es;

virga tua et baculus tuus ipsa mē consōlāta sunt.

⁵Parāstī in conspectū meō mensam

adversus eōs quī trībulant mē.

Inpinguāstī in oleō caput meum,

et calix meus inēbrians quam praeclārus est.

⁶Et misericordia tua subsequitur mē

omnibus diēbus vītae meae,

et ut inhabitem in domō Dominī

so that I also may dwell in the house of the Lord

in longitūdinem diērum.

for the length of [my] days.

Grammar

Third -*iō* Conjugation Verbs:

Congratulations. You have arrived at the Third -*iō* Conjugation, the final conjugation of Latin verbs! And it isn't even really a whole new conjugation; it's more of a hybrid between the Third and Fourth Conjugations. Therefore, some grammar books do not consider it its own separate thing and include it in with the Third (its verbs can also be referred to as Third Conjugation i-stems).

How is such a verb identified? By the principal parts, of course. Our example verb for this chapter is word #18, *iaciō, -ere, iēcī, iactum*, "I throw, cast, hurl." We go to the second principal part and take off the -*re*, and are left with *iace-*. Clearly, the short *e* of the stem indicates that it belongs to the Third Conjugation. However, we also must look at the first principal part, and there we see *iaciō*, which looks an awful lot like the first principal parts of all the Fourth Conjugation verbs we've learned. Thus we have a Third -*iō* verb.

Like verbs of the Third and Fourth conjugation, Third -*iō* verbs are only a bit tricky in the present system. They also use a vowel change for the future tense rather than -*bō*, -*bis*, -*bit*. Here is a review of the vowels used in the present tense in Third and Fourth conjugation verbs, with the new conjugation's vowels:

Present Vowels

	3RD CONJ. PRESENT ACTIVE		4TH CONJ. PRESENT ACTIVE		3RD CONJ. -*iō* PRESENT ACTIVE	
	SINGULAR	PLURAL	SINGULAR	PLURAL	SINGULAR	PLURAL
1ST	-ō	-i-	-iō	-ī-	-iō	-i-
2ND	-i-	-i-	-ī-	-ī-	-i-	-i-
3RD	-i-	-u-	-i-	-iu-	-i-	-iu-

	3RD CONJ. PRESENT PASSIVE		4TH CONJ. PRESENT PASSIVE		3RD CONJ. -IO PRESENT PASSIVE	
	SINGULAR	PLURAL	SINGULAR	PLURAL	SINGULAR	PLURAL
1ST	-o	-i-	-io	-ī-	-io	-i-
2ND	-e-	-i-	-ī-	-ī-	-e-	-i-
3RD	-i-	-u-	-ī-	-iu-	-i-	-iu-

As you can see, third -iō verbs follow the general ō, i, i, i, i, u pattern—they imitate the Third Conjugation in the second singular, third singular, first plural, and second plural. Like the Fourth Conjugation, however, they have an *-iō/-io* in the first person singular, and an *-iu-* in the third person plural. Here is *iaciō* fully conjugated in the present active and passive to give you a fuller picture of its vowels in their proper context:

iaciō, -ere, iēcī, iactum—I throw, cast, hurl

Present Active Indicative

	LATIN SINGULAR	ENGLISH SINGULAR	LATIN PLURAL	ENGLISH PLURAL
1ST	**iaciō**	I throw	**iacimus**	we throw
2ND	**iacis**	you throw	**iacitis**	you (pl.) throw
3RD	**iacit**	he/she/it throws	**iaciunt**	they throw

Present Passive Indicative

	LATIN SINGULAR	ENGLISH SINGULAR	LATIN PLURAL	ENGLISH PLURAL
1ST	**iacior**	I am (being) thrown	**iacimur**	we are (being) thrown
2ND	**iaceris**	you are (being) thrown	**iaciminī**	you (pl.) are (being) thrown
3RD	**iacitur**	he/she/it is (being) thrown	**iaciuntur**	they are (being) thrown

The imperfect of Third -iō verbs copies the Fourth Conjugation *-iē-* all the way down:

	3RD CONJ. IMPERF. ACT./PASS.		4TH CONJ. IMPERF. ACT./PASS.		3RD CONJ. -IO IMPERF. ACT./PASS.	
	SINGULAR	PLURAL	SINGULAR	PLURAL	SINGULAR	PLURAL
1ST	-ē-	-ē-	-iē-	-iē-	-iē-	-iē-
2ND	-ē-	-ē-	-iē-	-iē-	-iē-	-iē-
3RD	-ē-	-ē-	-iē-	-iē-	-iē-	-iē-

And here is *iaciō* conjugated in the imperfect active and passive, with English translation:

Imperfect Active Indicative

	LATIN SINGULAR	ENGLISH SINGULAR	LATIN PLURAL	ENGLISH PLURAL
1ST	**iaciēbam**	I was throwing	**iaciēbāmus**	we were throwing
2ND	**iaciēbās**	you were throwing	**iaciēbātis**	you (pl.) were throwing
3RD	**iaciēbat**	he/she/it was throwing	**iaciēbant**	they were throwing

Imperfect Passive Indicative

	LATIN SINGULAR	ENGLISH SINGULAR		LATIN PLURAL	ENGLISH PLURAL
1ST	iaciēbar	I was (being) thrown		iaciēbāmur	we were (being) thrown
2ND	iaciēbāris	you were (being) thrown		iaciēbāminī	you (pl.) were (being) thrown
3RD	iaciēbātur	he/she/it was (being) thrown		iaciēbantur	they were (being) thrown

In the future tense, third -iō verbs will generally follow the vowel change pattern of *a, ē, e, ē, ē, e* (rather than using the *-bō, -bis, -bit* endings). In both the active and passive, they imitate Fourth Conjugation verbs by inserting that extra i in front of the future vowel:

	3RD CONJ. FUTURE ACTIVE			4TH CONJ. FUTURE ACTIVE			3RD CONJ. -IO FUTURE ACTIVE	
	SINGULAR	PLURAL		SINGULAR	PLURAL		SINGULAR	PLURAL
1ST	-a-	-ē-		-ia-	-iē-		-ia-	-iē-
2ND	-ē-	-ē-		-iē-	-iē-		-iē-	-iē-
3RD	-e-	-e-		-ie-	-ie-		-ie-	-ie-

	3RD CONJ. FUTURE PASSIVE			4TH CONJ. FUTURE PASSIVE			3RD CONJ. -IO FUTURE PASSIVE	
	SINGULAR	PLURAL		SINGULAR	PLURAL		SINGULAR	PLURAL
1ST	-a-	-ē-		-ia-	-iē-		-ia-	-iē-
2ND	-ē-	-ē-		-iē-	-iē-		-iē-	-iē-
3RD	-ē-	-e-		-iē-	-ie-		-iē-	-ie-

And so here is our example verb fully conjugated in the future active and passive:

Future Active Indicative

	LATIN SINGULAR	ENGLISH SINGULAR		LATIN PLURAL	ENGLISH PLURAL
1ST	iaciam	I will throw		iaciēmus	we will throw
2ND	iaciēs	you will throw		iaciētis	you (pl.) will throw
3RD	iaciet	he/she/it will throw		iacient	they will throw

Future Passive Indicative

	LATIN SINGULAR	ENGLISH SINGULAR		LATIN PLURAL	ENGLISH PLURAL
1ST	iaciar	I will be thrown		iaciēmur	we will be thrown
2ND	iaciēris	you will be thrown		iaciēminī	you (pl.) will be thrown
3RD	iaciētur	he/she/it will be thrown		iacientur	they will be thrown

Although all of these minute vowel differences may seem a bit bewildering at the moment, these verbs are really quite easy to translate—in the midst of working on a sentence your mind will not have a panic attack about whether this particular verb is at this particular moment imitating a Third or Fourth Conjugation verb. Review them, and you'll find they're really intuitive.

Finally we come to our imperatives. Since Third -iō verbs have that short -e once the -re is removed, we should not wonder that they will imitate Third Conjugation imperatives (stem ending in -e) rather than Fourth (which end in -ī). Like the Third Conjugation, that short -e gets trimmed down to a short -i- when the plural -te ending is added:

3RD CONJ. IMPERATIVE		4TH CONJ. IMPERATIVE		3RD CONJ. -IO IMPERATIVE	
SINGULAR	PLURAL	SINGULAR	PLURAL	SINGULAR	PLURAL
2ND	-e	-ite	-ī	-īte	-e	-ite

Imperative

LATIN SINGULAR	ENGLISH SINGULAR	LATIN PLURAL	ENGLISH PLURAL
iace!	throw!	iacite!	throw!

Just in case you are reeling from this new conjugation, here is *iaciō* conjugated alongside a third and a Fourth Conjugation verb so that you can more easily spot the differences and similarities:

Comparison of Third, Fourth, and Third -iō Conjugations in the Present System

regō, impediō, and *iaciō*

	ACTIVE			PASSIVE		
	THIRD	FOURTH	THIRD -IŌ	THIRD	FOURTH	THIRD -IŌ
PRES.	regō	impediō	iaciō	regor	impedior	iacior
	regis	impedīs	iacis	regeris	impedīris	iaceris
	regit	impedit	iacit	regitur	impedītur	iacitur
	regimus	impedīmus	iacimus	regimur	impedīmur	iacimur
	regitis	impedītis	iacitis	regiminī	impedīminī	iaciminī
	regunt	impediunt	iaciunt	reguntur	impediuntur	iaciuntur
IMPF.	regēbam	impediēbam	iaciēbam	regēbar	impediēbar	iaciēbar
	regēbās	impediēbās	iaciēbās	regēbāris	impediēbāris	iaciēbāris
	regēbat	impediēbat	iaciēbat	regēbātur	impediēbātur	iaciēbātur
	regēbāmus	impediēbāmus	iaciēbāmus	regēbāmur	impediēbāmur	iaciēbāmur
	regēbātis	impediēbātis	iaciēbātis	regēbāminī	impediēbāminī	iaciēbāminī
	regēbant	impediēbant	iaciēbant	regēbantur	impediēbantur	iaciēbantur
FUT.	regam	impediam	iaciam	regar	impediar	iaciar
	regēs	impediēs	iaciēs	regēris	impediēris	iaciēris
	reget	impediet	iaciet	regētur	impediētur	iaciētur
	regēmus	impediēmus	iaciēmus	regēmur	impediēmur	iaciēmur
	regētis	impediētis	iaciētis	regēminī	impediēminī	iaciēminī
	regent	impedient	iacient	regentur	impedientur	iacientur
	IMPERATIVE SINGULAR			IMPERATIVE PLURAL		
	rege!	impedī!	iace!	regite!	impedīte!	iacite!

As for the perfect system of Third Conjugation -iō verbs, there is nothing new or tricky to be learned. Once you have the third and fourth principal parts (which very likely could be a bit irregular), they will conjugate in the perfect, pluperfect, and future perfect active and passive just like all the other verbs you have been using.

Irregular Verbs: *faciō* and *fiō*

The verb *faciō, -ere, fēcī, factum* means "I make, do," and is a very commonly used verb in Latin. And, like most commonly used words, it has some interesting aspects to it. For one thing, in the present system, the Romans did not conjugate it with regular passive endings (*facior, faceris, facitur*, etc.). Rather, they used another verb entirely to express the present, imperfect, and future passive of *faciō: fiō, fierī, factus sum. Fiō* means "I am made, am done, become, happen." Although it is active in form, some of its meanings are passive. *Fiō* lacks a perfect passive system, so it borrows from *faciō* just like *faciō* borrows from it in the present system.

Otherwise, *faciō* is conjugated like other "normal" third -iō verbs, and its full conjugation can be written out thus:

	ACTIVE		PASSIVE	
	LATIN	**ENGLISH**	**LATIN**	**ENGLISH**
PRES.	faciō	facimus	**fīō**	**fīmus**
	facis	facitis	**fīs**	**fītis**
	facit	faciunt	**fit**	**fīunt**
IMPF.	faciēbam	faciēbāmus	**fīēbam**	**fīēbāmus**
	faciēbās	faciēbātis	**fīēbās**	**fīēbātis**
	faciēbat	faciēbant	**fīēbat**	**fīēbant**
FUT.	faciam	faciēmus	**fīam**	**fīēmus**
	faciēs	faciētis	**fīēs**	**fīētis**
	faciet	facient	**fīet**	**fīent**
PERF.	fēcī	fēcimus	factus/a/um sum	factī/ae/a sumus
	fēcistī	fēcistis	factus/a/um es	factī/ae/a estis
	fēcit	fēcērunt	factus/a/um est	factī/ae/a sunt
PLUPF.	fēceram	fēcerāmus	factus/a/um eram	factī/ae/a erāmus
	fēcerās	fēcerātis	factus/a/um erās	factī/ae/a erātis
	fēcerat	fēcerant	factus/a/um erat	factī/ae/a erant
FT. PF.	fēcerō	fēcerimus	factus/a/um erō	factī/ae/a erimus
	fēceris	fēceritis	factus/a/um eris	factī/ae/a eritis
	fēcerit	fēcerint	factus/a/um erit	factī/ae/a erunt

A synopsis of *faciō* will be tricky, since in the present passive system a form of *fiō* will have to be used. For example, if you are asked for a synopsis of *faciō* in the third person singular, it would look like this:

	ACTIVE			PASSIVE	
	LATIN	ENGLISH		LATIN	ENGLISH
PRES.	facit	he/she/it makes/does		**fit**	it is (being) made/done
IMPF.	faciēbat	it was doing		**fīēbat**	it was (being) done
FUT.	faciet	it will do		**fīet**	it will be done
PERF.	fēcit	it did, has done		factus/a/um est	it was/has been done
PLUPF.	fēcerat	it had done		factus/a/um erat	it had been done
FT. PF.	fēcerit	it will have done		factus/a/um erit	it will have been done

Review

Quiz yourself on all the forms you know at this point. Surely there are some you're weak on. Practice those. At the very least keep drilling the demonstratives. Some of the forms are weird.

Conclusion

That's it! That is all the grammar you will learn in *Kraken Latin Book 1*. There are two more books and it includes some very important concepts to help you read Latin, but you know all the noun declensions, both types of adjectives, all the verb conjugations and tenses, as well as pronouns and demonstratives. Good work, and I hope you enjoyed this journey into Latin!

Lesson 31 Worksheet

A. Vocabulary

Translate the following words from Latin to English or English to Latin as appropriate. For the verbs, also fill in the missing principal parts. For each preposition, include which case(s) it takes.

1. sella: _____

2. perhaps: _____

3. interficiō, _____, _____, -_____: _____

4. I desire: _____, _____, _____, _____

5. accipiō, _____, _____, _____: _____

6. knee: _____

7. fenestra: _____

8. I make: _____, _____, _____, _____

9. porta: _____

10. capiō, _____, _____, _____: _____

11. fīō, _____, _____: _____

12. according to: _____

13. fugiō, _____, _____, _____: _____

14. flesh: _____

15. grex: _____

16. I throw: _____, _____, _____, _____

17. foreign: _____

18. gēns: _____

19. animus: _____

20. I snatch: _____, _____, _____, _____

21. gelidus: _____

22. hour: _____

23. I begin: _____, _____, _____, _____

24. mensa: _____

25. grātia: _____

B. Grammar

1. Give a synopsis of *capiō* in the third person singular and give its singular and plural imperatives.

	ACTIVE			PASSIVE	
	LATIN	ENGLISH		LATIN	ENGLISH
PRES.					
IMPF.					
FUT.					
PERF.					
PLUPF.					
F.T. PF.					

IMPERATIVE			
LATIN SINGULAR	ENGLISH SINGULAR	LATIN PLURAL	ENGLISH PLURAL

2. Give a synopsis of *vinciō* in the third person singular and give its singular and plural imperatives.

	ACTIVE		PASSIVE	
	LATIN	ENGLISH	LATIN	ENGLISH
PRES.				
IMPF.				
FUT.				
PERF.				
PLUPF.				
FT. PF.				

IMPERATIVE			
LATIN SINGULAR	ENGLISH SINGULAR	LATIN PLURAL	ENGLISH PLURAL

3. Give a synopsis of *dūcō* in the third person singular and give its singular and plural imperatives.

	ACTIVE		PASSIVE	
	LATIN	ENGLISH	LATIN	ENGLISH
PRES.				
IMPF.				
FUT.				
PERF.				
PLUPF.				
FT. PF.				

IMPERATIVE			
LATIN SINGULAR	ENGLISH SINGULAR	LATIN PLURAL	ENGLISH PLURAL

4. Decline *ille* in full.

	SINGULAR			PLURAL		
	MASCULINE	FEMININE	NEUTER	MASCULINE	FEMININE	NEUTER
NOM.						
GEN.						
DAT.						
ACC.						
ABL.						

C. Memorization

Fill in the blanks.

_____

_____

_____

_____

_____

_____

_____

_____

_____

_____

_____

_____

_____

_____ _____ oleō _____ meum,

et _____ _____ inēbrians _____ _____ est.

[6]Et _____ _____ subsequitur _____

_____ diēbus _____ _____,

et ut _____ in _____ Dominī

_____ _____ diērum.

D. English to Latin Translation

Translate each sentence from English to Latin.

1. The daughter of the goddess of grain was going to the fields of flowers and then she was snatched suddenly by that god and carried swiftly under the earth.

   _____

   _____

2. Light was made by God, and He also afterwards made the sun and moon.

   _____

   _____

3. These soldiers will hurl spears and rocks toward the enemy, but not all of them will be killed.

   _____

   _____

4. We are hungry and greatly desire much bread and meat and wine—put them on the table now!

   _____

   _____

   _____

5. At the seventh hour that wicked knight fled through the gates of the city and was received by the foreign tribe of the enemy.

   _____

   _____

6. The night was cold and the white stars shone, but then the fiery dragon carried off their flock of sheep.

   _____

   _____

7. Those leaders will throw the city's enemy from the window of the castle.

   _____

   _____

8. Many chairs have been placed next to the table; we will now begin to eat and drink.

   _____

   _____

9. I have sailed on the cold deep sea for many days and I greatly long for my wife and my native land.

   _____

   _____

10. You had seen the lions, and because of fear you turned and fled into the house.

E. Latin to English Translation

1 **Illud Ōrāculum**

Ōlim rex vetus septem fīliōs habēbat. Ille rēgīnaque hōs fīliōs ad illam vātem[1] in spēluncā dūxērunt quia ōrācula[2] dē eīs audīre cupīvērunt. Vātes nihil dē sex fīliīs maiōribus[3] dīxit, sed minimum[4] (modo īnfantem[5]) spectāvit et praedīxit:[6] "Ūnō diē ille īnfāns regnum dē perīculō magnō servābit et rex fīet."

5 Maximus[7] frāter, adulescens, dē hōc ōrāculō īrātus erat, itaque ūnā nocte īnfantem frātrem rapuit, eum ex castellō portāvit, eum in nāviculā[8] parvā pōsuit, et nāviculam in flūmine mīsit. Hic raptus[9] numquam inventus est, et post multōs annōs maximus frāter rex factus est.

Uxor pastōris veteris nāviculam parvam cum īnfante interim invēnerat, et illī duo puerum cūrābant et quoque eum fovēbat quod līberōs nōn habuērunt. Nōmen *Oswaldum* eī dedērunt. Ūnō diē, draco barbarus

10 super terram volāvit et omnia cremāre incēpit. Metus super omnēs cecidit. Rex novus dē dracōnibus nescīvit et magnoperē timuit. Iste draco multa animālia ex grege Oswaldī iam perdiderat; itaque is ad castellum iit et "Ego," āit, "tuus servus pastor sum, sed ego istum dracōnem occīdam." Rex eī dīxit, "Sī eum occīdēs, ego tibī multum aurum dabō et tē equitem faciam." Ergō Oswaldus ab castellum cessit, dracōnem appropinquāvit in spēluncam ātram eius, et eum gladiō antīquō pastōris interfēcit. Omnēs

15 laetī erant, et Oswaldum rēgem facere cupīvērunt quoniam is fortior[10] erat quam rex novus. Ille, "Sed quis,"[11] inquit, "est pater eius? Bonus rex erit? Pastor modo est." Oswaldus cōram rēge dīxit: "Ego modo pastor sum, sed meum patrem vērum nesciō. Quam īnfāns ego in nāviculā parvā ab pastōre veterī et uxōre eius inventus sum." Rex magnoperē timuit, tum enim suum[12] frātrem scīvit. "Tū vērus rex es," flēvit. "Ego tuus frāter maximus sum, et ego tē in illā nāviculā parvā istā nocte posuī propter ōrāculum.

20 Mē dīmitte!" Et Oswaldus rex deinde factus est, frātrem suum dīmīsit, et multōs annōs laetōs bene rexit.

Glossary
1. *vātes, -is* (m/f): prophet/prophetess
2. *ōrāculum, -ī* (n): oracle, prophecy
3. *māior, māius* (gen. *māioris*): greater; here, "older"
4. *minimus, -a, -um*: least; here, "youngest"
5. *īnfāns, -fantis* (adj. & noun, m/f): baby, infant
6. *praedicō, -ere, -dīxī, -dictum*: I predict, prophesy

7. *maximus, -a, -um*: greatest; here, "oldest"
8. *nāvicula, -ae* (f): boat
9. *raptus, -ūs* (m): kidnapping, abduction
10. *fortior, -tius* (gen. *fortioris*): braver
11. *quis*: who?
12. *suus, -a, -um*: his own, her own, its own

LESSON 32

Review & Test

Word List

No new word list this lesson. Review all the vocabulary from Lessons 25–31.

Memorization

No memorization this lesson. Review the entirety of *Psalmus XXIII*.

Grammar

This lesson brings you not only to the end of a unit, but the end of an entire year of Latinic study. Take time to correct any recurring grammatical errors or translational confusions. Review the following:

Verbs: how to conjugate first, second, third, fourth, and third *-iō* verbs in the active and passive

Nouns: fourth and fifth declensions especially, but brush up on the first, second, and third declensions as well

Pronouns: Demonstratives *hic, ille, iste;* review *is*

Adjectives: Review first/second and third declension adjectives, as well as numerals

Lesson 32 Worksheet

A. Vocabulary

Translate the following words from Latin to English or English to Latin as appropriate. Include case(s) with prepositions.

1. and, and also: _____

2. cito: _____

3. clam: _____

4. cōram: _____
_____

5. perhaps: _____

6. iterum: _____

7. iūxta: _____ _____

8. magnoperē: _____

9. modo: _____

10. afterwards: _____

11. propter: _____

12. quam: _____

13. how, in what way: _____

14. quoniam: _____

15. quoque: _____

16. enough: _____

17. secundum: _____ _____

18. sēū: _____

19. super: _____ _____

20. tamen: _____

21. together: _____

22. undique: _____

23. accipiō: _____

24. agō: _____

25. I open, expose: _____

26. appropinquō: _____

27. audiō: _____

28. cadō: _____

29. capiō: _____

30. I go, move, yield: _____

31. cōgō: _____

32. colō: _____

33. crēdō: _____

34. cupiō: _____

35. I run: _____

36. dēfendō: _____

37. dēligō: _____

38. dīcō: _____

39. dīmittō: _____
_____

40. I sleep: _____

41. dūcō: _____

42. eō: _____

43. faciō: _____

44. fīō: _____
_____

45. I cherish, love, esteem: _____

46. frangō: _____

47. I flee, run away: _____

48. gerō: _____

49. gubernō: _____

50. I throw, cast, hurl: _____

51. impediō: _____

52. incipiō: _____

53. interficiō: _____

54. inveniō: _____

55. I join, unite, yoke: _____

56. legō: _____

57. lūdō: _____

58. mittō: _____

59. nesciō: _____

60. occīdō: _____

61. I destroy, ruin, lose: _____

62. pōnō: _____

63. rapiō: _____

64. regō: _____

65. I abandon, leave behind: _____

66. resurgō: _____

67. sciō: _____

68. scrībō: _____

69. I (a)rise: _____

70. I touch, strike: _____

71. trahō: _____

72. vehō: _____

73. vertō: _____

74. veniō: _____

75. I bind, tie: _____

76. vincō: _____

77. vītō: _____

78. vīvō: _____

79. adulescens: _____

80. mind: _____

81. bow, arch, rainbow: _____

82. cantus: _____

83. caro: _____

84. cāsus: _____
_____

85. classis: _____
_____

86. cōnsilium: _____
_____

87. cornū: _____

88. day, period of time: _____

89. domus: _____

90. exercitus: _____

91. faciēs: _____

92. fenestra: _____

93. fidēs: _____

94. frūctus: _____

95. gēns: _____

96. knee: _____

97. grātia: _____

98. grex: _____

99. hour: _____

100. Iēsus: _____

101. lacus: _____

102. lingua: _____

103. littera: _____

104. manus: _____

105. table: _____

106. merīdiēs: _____

107. metus: _____

108. pānis: _____

109. poena: _____

110. porta: _____

111. port, harbor: _____

112. rēs: _____

113. saxum: _____

114. sella: _____

115. spēs: _____

116. spīritus: _____

117. weather, storm: _____

118. tonitrus: _____

119. wife: _____

120. vēritas: _____

121. versus: _____

122. vultus: _____

123. āridus: _____

124. barbarus: _____

125. blind: _____

126. dexter: _____

_____

127. ēgregius: _____

128. hungry: _____

129. gelidus: _____

130. grātus: _____

131. hic: _____

132. ille: _____

133. improbus: _____

134. iste: _____

135. middle, midst (of): _____

136. new: _____

137. salvus: _____

138. sanctus: _____

139. sinister: _____

140. old: _____

B. Grammar

1. Conjugate *vītō* in the future perfect passive indicative.

	LATIN SINGULAR	ENGLISH SINGULAR		LATIN PLURAL	ENGLISH PLURAL
1ST					
2ND					
3RD					

2. Conjugate *dīmittō* in the perfect passive indicative.

	LATIN SINGULAR	ENGLISH SINGULAR		LATIN PLURAL	ENGLISH PLURAL
1ST					
2ND					
3RD					

3. Conjugate *dormiō* in the imperfect active indicative.

	LATIN SINGULAR	ENGLISH SINGULAR		LATIN PLURAL	ENGLISH PLURAL
1ST					
2ND					
3RD					

4. Conjugate *gubernō* in the pluperfect passive indicative.

	LATIN SINGULAR	ENGLISH SINGULAR		LATIN PLURAL	ENGLISH PLURAL
1ST					
2ND					
3RD					

5. Conjugate *perdō* in the future active indicative.

	LATIN SINGULAR	ENGLISH SINGULAR		LATIN PLURAL	ENGLISH PLURAL
1ST					
2ND					
3RD					

6. Conjugate *rapiō* in the present passive indicative.

	LATIN SINGULAR	ENGLISH SINGULAR		LATIN PLURAL	ENGLISH PLURAL
1ST					
2ND					
3RD					

7. Conjugate *faciō* in the future passive indicative.

	LATIN SINGULAR	ENGLISH SINGULAR		LATIN PLURAL	ENGLISH PLURAL
1ST					
2ND					
3RD					

8. Conjugate *surgō* in the perfect active indicative.

	LATIN SINGULAR	ENGLISH SINGULAR		LATIN PLURAL	ENGLISH PLURAL
1ST					
2ND					
3RD					

9. Conjugate *eō* in the present active indicative.

	LATIN SINGULAR	ENGLISH SINGULAR	LATIN PLURAL	ENGLISH PLURAL
1ST				
2ND				
3RD				

10. Conjugate *vinciō* in the pluperfect active indicative.

	LATIN SINGULAR	ENGLISH SINGULAR	LATIN PLURAL	ENGLISH PLURAL
1ST				
2ND				
3RD				

11. Conjugate *foveō* in the imperfect passive indicative.

	LATIN SINGULAR	ENGLISH SINGULAR	LATIN PLURAL	ENGLISH PLURAL
1ST				
2ND				
3RD				

12. Conjugate *accipiō* in the future perfect active indicative.

	LATIN SINGULAR	ENGLISH SINGULAR	LATIN PLURAL	ENGLISH PLURAL
1ST				
2ND				
3RD				

13. Give the imperatives of the following verbs.

	VERB	LATIN SINGULAR	ENGLISH SINGULAR		LATIN PLURAL	ENGLISH PLURAL
1.	appropinquō					
2.	augeō					
3.	dūcō					
4.	audiō					
5.	capiō					

14. Decline *this old animal* (use *hic* and *vetus*).

	LATIN SINGULAR	LATIN PLURAL
NOM.		
GEN.		
DAT.		
ACC.		
ABL.		
VOC.		

15. Decline *that holy fear* (use *ille*).

	LATIN SINGULAR	LATIN PLURAL
NOM.		
GEN.		
DAT.		
ACC.		
ABL.		
VOC.		

16. Decline *such a savage face* (use *faciēs*).

	LATIN SINGULAR	LATIN PLURAL
NOM.		
GEN.		
DAT.		
ACC.		
ABL.		
VOC.		

C. Memorization

Below is the first word from each line of *Psalmus XXIII*. Fill in the rest. (Be prepared on the test to write out the entire psalm without any hints!)

¹Psalmus _____

 Dominus _____

²In _____

 super _____

³Animam _____

 Dēdūxit _____

 propter _____

⁴Nam _____

 nōn _____

 virga _____

⁵Parāstī _____

 adversus _____

 Inpinguāstī _____

 et _____

⁶Et _____

 omnibus _____

 et _____

 in _____

D. Latin to English Translation

1 **David* et Goliath***

(adapted from the Vulgate, 1 Samuel 17:12–54)

David autem erat unus ex octo filiis viris Isai* Ephrathei.[1] Et abierunt[2] tres filii maiores[3] post Saul* in proelium. David autem erat minimus,[4] et abiit David et pascebat[5] gregem patris sui[6] in Bethleem.* Dixit

5 autem Isai ad David filium suum, "Accipe fratribus tuis frumentum et decem panes istos, et curre in castra ad fratres tuos."

Surrexit itaque David mane[7] et venit ad exercitum, et invenit fratres suos, et dicebat eis. Deinde vir ille spurius,[8] Goliath nomine Philistheus[9] de Geth,* ex castris Philistheorum abiit et castra Israhelitarum[10] ad proelium provocavit.[11] Omnes autem Israhelitae viderunt virum et fugerunt a facie eius quod

10 eum magnopere timuerunt. Sed ait David ad viros: "Quis[12] est enim hic Philistheus incircumcisus?[13] Exprobravit[14] enim exercitum Dei vivi." Ergo ad Saul regem ductus est et dixit: "Ego servus tuus ibo et pugnabo contra Philistheum." Et ait Saul ad David, "Non vales vincere Philistheum istum nec pugnare contra eum quia puer es; hic autem vir bellator[15] ab adulescentia[16] sua."

Dixitque David ad Saul, "Pascebat servus tuus patris sui gregem et saepe veniebat leo vel[17] ursus[18]

15 rapiebatque arietem[19] de medio grege, et currebam ad eos et occidebam rapiebamque eum de ore eorum interficiebamque eos. Nam[20] et leonem et ursum interfeci ego servus tuus. Philistheum igitur hunc incircumcisum quoque vincere potero, quia exercitum Dei vivi reprobrare audebat." Et ait David, "Dominus me rapuit de manu leonis et de manu ursi, et is liberabit me de manu Philisthei huius." Dixit autem Saul ad David, "I et Dominus tecum[21] sit."[22]

20 Et David baculum[23] suum portavit, et quinque limpidissimos[24] lapides[25] de torrente[26] delegit et misit eos in peram[27] pastoralem[28] et fundam[29] manu gessit et iit contra Philistheum. Autem Philistheus David appropinquavit et eum vidit, etiam despexit[30] eum enim adulescens rufus[31] erat et pulcher facies erat. Et dixit Philistheus ad David: "Ego canis sum, quod[32] tu venis ad me cum baculo?" et maledixit[33] Philistheus David in diis suis.[34]

25 Dixitque ad David: "Veni ad me et dabo carnes tuas avibus caeli et bestiis terrae." Dixit autem David ad Philistheum: "Tu venis ad me cum gladio et hasta et clypeo;[35] ego autem venio ad te in nomine Domini exercituum. Hodie et dabit te Dominus in manum meam et percutiam[36] te et auferam[37] caput tuum a te. Et dabo cadaver[38] castrorum Philistheorum hodie avibus caeli et bestiis terrae, et sciet omnis terra quia[39] est Deus in Israhel,* et tradet[40] vos in manus nostras."

30 Ergo surrexit Philistheus et venit et appropinquavit contra David. Festinavit David et cucurrit ad Philistheum, et misit manum suam in peram tulitque[41] unum lapidem. Et funda iecit et percussit Philistheum in fronte[42] et infixus est[43] lapis in fronte eius et cecidit in faciem suam super terram. Cucurrit et stetit super Philistheum et tulit gladium eius et interfecit eum praeciditque[44] caput eius. Viderunt autem Philisthei eum mortuum fortissimum[45] eorum, et fugerunt. Et viri Israhel surgerunt

35 et clamaverunt et Philistheos persecuti sunt[46] cecideruntque. David autem caput Philisthei adsumpsit[47] et tulit illud in Hierusalem,* sed arma[48] eius posuit in tabernaculo[49] suo.

Glossary

*The following names are indeclinable: *David, Goliath, Isai* (Jesse), *Bethleem, Saul, Geth, Israhel, Hierusalem* (Jerusalem)

1. *Ephratheus, -ī* (m): an Ephramite
2. *abeō, -īre, -iī, -itum:* I go away, depart
3. *māior, māius* (gen. *māioris*): greater; here, "older"
4. *minimus, -a, -um:* least; here, "youngest"
5. *pascō, -ere, pāvī, pastum:* I feed, pasture
6. *suus, -a, -um:* his (own), her (own), its (own). This is a reflexive possessive adjective—it refers back to the subject.
7. *māne:* in the morning, early
8. *spurius, -a, -um:* spurious, false
9. *Philistheus, -ī:* (m) Philistine
10. *Israhelita, -ae:* (m) Israelite
11. *prōvocō* (1): I challenge
12. *quis:* who?
13. *incircumcisus, -a, -um:* uncircumcised
14. *exprobrō* (1): I reproach
15. *bellātor, -tōris* (m): warrior
16. *adulescentia, -ae* (f): youth
17. *vel:* or
18. *ursus, -ī* (m): bear
19. *ariēs, -ietis* (m): ram
20. *nam:* for
21. *tēcum = cum tē*
22. *sit:* third person singular present active subjunctive of *sum*; here, translate it as "may he be"
23. *baculum, -ī* (n): staff
24. *limpidissimus, -a, -um:* very bright, very clear
25. *lapis, -idis* (m): stone
26. *torrens, -ntis* (m): a torrent, stream
27. *pēra, -ae* (f): bag, satchel
28. *pastōrālis, -e:* of/belonging to a shepherd, pastoral
29. *funda, -ae* (f): sling
30. *dēspiciō, -ere, -spexī, -spectum:* I look down on, despise
31. *rūfus, -a, -um:* red, ruddy
32. *quod:* here, translate as "that"
33. *maledīcō, -ere, -dīxī, -dictum:* I curse, speak evil
34. *in diīs suīs = in deīs suīs;* here, translate "in" as "by"
35. *clypeum, -ī* (n): shield
36. *percutiō, -ere, -cussī, -cussum:* I strike down, cut down
37. *auferō, -ferre* (3rd conj. irreg.), *abstulī, ablatum:* I carry away/ off, remove
38. *cadāver, -veris* (n): dead body, carcass
39. *quia:* here, translate as "that"
40. *tradō, -ere, -didī, -ditum:* I hand over, surrender
41. *ferō, ferre* (irreg. 3rd conj.), *tulī, lātum:* I carry, bring (forth), bear
42. *frōns, -ontis:* (f) forehead
43. *infīgō, -ere, -fīxī, -fixum:* I fix in, fasten in
44. *praecīdō, -ere, -cīdī, -cīsum:* I cut off, lop
45. *fortissimus, -a, -um:* bravest, strongest
46. *persequor, -sequī, -secūtus sum:* I pursue (with hostile intent), hunt down; this is a deponent verb—it is active in meaning but has passive forms
47. *adsūmō, -ere, -sumpsī, -sumptum:* I take for myself
48. *arma, -ōrum* (n, pl.): arms, armor, weapons
49. *tabernāculum, -ī* (n): tent

APPENDICES

- Chant Charts
- Latin to English Glossary
- English to Latin Glossary
- Sources and Helps
- Verb Formation Chart

Chant Charts

VERBS

Present Active Indicative Verb Endings (*Lesson 1*)

	SINGULAR	PLURAL
1ST	-ō	-mus
2ND	-s	-tis
3RD	-t	-nt

	SINGULAR	PLURAL
	I am *verbing*, I *verb*	we are *verbing*
	you are *verbing*	you all are *verbing*
	he/she/it is *verbing*	they are *verbing*

Imperfect Active Indicative Verb Endings (*Lesson 6*)

	SINGULAR	PLURAL
1ST	-bam	-bāmus
2ND	-bās	-bātis
3RD	-bat	-bant

	SINGULAR	PLURAL
	I was *verbing*	we were *verbing*
	you were *verbing*	you all were *verbing*
	he/she/it was *verbing*	they were *verbing*

Future Active Indicative Verb Endings (*Lesson 6*)

	SINGULAR	PLURAL
1ST	-bō	-bimus
2ND	-bis	-bitis
3RD	-bit	-bunt

	SINGULAR	PLURAL
	I will *verb*	we will *verb*
	you will *verb*	you all will *verb*
	he/she/it will *verb*	they will *verb*

Perfect Active Indicative Verb Endings (*Lesson 14*)

	LATIN SINGULAR	ENGLISH SINGULAR
1ST	-ī	I *verbed*, have *verbed*
2ND	-istī	you *verbed*, have verbed
3RD	-it	he/she/it *verbed*, has *verbed*

	LATIN PLURAL	ENGLISH PLURAL
	-imus	we *verbed*, have *verbed*
	-istis	you (pl.) *verbed*, have *verbed*
	-ērunt	they *verbed*, have *verbed*

Pluperfect Active Indicative Verb Endings (*Lesson 15*)

	LATIN SINGULAR	ENGLISH SINGULAR
1ST	-eram	I had *verbed*
2ND	-erās	you had *verbed*
3RD	-erat	he/she/it had *verbed*

	LATIN PLURAL	ENGLISH PLURAL
	-erāmus	we had *verbed*
	-erātis	you (pl.) had *verbed*
	-erant	they had *verbed*

Future Perfect Active Indicative Verb Endings *(Lesson 15)*

	LATIN SINGULAR	ENGLISH SINGULAR		LATIN PLURAL	ENGLISH PLURAL
1ST	-erō	I will have *verbed*		-erimus	we will have *verbed*
2ND	-eris	you will have *verbed*		-eritis	you (pl.) will have *verbed*
3RD	-erit	he/she/it will have *verbed*		-erint	they will have *verbed*

Present Passive Indicative Verb Endings *(Lesson 20)*

	LATIN SINGULAR	ENGLISH SINGULAR		LATIN PLURAL	ENGLISH PLURAL
1ST	-r	I am (being) *verbed*		-mur	we are (being) *verbed*
2ND	-ris	you are (being) *verbed*		-minī	you (pl.) are (being) *verbed*
3RD	-tur	he/she/it is (being) *verbed*		-ntur	they are being *verbed*

Imperfect Passive Indicative Verb Endings *(Lesson 20)*

	LATIN SINGULAR	ENGLISH SINGULAR		LATIN PLURAL	ENGLISH PLURAL
1ST	-ba**r**	I was (being) *verbed*		-bā**mur**	we were (being) *verbed*
2ND	-bā**ris**	you were (being) *verbed*		-bā**minī**	you (pl.) were (being) *verbed*
3RD	-bā**tur**	he/she/it was (being) *verbed*		-ban**tur**	they were (being) *verbed*

Future Passive Indicative Verb Endings *(Lesson 20)*

	LATIN SINGULAR	ENGLISH SINGULAR		LATIN PLURAL	ENGLISH PLURAL
1ST	-bo**r**	I will be *verbed*		-bi**mur**	we will be *verbed*
2ND	-be**ris**	you will be *verbed*		-bi**minī**	you (pl.) will be *verbed*
3RD	-bi**tur**	he/she/it will be *verbed*		-bu**ntur**	they will be *verbed*

Perfect Passive Indicative *(Lesson 22)*

	LATIN SINGULAR	ENGLISH SINGULAR		LATIN PLURAL	ENGLISH PLURAL
1ST	4th principal part (sg.) + sum	I was/have been *verbed*		4th p.p. (pl.)+ sumus	we were/have been *verbed*
2ND	4th p.p. (sg.) + es	you were/have been *verbed*		4th p.p. (pl.)+ estis	you (pl.) were/have been *verbed*
3RD	4th p.p. (sg.) + est	he/she/it was/has been *verbed*		4th p.p. (pl.)+ sunt	they were/have been *verbed*

Pluperfect Passive Indicative *(Lesson 22)*

	LATIN SINGULAR	ENGLISH SINGULAR		LATIN PLURAL	ENGLISH PLURAL
1ST	4th principal part (sg.) + eram	I had been *verbed*		4th p.p. (pl.)+ erāmus	we had been *verbed*
2ND	4th p.p. (sg.) + erās	you had been *verbed*		4th p.p. (pl.)+ erātis	you (pl.) had been *verbed*
3RD	4th p.p. (sg.) + erat	he/she/it had been *verbed*		4th p.p. (pl.)+ erant	they had been *verbed*

Future Perfect Passive Indicative *(Lesson 22)*

	LATIN SINGULAR	ENGLISH SINGULAR		LATIN PLURAL	ENGLISH PLURAL
1ST	4th principal part (sg.) + erō	I will have been *verbed*		4th p.p. (pl.)+ erimus	we will have been *verbed*
2ND	4th p.p. (sg.) + eris	you will have been *verbed*		4th p.p. (pl.)+ eritis	you (pl.) will have been *verbed*
3RD	4th p.p. (sg.) + erit	he/she/it will have been *verbed*		4th p.p. (pl.)+ erunt	they will have been *verbed*

Irregular Verb: Sum, *I am*—Present Active *(Lesson 3)*

	LATIN SINGULAR	ENGLISH SINGULAR		LATIN PLURAL	ENGLISH PLURAL
1ST	sum	I am		sumus	we are
2ND	es	you are		estis	you all are
3RD	est	he/she/it is		sunt	they are

Irregular Verb: Eram, *I was*—Imperfect Active of *Sum (Lesson 10)*

	LATIN SINGULAR	ENGLISH SINGULAR		LATIN PLURAL	ENGLISH PLURAL
1ST	eram	I was		erāmus	we were
2ND	erās	you were		erātis	you all were
3RD	erat	he/she/it was		erant	they were

Irregular Verb: Erō, *I will be*—Future Active of *Sum (Lesson 10)*

	LATIN SINGULAR	ENGLISH SINGULAR		LATIN PLURAL	ENGLISH PLURAL
1ST	erō	erimus		I will be	we will be
2ND	eris	eritis		you will be	you all will be
3RD	erit	erunt		he/she/it will be	they will be

Irregular Verb: Fuī, *I was, have been*—Perfect Active Indicative of *Sum (Lesson 14)*

	LATIN SINGULAR	ENGLISH SINGULAR		LATIN PLURAL	ENGLISH PLURAL
1ST	fuī	I was, have been		fuimus	we were, have been
2ND	fuistī	you were, have been		fuistis	you (pl.) were, have been
3RD	fuit	he/she/it was, has been		fuērunt	they were, have been

Irregular Verb: Possum, *I am able*—Present Active Indicative *(Lesson 11)*

	LATIN SINGULAR	ENGLISH SINGULAR		LATIN PLURAL	ENGLISH PLURAL
1ST	possum	I am able		possumus	we are able
2ND	potes	you are able		potestis	you (pl.) are able
3RD	potest	he/she/it is able		possunt	they are able

Irregular Verb: Poteram, *I was able*—Imperfect Active Indicative of *Possum* (*Lesson 11*)

	LATIN SINGULAR	ENGLISH SINGULAR		LATIN PLURAL	ENGLISH PLURAL
1ST	poteram	I was able		poterāmus	we were able
2ND	poterās	you were able		poterātis	you (pl.) were able
3RD	poterat	he/she/it was able		poterant	they were able

Irregular Verb: Poterō, *I will be able*—Future Active Indicative of *Possum* (*Lesson 11*)

	LATIN SINGULAR	ENGLISH SINGULAR		LATIN PLURAL	ENGLISH PLURAL
1ST	poterō	I will be able		poterimus	we will be able
2ND	poteris	you will be able		poteritis	you (pl.) will be able
3RD	poterit	he/she/it will be able		poterunt	they will be able

Irregular Verb: Potuī, *I was able, have been able*—Perfect Active Indicative of *Possum* (*Lesson 14*)

	LATIN SINGULAR	ENGLISH SINGULAR		LATIN PLURAL	ENGLISH PLURAL
1ST	potuī	I was able, have been able		potuimus	we were able, have been able
2ND	potuistī	you were able, have been able		potuistis	you (pl.) were able, have been able
3RD	potuit	he/she/it was able, has been able		potuērunt	they were able, have been able

NOUNS

First Declension Feminine Noun Endings (*Lesson 2*)

	LATIN SG.	ENGLISH SG.		LATIN PL.	ENGLISH PL.
NOM.	-a	a/the *noun* [subject]		-ae	the *nouns* [subject]
GEN.	-ae	of the *noun*, the *noun's*		-ārum	of the *nouns*, the *nouns'*
DAT.	-ae	to/for the *noun*		-īs	to/for the *nouns*
ACC.	-am	a/the *noun* [direct object]		-ās	the *nouns* [direct object]
ABL.	-ā	by/with/from the *noun*		-īs	by/with/from the *nouns*
VOC.	-a	[O] *noun*!		-ae	[O] *nouns*!

Second Declension Masculine Noun Endings (*Lesson 4*)

	LATIN SG.	ENGLISH SG.		LATIN PL.	ENGLISH PL.
NOM.	-us/ -r	a/the *noun* [subject]		-ī	the *nouns* [subject]
GEN.	-ī	of the *noun*, the *noun's*		-ōrum	of the *nouns*, the *nouns'*
DAT.	-ō	to/for the *noun*		-īs	to/for the *nouns*
ACC.	-um	a/the *noun* [direct object]		-ōs	the *nouns* [direct object]
ABL.	-ō	by/with/from the *noun*		-īs	by/with/from the *nouns*
VOC.	-e/ -r	[O] *noun*!		-ī	[O] *nouns*!

Second Declension Neuter Noun Endings *(Lesson 5)*

	LATIN SG.	ENGLISH SG.		LATIN PL.	ENGLISH PL.
NOM.	-um	a/the *noun* [subject]		-a	the *nouns* [subject]
GEN.	-ī	of the *noun*, the *noun's*		-ōrum	of the *nouns*, the *nouns'*
DAT.	-ō	to/for the *noun*		-īs	to/for the *nouns*
ACC.	-um	a/the *noun* [direct object]		-a	the *nouns* [direct object]
ABL.	-ō	by/with/from the *noun*		-īs	by/with/from the *nouns*
VOC.	-um	[O] *noun*!		-a	[O] *nouns*!

Third Declension Masculine/Feminine Noun Endings *(Lesson 12)*

	LATIN SG.	ENGLISH SG.		LATIN PL.	ENGLISH PL.
NOM.	**X**	a/the *noun* [subject]		-ēs	the *nouns* [subject]
GEN.	-is	of the *noun*, the *noun's*		-um	of the *nouns*, the *nouns'*
DAT.	-ī	to/for the *noun*		-ibus	to/for the *nouns*
ACC.	-em	a/the *noun* [direct object]		-ēs	the *nouns* [direct object]
ABL.	-e	by/with/from the *noun*		-ibus	by/with/from the *nouns*
VOC.	**X**	[O] *noun*!		-ēs	[O] *nouns*!

Third Declension Neuter Noun Endings *(Lesson 13)*

	LATIN SG.	ENGLISH SG.		LATIN PL.	ENGLISH PL.
NOM.	**X**	a/the *noun* [subject]		-a	the *nouns* [subject]
GEN.	-is	of the *noun*, the *noun's*		-um	of the *nouns*, the *nouns'*
DAT.	-ī	to/for the *noun*		-ibus	to/for the *nouns*
ACC.	**X**	a/the *noun* [direct object]		-a	the *nouns* [direct object]
ABL.	-e	by/with/from the *noun*		-ibus	by/with/from the *nouns*
VOC.	**X**	[O] *noun*!		**-a**	[O] *nouns*!

Third Declension Masculine/Feminine i-Stem Noun Endings *(Lesson 18)*

	LATIN SG.	ENGLISH SG.		LATIN PL.	ENGLISH PL.
NOM.	**X**	a/the *noun* [subject]		-ēs	the *nouns* [subject]
GEN.	-is	of the *noun*, the *noun's*		-ium	of the *nouns*, the *nouns'*
DAT.	-ī	to/for the *noun*		-ibus	to/for the *nouns*
ACC.	-em	a/the *noun* [direct object]		-ēs	the *nouns* [direct object]
ABL.	-e/ī	by/with/from the *noun*		-ibus	by/with/from the *nouns*
VOC.	**X**	[O] *noun*!		-ēs	[O] *nouns*!

Third Declension Neuter i-Stem Noun Endings *(Lesson 18)*

	LATIN SG.	ENGLISH SG.
NOM.	**X**	a/the *noun* [subject]
GEN.	-is	of the *noun*, the *noun's*
DAT.	-ī	to/for the *noun*
ACC.	**X**	a/the *noun* [direct object]
ABL.	-ī	by/with/from the *noun*
VOC.	**X**	[O] *noun!*

	LATIN PL.	ENGLISH PL.
	-ia	the *nouns* [subject]
	-ium	of the *nouns*, the *nouns'*
	-ibus	to/for the *nouns*
	-ia	the *nouns* [direct object]
	-ibus	by/with/from the *nouns*
	-ia	[O] *nouns!*

Fourth Declension Masculine/Feminine Noun Endings *(Lesson 25)*

	LATIN SG.	ENGLISH SG.
NOM.	-us	a/the *noun* [subject]
GEN.	-ūs	of the *noun*, the *noun's*
DAT.	-uī	to/for the *noun*
ACC.	-um	a/the *noun* [direct object]
ABL.	-ū	by/with/from the *noun*
VOC.	**-us**	[O] *noun!*

	LATIN PL.	ENGLISH PL.
	-ūs	the *nouns* [subject]
	-uum	of the *nouns*, the *nouns'*
	-ibus	to/for the *nouns*
	-ūs	the *nouns* [direct object]
	-ibus	by/with/from the *nouns*
	-ūs	[O] *nouns!*

Fourth Declension Neuter Noun Endings *(Lesson 25)*

	LATIN SG.	ENGLISH SG.
NOM.	-ū	a/the *noun* [subject]
GEN.	-ūs	of the *noun*, the *noun's*
DAT.	-ū	to/for the *noun*
ACC.	-ū	a/the *noun* [direct object]
ABL.	-ū	by/with/from the *noun*
VOC.	**-ū**	[O] *noun!*

	LATIN PL.	ENGLISH PL.
	-ua	the *nouns* [subject]
	-uum	of the *nouns*, the *nouns'*
	-ibus	to/for the *nouns*
	-ua	the *nouns* [direct object]
	-ibus	by/with/from the *nouns*
	-ua	[O] *nouns!*

Fifth Declension Noun Endings *(Lesson 28)*

	SINGULAR	PLURAL
NOM.	-es	a/the *noun* [subject]
GEN.	-eī/-ēī	of the *noun*, the *noun's*
DAT.	-eī/-ēī	to/for the *noun*
ACC.	-em	a/the *noun* [direct object]
ABL.	-ē	by/with/from the *noun*
VOC.	-es	[O] *noun!*

	SINGULAR	PLURAL
	-ēs	the *nouns* [subject]
	-ērum	of the *nouns*, the *nouns'*
	-ēbus	to/for the *nouns*
	-ēs	the *nouns* [direct object]
	-ēbus	by/with/from the *nouns*
	-ēs	[O] *nouns!*

ADJECTIVES

First and Second Declension Adjective Endings *(Lesson 7)*

	SINGULAR				PLURAL		
	MASC.	FEM.	NEUT.		MASC.	FEM.	NEUT.
NOM.	-us / -r	-a	-um		-ī	-ae	-a
GEN.	-ī	-ae	-ī		-ōrum	-ārum	-ōrum
DAT.	-ō	-ae	-ō		-īs	-īs	-īs
ACC.	-um	-am	-um		-ōs	-ās	-a
ABL.	-ō	-ā	-ō		-īs	-īs	-īs
VOC.	-e/ -r	-a	-um		-ī	-ae	-a

Third Declension Adjectives   *(Lesson 19)*

	SINGULAR		PLURAL	
	MASC./FEM.	NEUTER	MASC./FEM.	NEUTER
NOM.	X	X	-ēs	-ia
GEN.	-is	-is	-ium	-ium
DAT.	-ī	-ī	-ibus	-ibus
ACC.	-em	X	-ēs	-ia
ABL.	-ī	-ī	-ibus	-ibus
VOC.	X	X	-ēs	-ia

Numerals *(Lesson 21)*

ūnus, ūna, ūnum, *one*

	SINGULAR		
	MASCULINE	FEMININE	NEUTER
NOM.	ūnus	ūna	ūnum
GEN.	ūnīus	ūnīus	ūnīus
DAT.	ūnī	ūnī	ūnī
ACC.	ūnum	ūnam	ūnum
ABL.	ūnō	ūnā	ūnō

duo, duae, duo, *two*

	PLURAL		
	MASCULINE	FEMININE	NEUTER
duo	duae	duo
duōrum	duārum	duōrum
duōbus	duābus	duōbus
duōs	duās	duo
duōbus	duābus	duōbus

trēs, tria, *three*

	PLURAL	
	M/F	**N**
NOM.	trēs	tria
GEN.	trium	trium
DAT.	tribus	tribus
ACC.	trēs	tria
ABL.	tribus	tribus

mille, *one thousand*

	SINGULAR	PLURAL
	M/F/N	**N**
mille	mīlia	
mille	mīlium	
mille	mīlibus	
mille	mīlia	
mille	mīlibus	

PRONOUNS

First Person Personal Pronouns (*Lesson 17*)

	LATIN SINGULAR	ENGLISH SINGULAR		LATIN PLURAL	ENGLISH PLURAL
NOMINATIVE	ego	I [subject]		nōs	we [subject]
GENITIVE	meī	of me		nostrum	of us
DATIVE	mihi	to/for me		nōbīs	to/for us
ACCUSATIVE	mē	me [direct object]		nōs	us [direct object]
ABLATIVE	mē	by/with/from me		nōbīs	by/with/from us

Second Person Personal Pronouns (*Lesson 17*)

	LATIN SINGULAR	ENGLISH SINGULAR		LATIN PLURAL	ENGLISH PLURAL
NOMINATIVE	tū	you [subject]		vōs	you (pl.) [subject]
GENITIVE	tuī	of you		vestrum	of you (pl.)
DATIVE	tibī	to/for you		vōbīs	to/for you (pl.)
ACCUSATIVE	tē	you [direct object]		vōs	you (pl.) [direct object]
ABLATIVE	tē	by/with/from you		vōbīs	by/with/from you (pl.)

Third Person Personal Pronouns—Singular (*Lesson 17*)

	MASCULINE	FEMININE	NEUTER	
	he/his/him	she/hers/her	it/its	**ENGLISH**
NOM.	is	ea	id	he/she/it (this/that, etc.)
GEN.	eius	eius	eius	of him/his, of her/hers, of it/its
DAT.	eī	eī	eī	to/for him, to/for her, to/for it
ACC.	eum	eam	id	him/her/it
ABL.	eō	eā	eō	by/with/from him/her/it

Third Person Personal Pronouns—Plural *(Lesson 17)*

	MASCULINE	FEMININE	NEUTER	ENGLISH
	they/their/them	they/their/them	they/their/them	
NOM.	eī	eae	ea	they (these/those, etc.)
GEN.	eōrum	eārum	eōrum	of them, their
DAT.	eīs	eīs	eīs	to/for them
ACC.	eōs	eās	ea	them
ABL.	eīs	eīs	eīs	by/with/from them

DEMONSTRATIVES

Various Demonstrative Pronouns *(Lesson 30)*

Hic, haec, hoc—this; (pl.) these

	SINGULAR			PLURAL		
	MASCULINE	FEMININE	NEUTER	MASCULINE	FEMININE	NEUTER
NOM.	hic	haec	hoc	hī	hae	haec
GEN.	huius	huius	huius	hōrum	hārum	hōrum
DAT.	huic	huic	huic	hīs	hīs	hīs
ACC.	hunc	hanc	hoc	hōs	hās	haec
ABL.	hōc	hāc	hōc	hīs	hīs	hīs

Ille, illa, illud—that; (pl.) those; that famous

	SINGULAR			PLURAL		
	MASCULINE	FEMININE	NEUTER	MASCULINE	FEMININE	NEUTER
NOM.	ille	illa	illud	illī	illae	illa
GEN.	illīus	illīus	illīus	illōrum	illārum	illōrum
DAT.	illī	illī	illī	illīs	illīs	illīs
ACC.	illum	illam	illud	illōs	illās	illa
ABL.	illō	illā	illō	illīs	illīs	illīs

Iste, ista, istud—that (of yours); such

	SINGULAR			PLURAL		
	MASCULINE	FEMININE	NEUTER	MASCULINE	FEMININE	NEUTER
NOM.	iste	ista	istud	istī	istae	ista
GEN.	istīus	istīus	istīus	istōrum	istārum	istōrum
DAT.	istī	istī	istī	istīs	istīs	istīs
ACC.	istum	istam	istud	istōs	istās	ista
ABL.	istō	istā	istō	istīs	istīs	istīs

Verb Memorization

Chants Applied to *amō, videō, dūcō, capiō,* and *audiō*

The chants in this section follow the conjugations of amō *(1st)*, videō *(2nd)*, dūcō *(3rd)*, capiō *(3rd -iō), and* audiō *(4th) through the present, imperfect, and future indicative tenses. Endings have been bolded.*

	1ST	2ND	3RD	3RD -iō	4TH
PRESENT ACTIVE	am**ō**	vide**ō**	dūc**ō**	capi**ō**	audi**ō**
	amā**s**	vidē**s**	dūci**s**	capi**s**	audī**s**
	ama**t**	vide**t**	dūci**t**	capi**t**	audi**t**
	amā**mus**	vidē**mus**	dūci**mus**	capi**mus**	audī**mus**
	amā**tis**	vidē**tis**	dūci**tis**	capi**tis**	audī**tis**
	ama**nt**	vide**nt**	dūcu**nt**	capiu**nt**	audiu**nt**
IMPERFECT ACTIVE	amā**bam**	vidē**bam**	dūcē**bam**	capiē**bam**	audiē**bam**
	amā**bās**	vidē**bās**	dūcē**bās**	capiē**bās**	audiē**bās**
	amā**bat**	vidē**bat**	dūcē**bat**	capiē**bat**	audiē**bat**
	amā**bāmus**	vidē**bāmus**	dūcē**bāmus**	capiē**bāmus**	audiē**bāmus**
	amā**bātis**	vidē**bātis**	dūcē**bātis**	capiē**bātis**	audiē**bātis**
	amā**bant**	vidē**bant**	dūcē**bant**	capiē**bant**	audiē**bant**
FUTURE ACTIVE	amā**bō**	vidē**bō**	dūc**am**	capi**am**	audi**am**
	amā**bis**	vidē**bis**	dūc**ēs**	capi**ēs**	audi**ēs**
	amā**bit**	vidē**bit**	dūc**et**	capi**et**	audi**et**
	amā**bimus**	vidē**bimus**	dūc**ēmus**	capi**ēmus**	audi**ēmus**
	amā**bitis**	vidē**bitis**	dūc**ētis**	capi**ētis**	audi**ētis**
	amā**bunt**	vidē**bunt**	dūc**ent**	capi**ent**	audi**ent**
PRESENT PASSIVE	am**or**	vide**or**	dūc**or**	capi**or**	audi**or**
	amā**ris**	vidē**ris**	dūce**ris**	cape**ris**	audī**ris**
	amā**tur**	vidē**tur**	dūci**tur**	capi**tur**	audī**tur**
	amā**mur**	vidē**mur**	dūci**mur**	capi**mur**	audī**mur**
	amā**minī**	vidē**minī**	dūci**minī**	capi**minī**	audī**minī**
	ama**ntur**	vide**ntur**	dūcu**ntur**	capiu**ntur**	audiu**ntur**
IMPERFECT PASSIVE	amā**bar**	vidē**bar**	dūcē**bar**	capiē**bar**	audiē**bar**
	amā**bāris**	vidē**bāris**	dūcē**bāris**	capiē**bāris**	audiē**bāris**
	amā**bātur**	vidē**bātur**	dūcē**bātur**	capiē**bātur**	audiē**bātur**
	amā**bāmur**	vidē**bāmur**	dūcē**bāmur**	capiē**bāmur**	audiē**bāmur**
	amā**bāminī**	vidē**bāminī**	dūcē**bāminī**	capiē**bāminī**	audiē**bāminī**
	amā**bantur**	vidē**bantur**	dūcē**bantur**	capiē**bantur**	audiē**bantur**

FUTURE PASSIVE	amā**bor**	vidē**bor**	dūc**ar**	capi**ar**	audi**ar**
	amā**beris**	vidē**bēris**	dūcē**ris**	capiē**ris**	audiē**ris**
	amā**bitur**	vidē**bitur**	dūcē**tur**	capiē**tur**	audiē**tur**
	amā**bimur**	vidē**bimur**	dūcē**mur**	capiē**mur**	audiē**mur**
	amā**biminī**	vidē**biminī**	dūcē**minī**	capiē**minī**	audiē**minī**
	amā**buntur**	vidē**buntur**	dūce**ntur**	capie**ntur**	audie**ntur**

The chants in this section follow the conjugations of amō *(1st)* , video *(2nd),* dūcō *(3rd),* capiō *(3rd -iō), and* audiō *(4th) through the perfect, pluperfect, and future perfect indicative tenses. Endings have been bolded.*

	1ST	2ND	3RD	3RD -IŌ	4TH
PERFECT ACTIVE	amāv**ī**	vīd**ī**	dūx**ī**	cēp**ī**	audīv**ī**
	amā**vistī**	vīd**istī**	dūx**istī**	cēp**istī**	audīv**istī**
	amā**vit**	vīd**it**	dūx**it**	cēp**it**	audīv**it**
	amā**vimus**	vīd**imus**	dūx**imus**	cēp**imus**	audīv**imus**
	amā**vistis**	vīd**istis**	dūx**istis**	cēp**istis**	audīv**istis**
	amā**vērunt**	vīd**ērunt**	dūx**ērunt**	cēp**ērunt**	audīv**ērunt**
PLUPERFECT ACTIVE	amāv**eram**	vīd**eram**	dūx**eram**	cēp**eram**	audīv**eram**
	amāv**erās**	vīd**erās**	dūx**erās**	cēp**erās**	audīv**erās**
	amāv**erat**	vīd**erat**	dūx**erat**	cēp**erat**	audīv**erat**
	amāv**erāmus**	vīd**erāmus**	dūx**erāmus**	cēp**erāmus**	audīv**erāmus**
	amāv**erātis**	vīd**erātis**	dūx**erātis**	cēp**erātis**	audīv**erātis**
	amāv**erant**	vīd**ērant**	dūx**erant**	cēp**erant**	audīv**erant**
FUTURE PERFECT ACTIVE	amāv**erō**	vīd**erō**	dūx**erō**	cēp**erō**	audīv**erō**
	amāv**eris**	vīd**eris**	dūx**eris**	cēp**eris**	audīv**eris**
	amāv**erit**	vīd**erit**	dūx**erit**	cēp**erit**	audīv**erit**
	amāv**erimus**	vīd**erimus**	dūx**erimus**	cēp**erimus**	audīv**erimus**
	amāv**eritis**	vīd**eritis**	dūx**eritis**	cēp**eritis**	audīv**eritis**
	amāv**erint**	vīd**ērint**	dūx**erint**	cēp**erint**	audīv**erint**
PERFECT PASSIVE	amāt**us sum**	vīs**us sum**	duct**us sum**	capt**us sum**	audit**us sum**
	amāt**us es**	vīs**us es**	duct**us es**	capt**us es**	audit**us es**
	amāt**us est**	vīs**us est**	duct**us est**	capt**us est**	audit**us est**
	amāt**ī sumus**	vīs**ī sumus**	duct**ī sumus**	capt**ī sumus**	audit**ī sumus**
	amāt**ī estis**	vīs**ī estis**	duct**ī estis**	capt**ī estis**	audit**ī sumus**
	amāt**ī sunt**	vīs**ī sunt**	duct**ī sunt**	capt**ī sunt**	audit**ī sunt**

PLUPERFECT PASSIVE	amāt**us eram**	vīs**us eram**	duct**us eram**	capt**us eram**	audit**us eram**
	amāt**us erās**	vīs**us erās**	duct**us erās**	capt**us erās**	audit**us erās**
	amāt**us erat**	vīs**us erat**	duct**us erat**	capt**us erat**	audit**us erat**
	amāt**ī erāmus**	vīs**ī erāmus**	duct**ī erāmus**	capt**ī erāmus**	audit**ī erāmus**
	amāt**ī erātis**	vīs**ī erātis**	duct**ī erātis**	capt**ī erātis**	audit**ī erātis**
	amāt**ī erant**	vīs**ī erant**	duct**ī erant**	capt**ī erant**	audit**ī erant**

FUTURE PERFECT PASSIVE	amāt**us erō**	vīs**us erō**	duct**us erō**	capt**us erō**	audit**us erō**
	amāt**us eris**	vīs**us eris**	duct**us eris**	capt**us eris**	audit**us eris**
	amāt**us erit**	vīs**us erit**	duct**us erit**	capt**us erit**	audit**us erit**
	amāt**ī erimus**	vīs**ī erimus**	duct**ī erimus**	capt**ī erimus**	audit**ī erimus**
	amāt**ī eritis**	vīs**ī eritis**	duct**ī eritis**	capt**ī eritis**	audit**ī eritis**
	amāt**ī erunt**	vīs**ī erunt**	duct**ī erunt**	capt**ī erunt**	audit**ī erunt**

ENGLISH-LATIN GLOSSARY

Here you will find the words for the English-Latin sections of your worksheets. When using any glossary, always keep in mind that two languages don't always mesh perfectly. For example, if you look up "land" you will find *patria*, *tellūs*, and *terra*. They all can mean "land," but you'll have to use good judgment to decide which is correct in a given context! In brackets you will find the number of the lesson (L) or worksheet (W) where each word is introduced.

A

abandon *relinquō, -ere, -līquī, -lictum* [L28]

abduction *raptus, -ūs (m)* [W31]

able (am able) *possum, posse, potuī, —— [L11]*

above *super (+ acc. & + abl.)* [L6]; *suprā (adv. & prep. + acc.)* [L14]

abundance *cōpia, -ae (f)* [L15]

accept *accipiō, -ere, -cēpī, -ceptum* [L31]

according to *secundum (adv. & prep. + acc.)* [L28]

accordingly *ergo (adv.)* [L18]

across *trans (+ acc.)* [L11]

act *agō, -ere, ēgi, actum* [L26]

advice *cōnsilium, -iī (n)* [L30]

Aegean *Aegeus, -a, -um* [W30]

Aegeus *Aegeus, -eī (m)* [W30]

affirm *āiō* [L14]

after (prep.) *post (+ acc.)* [L17]; *secundum (adv./prep. + acc.)* [L28]; *postquam (conj.)* [W15]

afterwards *postea* [L28]

again *iterum* [L25]

against *contrā (+ acc.)* [L11]; *in (+ acc.)* [L3]

aid *auxilium, -ī (n)* [L5]

alas! *heu (ēheu)* [L22]

alchemy *alchemia, -ae (f)* [W27]

alder *alnus, -ī (f)* [L4]

all *omnis, -e* [L19]

allow *permittō, -ere, -mīsī, -missum* [W30]

allowed (it is allowed) *licet* [W26]

almost *paene (adv.)* [L19]

already *iam* [L15]

also *et* [L1]; *etiam* [L22]; *quoque* [L29]

always *semper* [L5]

am (I am) *sum, esse, fuī, futūrum* [L3]

amazement *stupor, -ōris (m)* [W28]

among *inter (+ acc.)* [L19]

ancestor *avus, -ī (m)* [L22]

ancient *antīquus, -a, -um* [L7]

and *ac (atque)* [L27]; *et* [L1]; *-que (enclitic)* [L10]

and also *ac (atque)* [L27]

and not *nec (neque)* [L14]

and so *itaque* [L2]

anger *īra, -ae (f)* [L2]

angry *īrātus,-a, -um* [L15]

animal *animal, -ālis (n)* [L18]

announce *nuntiō (1)* [L14]

annoy *vexō (1)* [L19]

another *alius, alia, aliud* [W21]

answer *respondeō, -ēre, -spondī, -spōnsum* [L9]

anyone *ūllus, -a, -um* [W27]

anything *ūllus, -a, -um* [W27]

Apollo *Apollō, -inis (m)* [W20]

apostle *apostolus, -ī (m)* [L11]

apprentice *discipulus, -ī (m)* [L5]

approach *appropinquō (1)* [L25]

arch *arcus, -ūs (m)* [L27]

Argus *Argus, -ī (m)* [W21]

Ariadne *Ariadna, -ae (f)* [W30]

arise *surgō, -ere, surrēxī, surrēctum* [L28]

arm *bracchium, -ī (n)* [W13]

armor *arma, -ōrum (n, pl)* [W32]

arms *arma, -ōrum (n, pl)* [W32]

army *exercitus, -ūs (m)* [L25]

arrange *collocō (1)* [W21]

arrow *sagitta, -ae (f)* [L3]

as *quam* [L28]; *sīcut* [L20]

ask *rogō (1)* [L6]

assert *āiō* [L14]

astonishment *stupor, -ōris (m)* [W28]

at *ad (+ acc.)* [L3]

at that place *ibī* [L5]

at that time *tum* [L15]

at the foot of *sub (+ abl.)* [L14]

Athenian *Athēniensis, -is (m/f)* [W30]

Athens *Athēnae, -ārum (f, pl)* [W30]

attack *oppugnō (1)* [L4]

attempt *temptō (1)* [W27]

aunt *amita, -ae (f)* [L22]

avoid *vītō (1)* [L30]

away from *ā, ab (+ abl.)* [L3]

awful *horrendus, -a, -um* [L13]

B

baby *infāns, -fantis (adj. /noun, m/f)* [W31]

Bacchus *Bacchus, -ī (m)* [W27]

back(ward) *retrō* [W23]

bad *malus, -a, -um* [L7]

badly *male* [L1]

bag *pēra, -ae (f)* [W32]

ball *pila, -ae (f)* [W30]

barbarian *barbarus, -ī (m)* [L31]

barber *tonsor, -ōris (m)* [W28]

barrier *spīna, -ae (f)* [W23]

battle *proelium, -ī (n)* [L15]

be *sum, esse, fuī, futūrum* [L3]

behind *retrō* [W23]

be silent *taceō, ēre, -uī, -itum* [W26]

be strong *valeō, -ēre, -uī, valitūrum* [L9]

be well *salveō, -ēre, ——, ——* [L9]; *valeō, -ēre, -uī, valitūrum* [L9]

beach *harēna, -ae (f)* [L3]

bear (noun) *ursus, -ī (m)* [W32]

bear (verb) *gerō, -ere, gessī, gestum* [L28]; *ferō, ferre, tulī, lātum (irreg. 3rd conj.)* [W32]

beast *bēstia, -ae (f)* [L2]

beautiful *pulcher, -chra, -chrum* [L7]

because *quandō* [L12]; *quia (conj.)* [L18]; *quod* [L10]; *quoniam* [L26]

because of *propter (+ acc.)* [L25]

become *fīō, fierī, ——, factus sum* [L31]

before *ante (+ acc.)* [L17]; *cōram (+ abl.)* [L27]; *pro (+ abl.)* [L18]

begin *incipiō, -ere, -cēpī, -ceptum* [L31]

behind *post (+ acc.)* [L17]

behold! *ecce* [L17]

believe *crēdō, -ere, -didī, -ditum* [L26]

beloved *cārus, -a, -um* [L13]

below *sub (+ abl.)* [L14]

bereft *orbus, -a, -um* [L22]

beseige *obsideō, -ēre, -sēdī, -sessum* [L10]

besides *etiam* [L22]

Bethlehem *Bethleem (indecl.)* [W32]

better *melior, -ius* [W28]

between *inter (+ acc.)* [L19]

beware (of) *caveō, -ēre, cāvī, cautum* [L12]

beyond *super (+ acc./+ abl.)* [L26]

Bible (Holy Bible) *Biblia Sacra, Bibliae Sacrae (f)* [L11]

big *magnus, -a, -um* [L7]

billy goat *caper, -prī (m)* [L4]

bind *vinciō, -īre, vīnxī, vīnctum* [L30]

bird *avis, avis (f)* [L18]

bit by bit *minūtātim* [L20]

bite *mordeō, -ēre, momordī, morsum* [L9]

black (dead black) *āter, -tra, -trum* [L17]; **(shining black)** *niger, -gra, grum* [L17]

blaze *ardeō, ardēre, arsī, ——* [L20]

blessed *beātus, -a, -um* [L7]

blind *caecus, -a, -um* [L27]

blue *caeruleus, -a, -um* [L17]; *hyacinthinus, -a, -um* [L17]

boat *nāvicula, -ae (f)* [W31]

body *corpus, corporis (n)* [L13]; **(dead body)** *cadaver, -veris (n)* [W32]

bold *magnanimus, -a, -um* [W9]

book *liber, librī (m)* [L11]

both...and *et...et* [L1]

boundary *fīnis, -is (m)* [W4]

bow *arcus, -ūs (m)* [L27]

boy *puer, puerī (m)* [L5]

brave *fortis, -e* [L19]; *magnanimus, -a, -um* [W9]

braver *fortior, -tius (gen. fortioris)* [W31]

bravest *fortissimus, -a, -um* [W32]

bread *pānis, -is (m)* [L29]

break *frangō, -ere, frēgī, fractum* [L27]

breath *spīritus, -ūs (m)* [L25]

bridge *pōns, pontis (m)* [W19]

brief *brevis, -e* [L19]

bright (verb; am bright) *lūceō, lūcēre, lūxī, ——* [L11]

bright (adj.; very bright) *limpidissimus, -a, -um* [W32]

bring (forth) *ferō, ferre, tulī, lātum (irreg. 3rd conj.)* [W32]

broad *lātus, -a, -um* [L20]

brother *frāter, frātris (m)* [L12]; *germānus, -ī (m)* [L4]

brown (dark-brown) *purpureus, -a, -um* [L17]

bull *bōs, bovis (m)* [L19]

burden *onus, oneris (n)* [L13]

burn (intransit.) *ardeō, ardēre, arsī, ——* [L20]; *torreō, -ēre, torruī, tostum* [L17]

burn (transit.) *cremō (1)* [L2]

business (mind one's own business) *suum negōtium agere* [W29]

but *modo* [L27]; *sed* [L1]

by *iūxta (adv. & prep. + acc.)* [L28]

C

cabin (of a ship) *diaeta, -ae (f)* [W18]

call *appellō (1)* [L15]; *vocō (1)* [L1]

calm *placidus, -a, -um* [W29]

camel *camēlus, -ī (m/f)* [L4]

camp *castra, -ōrum (n, pl)* [L15]

can *possum, posse, potuī, ——* [L11]

capture *capiō, -ere, cēpī, captum* [L31]

carcass *cadaver, -veris (n)* [W32]

care for *cūrō (1)* [L15]

carry (off) *rapiō, -ere, rapuī, raptum* [L31]

carry away/off *auferō, -ferre, abstulī, ablatum (3rd conj. irreg.)* [W32]

carry *ferō, ferre, tulī, lātum (irreg. 3rd conj.)* [W32]; *portō (1)*; *vehō, -ere, vexī, vectum* [L27]

carry on *gerō, -ere, gessī, gestum* [L28]

cast *iaciō, -ere, iēcī, iactum* [L31]

cast down *dēiciō, -icere, -iēcī, iectum* [W23]

castle *castellum, -ī (n)* [L5]

cattle *plural of bōs, bovis (m/f)* [L19]

cavalryman *eques, -quitis (m)* [L20]

cave *spēlunca, -ae (f)* [L3]

centaur *centaurus, -ī (m)* [L10]

certainly *enim (postpositive conj.)* [L17]

chair *sella, -ae (f)* [L31]

challenge *provocō (1)*

change *mūtō (1)* [L20]; *vertō, -ere, vertī, versum* [L28]

chant *carmen, -inis (n)* [L13]

character *faciēs, -ēī (f)* [L28]

chariot (four-horse chariot) *quadrīgae, -ārum (f)* [W23]

charioteer *aurīga, -ae (m/f)* [W23]

cherish *foveō, -ēre, fōvī, fōtum* [L25]

chew *mandūcō (1)* [L6]

children *līberī, ōrum (m, pl)* [L10]

choice *optio, optiōnis (f)* [W12]

choose *dēligō, -ere, lēgī, -lēctum* [L28]; *legō, -ere, lēgī, lēctum* [L28]

Christ *Christus, -ī (m)* [L4]

church *ecclēsia, -ae (f)* [L11]

Circus Maximus *Circus Maximus, Circī Maximī (m)* [W23]

city *urbs, urbis (f)* [L18]

city walls *moenia, -ium (n, pl)* [L18]

clan *gens, -ntis (f)* [L31]

class *classis, -is (f)* [L30]

clear (very clear) *limpidissimus, -a, -um* [W32]

clemency *clēmentia, -ae (f)* [W21]

cliff *scopulus, -ī (m)* [W30]

close *iūxta (adv. & prep. + acc.)* [L28]

close to *sub (+ acc.)* [L14]

clothing *vestis, vestis (f)* [L18]

cloud *nūbēs, nūbis (f)* [L18]

coin *nummus, -ī (m)* [W22]

cold *gelidus, -a, -um* [L31]

come upon *inveniō, -īre, -vēnī, -ventum* [L29]

come *veniō, -īre, vēnī, ventum* [L29]

commence *incipiō, -ere, -cēpī, -ceptum* [L31]

compel *cōgō, -ere, -ēgī, -āctum* [L28]

complete *perficiō, -ere, -fēcī, -fectum* [W23]

conceal *occultō (1)* [L22]

concerning *dē (+ abl.)* [L4]

conquer *superō (1)* [L2]; *vincō, -ere, vīcī, victum* [L26]

consecrated *sanctus, -a, -um* [L25]

consequently *ergo (adv.)* [L18]

consume by fire *cremō (1)* [L2]

contest *certāmen, -minis (n)* [W23]

convey *vehō, -ere, vexī, vectum* [L27]

cookie *crustulum, -ī (n)* [L5]

counsel *cōnsilium, -iī (n)* [L30]

country house *villa, -ae (f)* [L2]

courage *virtūs, virtūtis (f)* [L12]

course *curriculum, -ī (n)* [W23]

cousin (on the father's side) *patruēlis, -is (m/f)* [L22]; **(on the mother's side)** *consōbrīna, -ae (f) & consōbrīnus, -ī (m)* [L22]

cow *bōs, bovis (m/f)* [L19]

crash *naufragium, -ī (n)* [W23]

crawl *reptō (1)* [L14]

create *creō (1)* [L6]

creep *reptō (1)* [L14]

Crete *Crēta, -ae (f)* [W30]

crops *plural of frūmentum, -ī (n)* [L15]

cross *crux, crucis (f)* [L15]

crowd *turba, -ae (f)* [L2]

crown *corōna, -ae (f)* [L2]

cry (noun) *clāmor, -oris (m)* [W20]

cultivate *colō, -ere, coluī, cultum* [L29]

Cupid *Cupīdo, -dinis (m)* [W20]

curse *maledīcō, -ere, -dīxī, -dictum* [W30]

cut down *occīdō, -ere, -cīdī, -cīsum* [L30]; *percutiō, -ere, -cussī, -cussum* [W32]

cut off *praecīdō, -ere, -cīdī, -cīsum* [W32]

D

Daedalus *Daedalus, -ī (m)* [W30]

dagger *sīca, -ae (f)* [L3]

danger *perīculum, -ī (n)* [L5]

Daphne *Daphne, -ēs (f)* [W20]

dare *audeō, -ēre, ——, ausus sum* [L11]

dark *āter, -tra, -trum* [L17]

dark-colored *niger, -gra, -grum* [L17]

darkness *tenēbrae, -ārum (f, pl)* [L11]

daughter *fīlia, -ae (f)* [L6]

David *David (indecl.)* [W32]

day *diēs, diēī (m/f)* [L28]

dead body *cadaver, -veris (n)* [W32]

dear *cārus, -a, -um* [L13]

death *mors, mortis (f)* [L18]

declare *dēclārō (1)* [L10]; *nuntiō (1)* [L14]

deep *altus, -a, -um* [L19]

deer *cervus, -ī (m)* [L10]

defeat *superō (1)* [L2]; *vincō, -ere, vīcī, victum* [L26]

defend *dēfendō, -ere, -fendī, -fēnsum* [L28]

depart *abeō, īre, -iī, -itum* [W32]

deprive of *viduō (1)* [W19]

deprived of parents/children *orbus, -a, -um* [L22]

deserve *mereō, -ēre, -uī, -itum* [L15]

desire *cupiō, -ere, cupīvī, cupītum* [L31]

despise *despiciō, -ere, -spexī, -spectum* [W32]

destroy *dēleō, -ēre, -lēvī, -lētum* [L9]; *interficiō, -ere, -fēcī, -fectum* [L31]; *perdō, -ere, perdidī, perditum* [L27]

devastate *vastō (1)* [L14]

Diana *Diāna, -ae (f)* [W20]

difficult *difficilis, -e* [L20]

dig *fodiō, -ere, fōdī, fossum* [W28]

dinner *cēna, -ae (f)* [L20]

direct *gubernō (1)* [L25]

disciple *discipula, -ae (f)*; *discipulus, -ī (m)* [L5]

dismal *trīstis, -e* [L20]

dismiss *dīmittō, -ere, -mīsī, -missum* [L30]

distant *longinquus, -a, -um* [L7]

do *agō, -ere, ēgī, actum* [L26]; *faciō, -ere, fēcī, factum* [L31]

dog *canis, canis (m/f)* [L18]

done (be done) *fīō, fierī, ——, factus sum* [L31]

donkey *asinus, -ī (m)* [L27]

door *porta, -ae (f)* [L31]

down from *dē (+ abl.)* [L4]

downfall *cāsus, -ūs (m)* [L28]

drag *trahō, -ere, trāxī, trāctum* [L30]

dragon *dracō, dracōnis (m)* [L12]

draw near *appropinquō (1)* [L25]

draw *trahō, -ere, trāxī, trāctum* [L30]

dread *metus, -ūs (m)* [L26]

dreadful *horrendus, -a, -um* [L13]

dream (verb) *somniō (1)* [W18]

drink (heavily), *pōtō, -āre, -āvī, pōtātum* or *pōtum* [L6]

drive *agō, -ere, ēgī, actum* [L26]

drive together *cōgō, -ere, -ēgī, -āctum* [L28]

driver *aurīga, -ae (m/f)* [W23]

drop *cadō, -ere, cecidī, casurum* [L27]

drunk *ēbrius, -a, -um* [W13]

dry *āridus, -a, -um* [L27]

dry up *torreō, -ēre, torruī, tostum* [L17]

dwell *habitō (1)* [L3]

E

eager *ācer, ācris, ācre* [L20]

eagerly *certātim* [L20]

ear *auris, -is (f)* [W28]

early *māne* [W19]

earn *mereō, -ēre, -uī, -itum* [L15]

earth *tellūs, tellūris (f)* [L14]; *terra, -ae (f)* [L4]

easy *facilis, -e* [L20]

eat *mandūcō (1)* [L6]

eight *octō* [L21]

eighteen *duodēvīgintī* [L21]

eighteenth *duodēvīcēsimus, -a, -um* [L23]

eighth *octāvus, -a, -um* [L23]

elephant *elephantus, -ī (m)* [L19]

eleven *ūndecim* [L21]

eleventh *ūndecimus, -a, -um* [L23]

end *fīnis, -is (m)* [W4]

enemy (of the state) *hostis, -is (m)* [L18]; **(personal enemy)** *inimīcus, -ī (m)* [L10]

enormous *ingēns, (gen.) -entis* [L19]

enough *satis (adv./indecl. adj./noun)* [L30]

enter *intrō (1)* [L9]

envy *invideō, -ēre, -vīdī, -vīsum* [W29]

Ephramite *Ephratheus, -ī (m)* [W32]

epistle *plural of littera, -ae (f)* [L26]

err *errō (1)* [L14]

escape *effugiō, -ere, -fūgī, -fugitum* [W10]

esteem *foveō, -ēre, fōvī, fōtum* [L25]

eternal *aeternus, -a, -um* [L15]

even *et* [L1]; *etiam* [L22]

evening star *vesper, vesperis (m)* [L14]

evening *vesper, vesperis (m)* [L14]

event *cāsus, -ūs (m)* [L28]

ever *quandō* [L12]

every *omnis, -e* [L19]

everywhere *ubīque* [W29]

evil *malus, -a, -um* [L7]

excellent *ēgregius, -a, -um* [L29]

exercise *exerceō, ēre, -uī, -itum* [L14]

expect *exspectō (1)* [L3]

explain *dēclārō (1)* [L10]

expose *aperiō, -īre, aperuī, apertum* [L29]

expression *vultus, -ūs (m)* [L25]

extend *extendō, -ere, -tendī, -tensum* [W26]

F

Fabius *Fabius, -iī (m)* [W19]

face *faciēs, -ēī (f)* [L28]; *vultus, -ūs (m)* [L25]

fair *iūstus, -a, -um* [L7]

faith *fidēs, -eī (f)* [L28]

faithful *fīdus, -a, -um* [L7]

fall *cadō, -ere, cecidī, cāsūrum* [L27]

fame *glōria, -ae* [L15]; *fāma, -ae* [W23]

family *familia, -ae* [L22]

famous (that famous) *ille, illa, illud* [L30]

far away *longinquus, -a, -um* [L7]

farmer *agricola, -ae (m)* [L3]

farmhouse *villa, -ae (f)* [L2]

fast *cito* [L27]

fasten in *infīgō, -ere, -fīxī, -fīxum* [W32]

fat *pinguis, -e* [W25]

fate *fātum, -ī (n)* [L5]

father *pater, patris (m)* [L12]

favor *grātia, -ae (f)* [L27]

favorable *dexter, -tra, -trum (or -tera, -terum)* [L30]

fear (noun) *metus, -ūs (m)* [L26]

fear (verb) *timeō, -ēre, -uī, ——* [L9]

fearful *horrendus, -a, -um* [L13]

feast *epulae, -ārum (f, pl)* [L20]

feed *pasco, -ere, pāvī, pastum* [W32]

few *paucī, -ae, -a* [L7]

field *ager, agrī (m)* [L4]

fierce *ācer, ācris, ācre* [L20]; *ferus, -a, -um* [L7]

fiery *caldus, -a, -um* [L7]

fifteen *quīndecim* [L21]

fifteenth *quīntus, -a, -um decimus, -a, -um* [L23]

fifth *quīntus, -a, -um* [L23]

fiftieth *quīnquāgēsimus, -a, -um* [L23]

fifty *quīnquāgintā* [L21]

fight *pugnō (1)* [L1]

finally *dēnique* [L10]

find *inveniō, -īre, -vēnī, -ventum* [L29]

finish *perficiō, -ere, -fēcī, -fectum* [W23]

fire *ignis, ignis* [L18]

first *prīmus, -a, -um* [L23]

fish (noun) *piscis, -is (m)* [L19]

fish (verb) *piscor, -ārī, ——, -ātus sum (deponent)* [W29]

five hundred *quīngentī* [L21]

five hundredth *quīngentēsimus, -a, -um* [L23]

five *quīnque* [L21]

fix in *infīgo, -ere, -fīxī, -fīxum* [W32]

flag (starting flag) *mappa, -ae (f)* [W23]

flee *fugiō, -ere, fūgī, fugitum* [L31]

fleet (of ships) *classis, -is (f)* [L30]

flesh *caro, carnis (f)* [L31]

flock *grex, gregis (m)* [L31]

flourish *flōreō, -ēre, -uī, —* [L17]

flower *flōs, flōris (m)* [L15]

fly *volō (1)* [L10]

follow *sequor, sequī, ——, secūtus sum (deponent)* [W30]

folly *stultitia, -ae (f)* [W27]

food *cibus, -ī (m)* [L4]

foolish *stultus, -a, -um* [L7]

foolishness *stultitia, -ae (f)* [W27]

foot (at the foot of) *sub (+ abl.)* [L14]

for (the sake of) *pro (+ abl.)* [L18]

for a long time *diū* [L13]

for *enim (postpositive conj.)* [L17]; *nam* [W32]

force *cōgō, -ere, -ēgī, -āctum* [L28]

forehead *frōns, -ntis (f)* [W32]

foreign *barbarus, -a, -um* [L31]

foreigner *barbarus, -ī (m)* [L31]

forest *silva, -ae (f)* [L3]

forgive *dīmittō, -ere, -mīsī, -missum* [L30]

form *faciēs, -ēī (f)* [L28]

formerly *ōlim* [L6]

fortifications *moenia, -ium (n, pl)* [L18]

fortunate *fēlix, (gen.) -līcis* [L19]

four *quattuor* [L21]

four-horse chariot *quadrīgae, -ārum (f)* [W23]

fourteen *quattuordecim* [L21]

fourteenth *quārtus, -a, -um decimus, -a, -um* [L23]

fourth *quārtus, -a, -um* [L23]

free *līberō (1)* [L1]

fresh *viridis, -e* [L17]

friend *amīca, -ae (f)* [L15]; *amīcus, -ī (m)* [L15]

frighten *terreō, -ēre, -uī, -itum* [L9]

from *ā, ab (+ abl.)* [L3]; *dē (+ abl.)* [L4]; *ē, ex (+ abl.)* [L3]

from all sides *undique* [L30]

from every direction *undique* [L30]

from that place *deinde* [L24]

fruit *frūctus, -ūs (m)* [L25]

funeral pyre *pyra, -ae (f)* [W8]

furrow *versus, -ūs (m)* [L27]

G

garment *vestis, vestis (f)* [L18]

gate *porta, -ae (f)* [L31]

gates (starting gates of a horse race) *plural of carcer, -eris (m)* [W23]

general *dux, ducis (m)* [L14]

generation *saeculum, -ī (n)* [L6]

giant *gigās, gigantis (m)* [L15]

gift *dōnum, -ī (n)* [L5]

girl *puella, -ae (f)* [L3]

give *dō, dare, dedī, datum* [L1]

give thanks *grātiās agō (+ dat.)* [L27]

glad *laetus, -a, -um* [L7]

gloom *nūbēs, nūbis (f)* [L18]

gloomy place *tenēbrae, -ārum (f, pl)* [L11]

gloomy *trīstis, -e* [L20]

glory *glōria, -ae* [L15]

go away *abeō, īre, -iī, -itum* [W32]

go *cēdō, -ere, cessī, cessum* [L28]; *eō, īre, iī (īvī), itum* [L29]

goal *mēta, -ae (f)* [W23]

goat *caper, -prī (m)* [L4]

goblet *calix, calicis (m)* [W13]

god *deus, -i (m)* [L4]

God *Deus, -ī (m)* [L4]

goddess *dea, -ae (f)* [L6]

gold (noun) *aurum, -ī (n)* [L5]

gold(en) *aureus, -a, -um* [L17]

good *bonus, -a, -um* [L7]

Good day! *salvē(te)* [L9]

good news *ēvangelium, -ī* [L5]

Goodbye! *valē(te)* [L9]

gospel *ēvangelium, -ī* [L5]

govern *gubernō (1)* [L25]; *regnō (1)* [L6]

grace *grātia, -ae (f)* [L27]

gradually *minūtātim* [L20]

grain *frūmentum, -ī (n)* [L15]

grandfather *avus, -ī (m)* [L22]

grandmother *avia, -ae (f)* [L22]

grass *grāmen, grāminis (n)* [L13]

grateful *grātus, -a, -um* [L27]

greater *māior, māius (gen. māioris)* [W31]

greatest *māximus, -a, -um* [W31]

greatly *magnopere* [L29]

greedy *avārus, -a, -um* [L7]

green *viridis, -e* [L17]

greenery *grāmen, grāminis (n)* [L13]

ground *tellūs, tellūris (f)* [L14]

group *classis, -is (f)* [L30]

guard against *caveō, -ēre, cāvī, cautum* [L12]

guide *(verb), dūcō, -ere, duxī, ductum* [L26]

guide *(noun), dux, ducis (m)* [L14]

H

hall *aula, -ae (f)* [W13]

hand *manus, -ūs (f)* [L25]; *palma, -ae (f)* [W13]

hand over *trādō, -ere, -didī, -ditum* [W13]

handsome *pulcher, -chra, -chrum* [L7]

happen *fīō, fierī, ——, factus sum* [L31]

happily ever after *fēlīciter in aeternum* [W6]

happiness *gaudium, -ī (n)* [L5]

happy *beātus, -a, -um* [L7]; *fēlix, (gen.) -līcis* [L19]; *laetus, -a, -um* [L7]

harbor *portus, -ūs (m)* [L25]

hardship *labor, labōris (m)* [L12]

hasten *festīnō (1)* [L9]

haughty *superbus, -a, -um* [W18]

have *habeō, -ēre, -uī, -itum* [L9]

he *is, ea, id* [L17]

head *caput, -itis (n)* [L13]

hear *audiō, -īre, -īvī, -ītum* [L29]

heart *cor, cordis (n)* [L13]

heaven *caelum, -ī (n)* [L5]

Hello! *salvē(te)* [L9]

help (noun) *auxilium, -ī (n)* [L5]

help (verb) *iuvō, -āre, iūvī, iūtum* [L22]

her (own) *suus, -a, -um (reflexive possessive adj.)* [W31]

herd *grex, gregis (m)* [L31]

herself *sē (acc. reflexive pronoun)* [W8]

hide *occultō (1)* [L22]; *celō* [W28]

high *altus, -a, -um* [L19]

himself *sē (acc. reflexive pronoun)* [W8]

hinder *impediō, -īre, -īvī, -ītum* [L29]

his (own) *suus, -a, -um (reflexive possessive adj.)* [W31]

hold *habeō, -ēre, -uī, -itum* [L9]; *teneō, -ēre, tenuī, tentum* [L9]

hollow *lacus, -ūs (m)* [L27]

Holy Bible *Biblia Sacra, Bibliae Sacrae (f)* [L11]

holy *sanctus, -a, -um* [L25]

home *domus, -ūs (f)* [L25]

hope *spēs, speī (f)* [L28]

horn *cornū, -ūs (n)* [L25]

horrible *foedus, -a, -um* [L7]

horse *equus, -ī (m)* [L4]

horseman *eques, -quitis (m)* [L20]

hot *caldus, -a, -um* [L7]

hour *hōra, -ae (f)* [L31]

house *domus, -ūs (f)* [L25]; *(country house) villa, -ae (f)* [L2]

household *familia, -ae* [L22]

how (?) *quam* [L28]; *quōmodo* [L25]

however *autem (postposit. conj.)* [L12]

howl *ululō (1)* [L6]

huge *ingēns, (gen.) -entis* [L19]

human being *homō, hominis (m)* [L12]

hungry *famēlicus, -a, -um* [L29]

hunt *captō (1)* [L10]

hunt down *persequor, -sequī, ——, -secutus sum (deponent)* [W32]

hurl down *dēicio, -icere, -iēcī, -iectum* [W23]

hurl *iaciō, -ere, iēcī, iactum* [L31]

hurry *festīnō (1)* [L9]; *properō (1)* [L20]

husband *coniunx, -iugis (m)* [L22]

I

I *ego (sg)* [L17]

icy *gelidus, -a, -um* [L31]

if *sī (conj.)* [L16]

ill *male* [L1]

immediately *statim* [L13]

impartial *iūstus, -a, -um* [L7]

in *in (+ abl.)* [L3]

in front of *pro (+ abl.)* [L18]

in one *ūnā* [L29]

in the presence of *cōram (+ abl.)* [L27]

in what way *quōmodo* [L25]

Inachus *Īnachus, -ī (m)* [W21]

inauspicious *sinister, -stra, -strum* [L30]

incident *cāsus, -ūs (m)* [L28]

increase *augeō -ēre, auxī, auctum* [L19]

indeed *enim (postpositive conj.)* [L17]

infant *īnfāns, -fantis (adj. & noun, m/f)* [W31]

inhabit *colō, -ere, coluī, cultum* [L29]; *habitō (1)* [L3]

inner court *aula, -ae (f)* [W13]

instead of *prō (+ abl.)* [L18]

into *in (+ acc.)* [L3]

intoxicated *ēbrius, -a, -um* [W13]

invite *vocō (1)* [L1]

Io *Īō, -ōnis (f)* [W21]

island *īnsula, -ae (f)* [L3]

Israel *Israhel (indecl.)* [W32]

Israelite *Israhelita, -ae (m)* [W32]

it *is, ea, id* [L17]

Italy *Ītalia, -ae (f)* [W8]

its (own) *suus, -a, -um (reflexive possessive adj.)* [W31]

itself *sē (acc. reflexive pronoun)* [W8]

Iulia *Iūlia, -ae (f)* [W11]

Iulius *Iūlius, -iī (m)* [W19]

Iunia *Iūnia, -ae (f)* [W11]

J

Jerusalem *Hierusalem (indecl.)* [W32]

Jesse *Isai (indecl.)* [W32]

Jesus *Iēsus, -ūs (m)* [L25]

join *iungō, -ere, iūnxī, iunctum* [L27]

journey *iter, itineris (n)* [L13]

Jove *Iuppiter, Iovis (m)* [W21]

joy *gaudium, -ī (n)* [L5]

joyful *laetus, -a, -um* [L7]

judge *iūdex, -dicis (m)* [W28]

Julia *Iūlia, -ae (f)* [W11]

Julius *Iūlius, -iī (m)* [W19]

jump *saliō, -īre, saluī, saltum* [W29]

Junia *Iūnia, -ae (f)* [W11]

Juno *Iūno, -ōnis (f)* [W21]

Jupiter *Iuppiter, Iovis (m)* [W21]

just as *sīcut* [L20]

just (adj.) *iūstus, -a, -um* [L7]

just (adv.) *modo* [L27]

K

kidnapping *raptus, -ūs (m)* [W31]

kill *interficiō, -ere, -fēcī, -fectum* [L31]; *necō (1)* [L1]; *occīdō, -ere, -cīdī, -cīsum* [L30]

kindness *grātia, -ae (f)*

king *rēx, rēgis (m)* [L12]

kingdom *regnum, -ī (n)* [L5]

knee *genū, -ūs (n)* [L25]

knight *eques, -quitis (m)* [L20]

know *sciō, -īre, sciī (scīvī), scītum* [L29]

kraken *cētus, -ī (m)* [L10]

L

labor (noun) *labor, labōris (m)* [L12]

labyrinth *labyrinthus, -ī (m)* [W30]

lake *lacus, -ūs (m)* [L27]

land *tellūs, tellūris (f)* [L14]; *terra, -ae (f)* [L4]; **(native land)** *patria, -ae (f)* [L3]

language *lingua, -ae* [L26]

lap (of a race) *curriculum, -ī (n)* [W23]

large *magnus, -a, -um* [L7]

laugh *rīdeō, -ēre, rīsī, rīsum* [L9]

laurel (tree) *laurus, -ī (f)* [W20]

lay waste *vastō (1)* [L14]

lead (of lead) *plumbeus, -a, -um* [W20]

lead (verb) *dūcō, -ere, duxī, ductum* [L26]

leaden *plumbeus, -a, -um* [W20]

leader *dux, ducis (m)* [L14]

leaf *folium, -ī (n)* [W20]

leaky *pertūsus, -a, -um* [W29]

leap *saliō, -īre, -uī, saltum* [W29]

learned *doctus, -a, -um* [L13]

least *minimus, -a, -um* [W31]

leave behind *relinquō, -ere, -līquī, -lictum* [L28]

left(-handed) *sinister, -stra, -strum* [L30]

leg *crūs, crūris (n)* [W19]

legend *fābula, -ae (f)* [L2]

let go *mittō, -ere, mīsī, missum* [L26]

letter (of the alphabet) *littera, -ae (f)* [L26]

letter *plural of littera, -ae (f)* [L26]

lie *iaceō, -ēre, -uī, ——* [L9]

lie down *iaceō, -ēre, -uī, ——* [L9]

lie flat *iaceō, -ēre, -uī, ——* [L9]

life *vīta, -ae* [L11]

lift up *tollō, -ere, sustulī, sublātum* [W25]

light *lux, lūcis (f)* [L12]

lightning *fulgur, -uris (n)* [W25]

like *sīcut* [L20]

limit *fīnis, -is (m)* [W4]

line (of poetry) *versus, -ūs (m)* [L27]

lion *leō, leōnis (m)* [L12]

listen to *audiō, -īre, -īvī, -ītum* [L29]

little *parvus, -a, -um* [L7]

live *habitō (1)* [L3]; *vīvō, -ere, vīxī, victum* [L27]

living *vīvus, -a, -um* [L20]

load *onus, oneris (n)* [L13]

lofty *altus, -a, -um* [L19]

long (for) (verb) *cupiō, -ere, cupīvī, cupītum* [L31]

long (adj.) *longus, -a, -um* [L20]

look at *spectō (1)* [L1]

look down on *despiciō, -ere, -spexī, -spectum* [W32]

lop *praecīdō, -ere, -cīdī, -cīsum* [W32]

lord *dominus, -ī (m)* [L4]

lose *perdō, -ere, perdidī, perditum* [L27]

love (noun) *amor, amōris (m)* [L14]

love (verb) *amō (1)* [L1]; *foveō, -ēre, fōvī, fōtum* [L25]

lucky *fēlix, (gen.) -līcis* [L19]

lyre *lyra, -ae (f)* [W28]

M

made (am made) *fīō, fierī, ——, factus sum* [L31]

maiden *virgō, virginis (f)* [L12]

make clear *dēclārō (1)* [L10]

make *faciō, -ere, fēcī, factum* [L31]

man (as opposed to animal) *homō, hominis (m)* [L12]; **(as opposed to woman)** *vir, virī (m)* [L4]

manliness *virtūs, virtūtis (f)* [L12]

many *multus, -a, -um* [L7]

marriage *mātrimōnium, -ī (n)* [L20]

master *dominus, -ī (m)* [L4]

maze *labyrinthus, -ī (m)* [W30]

meal *cēna, -ae (f)* [L20]

meantime (in the meantime) *interim* [L9]

meanwhile *interim* [L9]

meat *caro, carnis (f)* [L31]

Mercury *Mercurius, -ī (m)* [W21]

mercy *clēmentia, -ae (f)* [W21]

merely *modo* [L27]

Midas *Midās, -ae (m)* [W27]

middle (of) *medius, -a, -um* [L26]

midst (of) *medius, -a, -um* [L26]

milk *lac, lactis (n)* [L13]

mind *animus, -ī (m)* [L29]

mind one's own business *suum negōtium agere* [W29]

mine *meus, -a, -um* [L11]

Minos *Mīnōs, -ōnis (m)* [W30]

Minotaur *Mīnōtaurus, -ī (m)* [W30]

miserable *infēlix, (gen.) -līcis* [L19]; *miser, -era, -erum* [L7]

misfortune *cāsus, -ūs (m)* [L28]

mistaken (am mistaken) *errō (1)* [L14]

mob *turba, -ae (f)* [L2]

money *argentum, -ī (n)* [L5]; *peccnia, -ae (f)* [L3]

monster *mōnstrum* [W30]

moon *lūna, -ae* [L2]

moreover *autem (postposit. conj.)* [L12]

morning (in the morning) *māne* [W19]

mother *māter, mātris (f)* [L12]

mountain *mōns, montis* [L18]

mouth *ōs, ōris (n)* [L13]

move (intransit.) *cēdō, -ere, cessī, cessum* [L28]

move (transit.) *moveō, -ēre, mōvī, mōtum* [L14]

much *multus, -a, -um* [L7]

musician *musicus, -ī (m)* [W28]

my *meus, -a, -um* [L11]

N

name (verb) *appellō (1)* [L15]

name (noun) *nōmen, nōminis (n)* [L13]

napkin *mappa, -ae (f)* [W23]

nation *gens, -ntis (f)* [L31]; *populus, -ī (m)* [L11]

native land *patria, -ae (f)* [L3]

near (to) *iūxta (adv. & prep. + acc.)* [L28]

near *ad (+ acc.)* [L3]; *prope (adv. & prep. + acc.)* [L19]; *propter (+ acc.)* [L25]

neither...nor *nec...nec* [L14]

never *numquam* [L5]

nevertheless *tamen* [L30]

new *novus, -a, -um* [L26]

next *deinde* [L22]; *tum* [L15]

next to *prope (adv. & prep. + acc.)* [L19]

night *nox, noctis (f)* [L18]

nine *novem* [L21]

nineteen *ūndēvīgintī* [L21]

nineteenth *ūndēvīcēsimus, -a, -um* [L23]

ninth *nōnus, -a, -um* [L23]

no longer *nōn iam* [L15]

noble *magnanimus, -a, -um* [W9]

noon *merīdiēs, -ēī (m)* [L28]

nor *nec (neque)* [L14]

not at all *nihil (n. indecl.)* [L6]

not know *nesciō, -īre, -īvī, -ītum* [L30]

not *nōn* [L1]; *nec (neque)* [L14]

nothing *nihil (n, indecl.)* [L6]

now *iam* [L15]; *nunc* [L1]

nymph *nympha, -ae (f)* [W20]

O

ocean *ōceanus, -ī (m)* [L4]

of/belonging to a shepherd *pastoralis, -e* [W32]

often *saepe* [L6]

oh! *heu (ēheu)* [L22]

old man *senex, senis (m)* [L14]

old *vetus, -teris* [L30]

older *māior, māius (gen. māioris)* [W31]

oldest (son) *postnatus, -ī (m)* [W19]

oldest *māximus, -a, -um* [W31]

on *in (+ abl.)* [L3]

on account of *propter (+ acc.)* [L25]

on all sides *undique* [L30]

once upon a time *ōlim* [L6]

one (in one) *ūnā* [L29]

one another *invicem* [W26]

one hundred *centum* [L21]

one hundredth *centēsimus* [L23]

one *ūnicus, -a, -um* [W22]; *ūnus, -a, -um* [L21]

only (adv.) *modo* [L27]

only (adj.) *sōlus, -a, -um* [W12]; *ūnicus, -a, -um* [W22]

open *aperiō, -īre, -uī, apertum* [L29]

openly *cōram* [L27]

or *aut* [L1]; *sīve (sēū)* [L30]

oracle *ōrāculum, -ī (n)* [W31]

ordinary *mediōcris, -e* [L19]

orphan *orba, -ae (f)/orbus, -ī (m)* [L22]

Oswald *Oswaldus, -ī (m)* [W19]

other *alius, alia, aliud* [W21]

ought *dēbeō, -ēre, -uī, -itum* [L11]

our(W) *noster, -stra, -strum* [L11]

out of *ē, ex (+ abl.)* [L3]

outstanding *ēgregius, -a, -um* [L29]

over *super (+ acc./+ abl.)* [L26]; *suprā (adv./prep. + acc.)* [L14]

owe *dēbeō, -ēre, -uī, -itum* [L11]

ox *bōs, bovis (m/f)* [L19]

P

Pactolus *Pactōlus, -ī (m)* [W27]

palace *rēgia, -ae (f)* [L2]

Pan *Pān, Pānos (acc. Pāna) (m)* [W28]

pan pipe *avēna, -ae (f)* [W21]

parch *torreō, -ēre, torruī, tostum* [L17]

parent *parens, -ntis (m/f)* [W11]

pastoral *pastoralis, -e* [W32]

pasture *pasco, -ere, pāvī, pastum* [W32]

pay the penalty *poenās dō* [L27]

peace *pāx, pācis (f)* [L15]

peacock *pāvo, -ōnis (m)* [W21]

penalty *poena, -ae (f)* [L27]

people *populus, -ī (m)* [L11]

perhaps *fortasse* [L26]

period of time *diēs, diēī (m/f)* [L28]

permit *permittō, -ere, -mīsī, -missum* [W30]

permitted (it is permitted) *licet* [W26]

personally *cōram* [L27]

persuade *persuādeō, -ere, -suāsī, -suāsum (+ dat.)* [W15]

Philistine *Philistheus, -ī (m)*

Phrygia *Phrygia, -ae (f)* [W27]

pick *dēligō, -ere, lēgī, -lēctum* [L28]

pig *porcus, -ī (m)* [L10]

pig-sty *hara, -ae (f)* [W25]

pipe (reed-pipe) *calamus, -ī (m)* [W28]

pirate *pīrāta, -ae (m)* [L2]

place (verb) *collocō (1)* [W21]; *pōnō, -ere, posuī, positum* [L26]

plan *cōnsilium, -iī (n)* [L30]

play (music) *cantō (1)* [L1]

play *lūdō, lūdere, lūsī, lūsum* [L26]

pleasing *grātus, -a, -um* [L27]

plenty *cōpia, -ae (f)* [L15]

poem *carmen, -inis (n)* [L13]

poet *poēta, -ae* [L2]

poison *venēnum, -ī (n)* [L10]

polite *urbānus, -a, -um* [W29]

port *portus, -ūs (m)* [L25]

possess *teneō, -ēre, tenuī, tentum* [L9]

powerful *potēns, (gen.) -entis* [L19]

praise (noun) *laus, laudis (f)* [L15]

praise (verb) *laudō (1)* [L1]

pray *ōrō (1) (takes double acc.)* [L6]

predict *cantō (1)* [L1]; *praedīcō, -ere, -dīxī, -dictum* [W31]

prepare *parō (1)* [L14]

presence (in the presence of) *cōram (+ abl.)* [L27]

prison *carcer, -eris (m)* [W23]

profit *frūctus, -ūs (m)* [L25]

prophecy *carmen, -inis (n)* [L13]; *ōrāculum, -ī (n)*

prophesy *praedīcō, -ere, -dīxī, -dictum* [W31]

prophet *vātēs, -is (m)* [W31]

prophetess *vātēs, -is (f)* [W31]

proud *superbus, -a, -um* [W18]

punishment *poena, -ae (f)* [L27]

purple *purpureus, -a, -um* [L17]

purplish-blue *hyacinthinus, -a, -um* [L17]

pursue (with hostile intent) *persequor, -sequī, ——, -secutus sum (deponent)* [W32]

put *pōnō, -ere, posuī, positum* [L26]

pyre *pyra, -ae (f)* [W8]

Q

quake *tremō, -ere, -uī, ——* [W25]

queen *rēgīna, -ae (f)* [L2]

quick *celer, celeris, celere* [L19]

quickly *cito* [L27]

quiet *placidus, -a, -um* [W29]

R

race *certāmen, -minis (n)* [W23]

rainbow *arcus, -ūs (m)* [L27]

raise *tollō, -ere, sustulī, sublātum* [W25]

ram *ariēs, -ietis (m)* [W32]

ravage *vexō (1)* [L19]

read *legō, -ere, lēgī, lēctum* [L28]

receive *accipiō, -ere, -cēpī, ceptum* [L31]

reciprocally *invicem* [W26]

recount *narrō (1)* [L2]

red *ruber, -bra, -brum* [L17]; *rūfus, -a, -um* [W32]; **(dark-red)** *purpureus, -a, -um* [L17]

reed *calamus, -ī (m)* [W28]

reign *regnō (1)* [L6]

rejoice *gaudeō, -ēre, ——, gāvīsus sum* [L22]

relate *narrō (1)* [L2]

remain *maneō, -ēre, mansī, mansum* [L10]

remain near *obsideō, -ēre, -sēdī, -sessum* [L10]

remove *auferō, -ferre, abstulī, ablatum (3rd conj. irreg.)* [W32]; *removeō, -ēre, -mōvī, -mōtum* [L14]

repair *reficiō, -ere, -fēcī, -fectum* [W29]

report *fāma, -ae (f)* [W23]

reproach *exprobrō (1)* [W32]

reputation *fāma, -ae (f)* [W23]

respond *respondeō, -ēre, -spondī, -spōnsum* [L9]

reward *praemium, -ī (n)* [W27]

riches *dīvitiae, -ārum (f, pl)* [L2]

riddle *enigma, -matis (n)* [W19]

ride *vehō, -ere, vexī, vectum* [L27]

right *iūstus, -a, -um* [L7]

right(-handed) *dexter, -tra, -trum (or -tera, -terum)* [L30]

righteous *iūstus, -a, -um* [L7]

rise again *resurgō, -ere, -surrēxī, -surrēctum* [L29]

rise *surgō, -ere, surrēxī, surrēctum* [L28]

river *flūmen, flūminis (n)* [L13]

road *iter, itineris (n)* [L13]; *via, -ae (f)* [L11]

rock *saxum, -ī (n)* [L29]

route *iter, itineris (n)* [L13]

row *versus, -ūs (m)* [L27]

royal court *aula, -ae (f)* [W13]

ruddy *ruber, -bra, -brum* [L17]; *rūfus, -a, -um* [W32]

ruin *perdō, -ere, perdidī, perditum* [L27]

rule *regnō (1)* [L6]; *regō, -ere, rexī, rectum* [L26]

run away *fugiō, -ere, fūgī, fugitum* [L31]

run *currō, -ere, cūcurrī, cursum* [L26]

rush *properō (1)* [L20]

S

Sabbath *sabbata, -ōrum (n, pl)* [W26]

sacred *sanctus, -a, -um* [L25]

sad *trīstis, -e* [L20]

safe *salvus, -a, -um* [L25]

sail (noun) *vēlum, -ī (n)* [W30]

sail (verb) *nāvigō (1)* [L4]

sailor *nauta, -ae (m)* [L3]

sand *harēna, -ae (f)* [L3]

satchel *pēra, -ae (f)* [W32]

Saul *Saul (indecl.)* [W32]

savage *barbarus, -a, -um* [L31]

save *servō (1)* [L6]

saved *salvus, -a, -um* [L25]

say *āiō* [L14]; *dīcō, -ere, dīxī, dictum* [L26]

scream *ululō (1)* [L6]

sea *mare, maris (n)* [L18]

sea serpent *hydrus, -ī (m)*

seat *sella, -ae (f)* [L31]

second (adv.; a second time) *iterum* [L25]

second (adj.) *secundus, -a, -um* [L23]

secret *sēcrētum, -ī (n)* [W28]

secretly *clam* [L29]

see *videō, -ēre, vīdī, vīsum* [L9]

seize *capiō, -ere, cēpī, captum* [L31]; *occupō (1)* [L6]; *rapiō, -ere, rapuī, raptum* [L31]

send away *dīmittō, -ere, -mīsī, -missum* [L30]

send *mittō, -ere, mīsī, missum* [L26]

servant *serva, -ae (f)* [L4]; *servus, -ī (m)* [L4]

set *collocō (1)* [W21]

set free *līberō (1)* [L1]

seven *septem* [L21]

seventeen *septendecim* [L21]

seventeenth *septimus, -a, -um decimus, -a, -um* [L23]

seventh *septimus, -a, -um* [L23]

shadows *tenēbrae, -ārum (f, pl)* [L11]

shape *faciēs, -ēī (f)* [L28]

sharp *ācer, ācris, ācre* [L20]

shatter *frangō, -ere, frēgī, fractum* [L27]

she *is, ea, id* [L17]

shepherd (of/belonging to a shepherd) *pastorālis, -e* [W32]

shepherd *pastor, pastōris (m)* [L20]

shepherd's pipe *avēna, -ae (f)* [W21]

shield *clypeum, -ī (n)* [W32]; *scūtum, -ī (m)* [L10]

shine *lūceō, lūcēre, lūxī, ——* [L11]

ship *nāvis, -is (f)* [L18]; *alnus, -ī (f)* [L4]

shipwreck *naufragium, -ī (n)* [W23]

shoot *petō, -ere, -īvī, -ītum* [W20]

shore *lītus, lītoris (n)* [L13]; *ōra, -ae (f)* [L13]

shoreline *lītus, lītoris (n)* [L13]

short *brevis, -e* [L19]

shout (noun) *clāmor, -ōris (m)* [W20]

shout (verb) *clāmō (1)* [L1]

shrine *templum, -ī (n)* [W25]

shun *vītō (1)* [L30]

silent (be silent) *taceō, ēre, -uī, -itum* [W26]

Silenus *Sīlēnus, -ī (m)* [W27]

silver (adj.) *argenteus, -a, -um* [L17]

silver (noun) *argentum, -ī (n)* [L5]

since *quandō* [L12]; *quia* [L18]; *quoniam* [L26]

sing *cantō (1)* [L1]

singing *cantus, -ūs (m)* [L25]

single *sōlus, -a, -um* [W12]

sink *cadō, -ere, cecidī, cāsūrum* [L27]

sister *germāna, -ae (f)* [L4]; *soror, sorōris (f)* [L12]

sit *sedeō, -ēre, sēdī, sessum* [L9]

six *sex* [L21]

sixteen *sēdecim* [L21]

sixteenth *sextus, -a, -um decimus, -a, -um* [L23]

sixth *sextus, -a, -um* [L23]

skilled *dexter, -tra, -trum (or -tera, -terum)* [L30]; *doctus, -a, -um* [L13]

sky *caelum, -ī (n)* [L5]

slave *serva, -ae (f)* [L4]; *servus, -ī (m)* [L4]

slay *interficiō, -ere, -fēcī, -fectum* [L31]; *necō (1)* [L1]; *occīdō, -ere, -cīdī, -cīsum* [L30]

sleep *dormiō, -īre, -īvī, -ītum* [L29]

sling *funda, -ae (f)* [W32]

small *brevis, -e* [L19]; *parvus, -a, -um* [L7]

small cake *crustulum, -ī (n)* [L5]

smash *frangō, -ere, frēgī, fractum* [L27]

smile *rīdeō, -ēre, rīsī, rīsum* [L9]

snatch *rapiō, -ere, rapuī, raptum* [L31]

soldier *mīles, mīlitis (m)* [L12]

sole *ūnicus, -a, -um* [W22]

son *fīlius, -ī (m)* [L4]

song *cantus, -ūs (m)* [L25]; *carmen, -inis (n)* [L13]

soon *mox* [L15]

sound (adj.) *salvus, -a, -um* [L25]

speak *dīcō, -ere, dīxī, dictum* [L26]; *ōrō (1) (takes double acc.)* [L6]

speak ill *maledīcō, -ere, -dixī, -dictum* [W30]

spear *hasta, -ae (f)* [L3]

speedily *cito* [L27]

spine *spīna, -ae (f)* [W23]

spirit of the age *saeculum, -ī (n)* [L6]

spirit *spīritus, -ūs (m)* [L25]

spurious *spurius, -a, -um* [W32]

staff *baculum, -ī (n)* [W32]

stag *cervus, -ī (m)* [L10]

stand *stō, stāre, stetī, statum* [L1]

star *stella, -ae* [L11]

starting gates (of a horse race) *plural of carcer, -eris (m)* [W23]

statue *simulacrum, -ī (n)* [W25]

steer *gubernō (1)* [L25]

step-mother *noverca, -ae (f)* [W22]

still *etiam* [L22]; *tamen* [L30]

sting *mordeō, -ēre, momordī, morsum* [L9]

stone *lapis, -idis (m)* [W27]

storm *tempestās, -tātis (f)* [L26]

story *fābula, -ae (f)* [L2]

strange *barbarus, -a, -um* [L31]; *mīrus, -a, -um* [L7]

stream *torrens, -ntis (m)* [W32]

strength *virtūs, virtūtis (f)* [L12]

stretch out *extendō, -ere, -tendī, -tensum* [W26]

strike down *percutiō, -ere, -cussī, -cussum* [W32]

strike *tangō, -ere, tetigī, tactum* [L27]

string *filum, -ī (n)* [W30]

strong *fortis, -e* [L19]

strongest *fortissimus, -a, -um* [W32]

student (female) *discipula, -ae (f) &* **(male)** *discipulus, -ī (m)* [L5]

subdue *domō, -āre, domuī, domitum* [L12]

such *iste, ista, istud* [L30]

suddenly *repentē* [L10]

sufficient(ly) *satis (adv. & indecl. adj./noun)* [L30]

summon *vocō (1)* [L1]

sun *sōl, sōlis (m)* [L12]

supply *cōpia, -ae (f)* [L15]

surrender *trādō, -ere, -didī, -ditum* [W13]

suspicious *suspīciōsus, -a, -um* [W21]

swamp *palus, palūdis (f)* [W13]

sweet *dulcis, -e* [L19]

swift *celer, celeris, celere* [L19]

swim *nō (1)* [L14]

sword *gladius, -ī (m)* [L4]

synagogue *synagōga, -ae (f)* [W26]

T

table *mensa, -ae (f)* [L31]

tail *cauda, -ae (f)* [W21]

take *accipiō, -ere, -cēpī, ceptum* [L31]; *capiō, -ere, cēpī, captum* [L31]

take away *removeō, -ēre, -mōvī, -mōtum* [L14]

take for myself *adsūmō, -ere, -sumpsī, -sumptum* [W32]

tale *fābula, -ae (f)* [L2]

tame *domō, -āre, domuī, domitum* [L12]

tax *tribūtum, -ī (n)* [W30]

teach *doceō, -ēre, docuī, doctum* [L9]

teacher (female) *magistra, -ae (f)*/(male) *magister, -strī (m)* [L6]

tease *lūdō, lūdere, lūsī, lūsum* [L26]

tell *narrō (1)* [L2]

temple *templum, -ī (n)* [W25]

ten *decem* [L21]

tent *tabernāculum, -ī (n)* [W32]

tenth *decimus, -a, -um* [L23]

terrify *terreō, -ēre, -uī, -itum* [L9]

than *quam* [L28]

thank *grātiās agō (+ dat.)* [L27]

thanks *grātia, -ae (f)* [L27]

that (of yours) *iste, ista, istud* [L30]

that (adj./pron.) *ille, illa, illud* [L30]; *is, ea, id* [L17]

that (conj.) *quia* [L18]; *quod* [L10]

then (therefore) *deinde* [L22]; *ergo (adv.)* [L18]; (of time) *ibī* [L5]; *ōlim* [L6]; *tum* [L15]

there *ibī* [L5]

therefore *ergo (adv.)* [L18]; *itaque* [L2]

thereupon *deinde* [L22]; *tum* [L15]

these *plural of hic, haec, hoc* [L30]

Theseus *Thēsēus, -eī (m)* [W30]

they *is, ea, id* [L9]

thing *rēs, reī (f)* [L28]

think *cōgitō (1)* [L6]

third *tertius, -a, -um* [L23]

thirteen *tredecim* [L21]

thirteenth *tertius, -a, -um decimus, -a, -um* [L23]

this *hic, haec, hoc* [L30]; *is, ea, id* [L17]

those *plural of ille, illa, illud* [L30]

thousand *mīlle* [L21]

thousandth (one thousandth) *mīllēsimus, -a, -um* [L23]

thread *fīlum, -ī (n)* [W30]

three *trēs, tria* [L21]

throng *turba, -ae (f)* [L2]

through *per (+ acc.)* [L3]

throw down *dēiciō, -icere, -iēcī, -iectum* [W23]

throw *iaciō, -ere, iēcī, iactum* [L31]

thunder *tonitrus, -ūs (m)* [L25]

tie *vinciō, -īre, vīnxī, vīnctum* [L30]

tiger *tigris, tigridis (m/f)* [L12]

time *tempus, temporis (n)* [L13]

times (the times) *saeculum, -ī (n)* [L6]

tired *fessus, -a, -um* [L20]

Tmolus *Tmōlus, -ī (m)* [W28]

to *ad (+ acc.)* [L3]

today *hodiē* [L2]

together *ūnā* [L29]

toil (noun) *labor, labōris (m)* [L28]

tomorrow *crās* [L6]

tongue *lingua, -ae (f)* [L26]

too *quoque* [L29]

torrent *torrens, -ntis (m)* [W32]

touch (noun) *tactus, -ūs (m)* [W28]

touch (verb) *tangō, -ere, tetigī, tactum* [L27]

toward *ad (+ acc.)* [L3]

tower *turris, turris (f)* [L18]

town *oppidum, -ī (n)* [L5]

tragedy *tragoedia, -ae (f)* [W4]

train *exerceō, -ēre, -uī, -itum* [L14]

tree *arbor, arboris (f)* [L20]

trek *iter, itineris (n)* [L13]

tremble *tremō, -ere, -uī, ——* [W25]

tribe *gens, -ntis (f)* [L31]

tribute *tribūtum, -ī (n)* [W30]

trick *lūdō, lūdere, lūsī, lūsum* [L26]

troops *plural of cōpia, -ae (f)* [L15]

true *vērus, -a, -um* [L22]

truly *enim (postpositive conj.)* [L17]

trustworthy *fīdus, -a, -um* [L7]

truth *veritas, -tatis (f)* [L27]

tub *lacus, -ūs (m)* [L27]

turban *mītra, -ae (f)* [W28]

turn *vertō, -ere, vertī, versum* [L28]

turning-post *mēta, -ae (f)* [W23]

turret *turris, turris (f)* [L18]

twelfth *duodecimus, -a, -um* [L23]

twelve *duodecim* [L21]

twentieth *vīcēsimus, -a, -um* [L23]

twenty *vīgintī* [L21]

twenty-first *vīcēsimus, -a, -um prīmus, -a, -um* [L23]

twenty-one *vīgintī ūnus, -a, -um (ūnus et vīgintī)* [L21]

twin *geminus, -ī (m)* [L10]

two *duo, duae, duo* [L21]

U

ugly *foedus, -a, -um* [L7]

uncircumcised *incircumcisus, -a, -um* [W32]

uncle (father's brother) *patruus, -ī (m)* [L22]; **(mother's brother)** *avunculus, -ī (m)* [L22]

under *sub (+ acc.)* [L24]

under(neath) *sub (+ abl.)* [L14]

unfortunate *infēlix, (gen.) -līcis* [L19]

unhappy *miser, -era, -erum* [L7]

unimportant *parvus, -a, -um* [L7]

unite *iungō, -ere, iūnxī, iunctum* [L27]

universe *mundus, -ī (m)* [L6]

unlucky *infēlix, (gen.) -līcis* [L19]

up under *sub (+ acc.)* [L14]

V

vale *vallēs, vallis (f)* [L18]

valley *vallēs, vallis (f)* [L18]

vast *ingēns, (gen.) -entis* [L19]

very much *magnoperē* [L29]

vex *vexō (1)* [L19]

victory *victōria, -ae (f)* [L11]

vigorous *viridis, -e* [L17]

violet *hyacinthinus, -a, -um* [L17]; **(dark-violet)** *purpureus, -a, -um* [L17]

voice *vōx, vōcis (f)* [L14]

W

wage war *bellum gerō* [L28]

wait for *exspectō (1)* [L3]

walk *ambulō (1)* [L1]

walls (city walls) *moenia, -ium (n, pl)* [L18]

wander *errō (1)* [L14]

war *bellum, -ī (n)* [L15]

warm *caldus, -a, -um* [L7]

warn *moneō, -ēre, -uī, -itum* [L9]

warrior *bellator, -toris (m)* [W32]

wash *lavō, -āre, lāvī, lōtum/lavātum* [W27]

watch *spectō (1)* [L1]

water *aqua, -ae (f)* [L2]

wave *unda, -ae (f)* [L10]

way *via, -ae (f)* [L11]

we *nōs (pl.)* [L17]

wealth *dīvitiae, -ārum (f, pl)* [L2]

weapons *arma, -ōrum (n, pl)* [W32]

weary *fessus, -a, -um* [L20]

weather *tempestās, -tātis (f)* [L26]

weep *fleō, -ēre, flēvī, flētum* [L14]

weight *onus, oneris (n)* [L13]

well (adj.) *salvus, -a, -um* [L25]

well (verb; be well) *salveō, -ēre, ——, ——* [L9]; *valeō, -ēre, valuī, valitūrum* [L9]

well (adv.) *bene* [L1]

wet (sopping) *aquōsus, -a, -um* [W29]

what? *quid* [W19]

when (?) *quandō* [L12]; *ubi* [L12]

where (?) *ubi* [L12]

whether...or *sīve/sēū... sīve/sēū* [L30]

whisper *susurrō (1)* [W28]

white (dead) *albus, -a, -um* [L17]; **(glittering)** *candidus, -a, -um* [L17]

who (?) *quis* [W31]

why *cūr* [L2]

wicked *improbus, -a, -um* [L29]

wide *lātus, -a, -um* [L20]

widow *vidua, -ae (f)* [L22]

widowed *viduāta, -ae* [W19]

wife *coniūnx, -iugis (f)* [L22]; *uxor, -ōris (f)* [L30]

wild *ferus, -a, -um* [L7]

wind *ventus, -ī (m)* [W28]

window *fenestra, ae (f)* [L31]

wine *vīnum, -ī (n)* [L5]

wing *āla, -ae (f)* [L10]

wisdom *cōnsilium, -iī (n)* [L30]

wise *doctus, -a, -um* [L13]

wish (for) *cupiō, -ere, cupīvī, cupītum* [L31]

with *cum (+ abl.)* [L9]

withered *āridus, -a, -um* [L27]

without *sine (+ abl.)* [L9]

woman *fēmina, -ae* [L2]; *mulier, mulieris (f)* [L22]; **(young woman)** *virgō, virginis (f)* [L12]

wonderful *mīrus, -a, -um* [L7]

word *verbum, -ī* [L5]

work (noun) *labor, labōris (m)* [L12]

work (verb) *labōrō (1)* [L22]

world *mundus, -ī (m)* [L6]

worship *colō, -ere, coluī, cultum* [L29]

worthy (am worthy of) *mereō, -ēre, -uī, -itum* [L23]

wound (noun) *vulnus, vulneris (n)* [L13]

wound (verb) *vulnerō (1)* [L1]

wrathful *īrātus,-a, -um* [L15]

wreck *naufragium, -ī (n)* [W23]

wretched *miser, -era, -erum* [L7]

write *scrībō, -ere, scrīpsī, scriptum* [L26]

wrongly *male* [L1]

Y

yesterday *herī* [L6]

yet *tamen* [L30]

yield *cēdō, -ere, cessī, cessum* [L28]

yoke *iungō, -ere, iūnxi, iunctum* [L27]

you (sg.) *tū* [L17]; **(pl.)** *vōs* [L17]

young man *adulescens, -entis (m)* [L30]

young *viridis, -e* [L17]

young woman *adulescens, -entis (f)* [L30]; *virgō, virginis (f)* [L12]

younger *minimus, -a, -um* [W31]

youngest *iuvenissimus, -a, -um* [W19]

your (sg.) *tuus, -a, -um* [L11]; **(pl.)** *vester, -stra, -strum* [L11]

yours (sg.) *tuus, -a, -um* [L11]; **(pl.)** *vester, -stra, -strum* [L11]

youth *adulescentia, -ae (f)* [W32]

Latin-English Glossary

A

ā, ab, (+ abl.) *from, away from* [L3]

abeō, -īre, -iī, -itum *I go away, depart* [W32]

ac (atque) *and, and also* [L27]

accipiō, -ere, -cēpī, -ceptum *I accept, receive, take* [L31]

ācer, ācris, ācre *sharp, eager; fierce* [L20]

ad (+ acc.) *to, toward, at, near* [L3]

adsūmō, -ere, -sumpsī, -sumptum *I take for myself* [W32]

adulescens, -entis (m/f) *young man/ woman* [L30]

adulescentia, -ae (f) *youth* [W32]

Aegeus, -a, -um *Aegean* [W30]

Aegeus, -eī (m) *Aegeus* [W30]

aeternus, -a, -um *eternal* [L15]

ager, agrī (m) *field* [L4]

agō, -ere, ēgī, actum *I do, act, drive* [L26]

agricola, -ae (m) *farmer* [L3]

āiō (defective) *I say, assert, affirm* [L14]

āla, -ae (f) *wing* [L10]

albus, -a, -um *(dead) white* [L17]

alchemia, -ae (f) *alchemy* [W27]

alius, alia, aliud *another, other* [W21]

alnus, -ī (f) *ship, alder (wood)* [L4]

altus, -a, -um *high, lofty, deep* [L19]

ambulō (1) *I walk* [L1]

amīca, -ae (f) *(female) friend* [L15]

amīcus, -ī (m) *(male) friend* [L15]

amita, -ae (f) *aunt* [L22]

amō (1) *I love* [L1]

amor, amōris (m) *love* [L14]

animal, -ālis (n) *animal* [L18]

animus, -ī (m) *mind* [L29]

ante (+ acc.) *before* [L17]

antīquus, -a, -um *ancient* [L7]

aperiō, -īre, -uī, apertum *I open, expose* [L29]

Apollo, -inis (m) *Apollo (god of prophesy, music, archery, the sun, etc.)* [W20]

apostolus, -ī (m) *apostle* [L11]

appellō (1) *I name, call* [L15]

appropinquō (1) *I approach, draw near* [L25]

aqua, -ae (f) *water* [L2]

aquōsus, -a, -um *sopping wet* [W29]

arbor, arboris (f) *tree* [L20]

arcus, -ūs (m) *bow, arch, rainbow* [L27]

ardeō, ardēre, arsī, —— *I burn, blaze* [L20]

argenteus, -a, -um *silver(y)* [L17]

argentum, -ī (n) *silver, money* [L5]

Argus, -ī (m) *Argus, a hundred-eyed giant* [W21]

Ariadna, -ae (f) *Ariadne* [W30]

āridus, -a, -um *dry, withered* [L27]

ariēs, -ietis (m) *ram* [W32]

arma, -ōrum (n, pl) *arms, armor, weapons* [W32]

asinus, -ī (m) *donkey* [L19]

āter, -tra, -trum *(dead) black, dark* [L17]

Athēnae, -ārum (f, pl) *Athens* [W30]

Athēniensis, -is (m/f) *an Athenian* [W30]

atque (ac) *and, and also* [L27]

audeō, -ēre, ——, ausus sum *I dare* [L11]

audiō, -īre, -īvī, -ītum *I hear, listen to* [L29]

auferō, -ferre, abstulī, ablatum *(3rd conj. irreg.) I carry away/off, remove* [W32]

augeō, -ēre, auxī, auctum *I increase* [L19]

aula, -ae (f) *hall, inner/royal court* [W13]

aureus, -a, -um *golden, gold* [L17]

aurīga, -ae (m/f) *charioteer, driver* [W23]

auris, -is (f) *ear* [W28]

aurum, -ī (n) *gold* [L5]

aut *or* [L1]

autem (postpositive conj.) *however, moreover* [L12]

auxilium, -ī (n) *help, aid* [L5]

avārus, -a, -um *greedy* [L7]

avēna, -ae (f) *pan pipe, shepherd's pipe* [W21]

avia, -ae (f) *grandmother* [L22]

avis, avis (f) *bird* [L18]

avunculus, -ī (m) *uncle (mother's brother)* [L22]

avus, -ī (m) *grandfather, ancestor* [L22]

B

Bacchus, -ī (m) *Bacchus, the god of wine* [W27]

baculum, -ī (n) *staff* [W32]

barbarus, -a, -um *foreign, strange, savage* [L31]

barbarus, -ī (m) *foreigner, barbarian* [L31]

beātus, -a, -um *happy, blessed* [L7]

bellator, -toris (m) *warrior* [W32]

bellum, -ī (n) *war* [L15]; **bellum gerō** *I wage war* [L28]

bene *well* [L1]

bēstia, -ae (f) *beast* [L2]

Bethleem (indecl.) *Bethlehem* [W32]

Biblia Sacra, Bibliae Sacrae (f) *Holy Bible* [L11]

bonus, -a, -um *good* [L7]

bōs, bovis (m/f) *cow, bull, ox (pl.) cattle* [L19]

bracchium, -ī (n) *arm* [W13]

brevis, -e *short, small, brief* [L19]

C

cadaver, -veris (n) *dead body, carcass* [W32]

cadō, -ere, cecidī, cāsum *I fall, sink, drop* [L27]

caecus, -a, -um *blind* [L27]

caelum, -ī (n) *sky, heaven* [L5]

caeruleus, -a, -um *blue* [L17]

calamus, -ī (m) *reed, reed-pipe* [W28]

caldus, -a, -um *warm, hot, fiery* [L7]

calix, calicis (m) *goblet* [W13]

camēlus, -ī (m/f) *camel* [L4]

candidus, -a, -um *(glittering) white* [L17]

canis, canis (m/f) *dog* [L18]

cantō (1) *I sing, play (music), predict* [L1]

cantus, -ūs (m) *song, singing* [L25]

caper, -prī (m) *(billy) goat* [L4]

capiō, -ere, cēpī, captum *I take, capture, seize* [L31]

captō (1) *I hunt* [L10]

caput, -itis (n) *head* [L13]

carcer, -eris (m) *prison; (generally in pl.) starting gates (of a horse race)* [W23]

carmen, -inis (n) *song, chant, poem, prophecy* [L13]

caro, carnis (f) *flesh, meat* [L31]

cārus, -a, -um *dear, beloved* [L13]

castellum, -ī (n) *castle* [L5]

castra, -ōrum (n, pl) *camp* [L15]

cāsus, -ūs (m) *event, incident; misfortune, downfall* [L28]

cauda, -ae (f) *tail* [W21]

caveō, -ēre, cāvī, cautum *I guard against, beware (of)* [L12]

cēdō, -ere, cessī, cessum *I go, move, yield* [L28]

celer, celeris, celere *swift, quick* [L19]

celō (1) *I hide* [W28]

cēna, -ae (f) *dinner, meal* [L20]

centaurus, -ī (m) *centaur* [L10]

centēsimus, -a, -um *one hundredth* [L23]

centum *one hundred* [L21]

certāmen, -minis (n) *contest, race* [W23]

certātim *eagerly* [L20]

cervus, -ī (m) *stag, deer* [L10]

cētus, -ī (m) *sea monster, kraken, whale* [L10]

Christus, -ī (m) *Christ* [L4]

cibus, -ī (m) *food* [L4]

Circus Maximus, Circī Maximī (m) *the Circus Maximus, a famous racetrack at the foot of the Palatine Hill in Rome* [W23]

cito *quickly, fast, speedily* [L27]

clam *secretly* [L29]

clāmō (1) *I shout* [L1]

clāmor, -oris (m) *shout, cry* [W20]

classis, -is (f) *group, class, fleet (of ships)* [L30]

clēmentia, -ae (f) *mercy, clemency* [W21]

clypeum, -ī (n) *shield* [W32]

cōgitō (1) *I think* [L6]

cōgō, -ere, -ēgī, -āctum *I drive together, force, compel* [L28]

collocō (1) *I place, set, arrange* [W21]

colō, -ere, coluī, cultum *I cultivate, inhabit, worship* [L29]

coniunx, -iugis (m/f) *husband or wife* [L22]

cōnsilium, -iī (n) *plan, counsel, advice; wisdom* [L30]

consōbrīna, -ae (f) *cousin (female, mother's side)* [L22]

consōbrīnus, -ī (m) *cousin (male, mother's side)* [L22]

contrā (+ acc.) *against* [L11]

cōpia, -ae (f) *supply, plenty, abundance; (pl.) troops* [L15]

cor, cordis (n) *heart* [L13]

cōram (+ abl.) *in the presence of, before; (adv.) personally, openly* [L27]

cornū, -ūs (n) *horn* [L25]

corōna, -ae (f) *crown* [L2]

corpus, corporis (n) *body* [L13]

crās *tomorrow* [L6]

crēdō, -ere, -didī, -ditum *I believe* [L26]

cremō (1) *I burn, consume by fire* [L2]

creō (1) *I create* [L6]

Crēta, -ae (f) *Crete* [W30]

crūs, crūris (n) *leg* [W19]

crustulum, -ī (n) *cookie, small cake* [L5]

crux, crucis (f) *cross* [L15]

cum (+ abl.) *with* [L9]

Cupīdo, -dinis (m) *Cupid (son of Venus and god of love)* [W20]

cupiō, -ere, cupīvī, cupītum *I wish (for), desire, long (for)* [L31]

cūr *why?* [L2]

cūrō (1) *I care for* [L15]

curriculum, -ī (n) *lap (of a race), course* [W23]

currō, -ere, cūcurrī, cursum *I run* [L26]

D

Daedalus, -ī (m) *Daedalus (a skilled inventor and craftsman)* [W30]

Daphne, -ēs (f) *Daphne* [W20]

David (indecl.) *David* [W32]

dē (+ abl.) *from, down from, concerning* [L4]

dea, -ae (f) *goddess; dat. and abl. pl. usually* **deābus** [L6]

dēbeō, -ēre, -uī, -itum *I owe, ought* [L11]

decem *ten* [L21]

decimus, -a, -um *tenth* [L23]

dēclārō (1) *I declare, make clear, explain* [L10]

dēfendō, -ere, -fendī, -fēnsum *I defend* [L28]

dēiciō, -icere, -iēcī, -iectum *I throw down, cast down, hurl down* [W23]

deinde *from that place, then, thereupon, next* [L24]

dēleō, -ēre, -lēvī, -lētum *I destroy* [L9]

dēligō, -ere, lēgī, -lēctum *I pick, choose* [L28]

dēnique *finally* [L10]

dēspiciō, -ere, -spexī, -spectum *I look down on, despise* [W32]

Deus, -ī (m) *God;* **deus, -ī (m)** *a god* [L4]

dexter, -tra, -trum (or –tera, -terum) *right(-handed); skilled, favorable* [L30]

diaeta, -ae (f) *cabin (of a ship)* [W18]

Diāna, -ae (f) *Diana (virgin goddess of the moon and hunting)* [W20]

dīcō, -ere, dīxī, dictum *I say, speak* [L26]

diēs, diēī (m/f) *day, period of time* [L28]

difficilis, -e *difficult* [L20]

dīmittō, -ere, -mīsī, -missum *I send away, dismiss, forgive* [L30]

discipula, -ae (f) *student (female), disciple* [L5]

discipulus, -ī (m) *student (male), apprentice, disciple* [L5]

diū *for a long time* [L13]

dīvitiae, -ārum (f, pl) *riches, wealth* [L2]

dō, dare, dedī, datum *I give* [L1]

doceō, -ēre, docuī, doctum *I teach* [L9]

doctus, -a, -um *learned, wise, skilled* [L13]

dominus, -ī (m) *lord, master* [L4]

dōmō, -āre, domuī, domitum *I tame, subdue* [L12]

domus, -ūs (f) *house, home* [L25]

dōnum, -ī (n) *gift* [L5]

dormiō, -īre, -īvī, -ītum *I sleep* [L29]

draco, dracōnis (m) *dragon* [L12]

dūcō, -ere, duxī, ductum *I lead, guide* [L26]

dulcis, -e *sweet* [L19]

duo, duae, duo *two* [L21]

duodecim *twelve* [L21]

duodecimus, -a, -um *twelfth* [L23]

duodēvīcēsimus, -a, -um *eighteenth* [L23]

duodēvīgintī *eighteen* [L21]

dux, ducis (m) *leader, guide, general* [L14]

E

ē *see* **ex**

ēbrius, -a, -um *drunk, intoxicated* [W13]

ecce *behold!* [L17]

ecclēsia, -ae (f) *church* [L11]

effugiō, -ere, -fūgī, -fugitum *I escape* [W10]

ego (sg.) *I* [L17]

ēgregius, -a, -um *outstanding, excellent* [L29]

ēheu (heu) *alas! oh! (expressing grief or pain)* [L22]

elephantus, -ī (m) *elephant* [L19]

enigma, -matis (n) *riddle* [W19]

enim (postpositive conj.) *indeed, truly, certainly; for* [L17]

eō, -īre, iī (īvī), itum *I go* [L29]

Ephratheus, -ī (m) *an Ephramite* [W32]

epulae, -ārum (f, pl) *feast* [L20]

eques, -quitis (m) *knight, horseman, cavalryman* [L20]

equus, -ī (m) *horse* [L4]

ergō *therefore, then, consequently, accordingly* [L18]

errō (1) *I wander, err, am mistaken* [L14]

et *and, even, also;* **et...et** *both...and* [L1]

etiam *even, also, besides, still* [L22]

ēvangelium, -ī (n) *good news, gospel* [L5]

ex, ē (+ abl.) *out of, from* [L3]

exerceō, -ēre, -uī, -itum *I train, exercise* [L14]

exercitus, -ūs (m) *army* [L25]

exprobrō (1) *I reproach* [W32]

exspectō (1) *I wait for, expect* [L3]

extendō, -ere, -tendī, -tensum *I stretch out, extend* [W26]

F

Fabius, -ī (m) *Fabius* [W19]

fābula, -ae (f) *story, legend, tale* [L2]

faciēs, -ēī (f) *shape, form; face; character* [L28]

facilis, -e *easy* [L20]

faciō, -ere, fēcī, factum *I make, do (for present passive system, use* **fīō**) [L31]

fāma, -ae *report, reputation, fame* [W23]

famēlicus, -a, -um *hungry* [L29]

familia, -ae *household, family* [L22]

fātum, -ī (n) *fate* [L5]

felīciter in aeternum *happily ever after* [W6]

fēlix, (gen.) -līcis *lucky, fortunate, happy* [L19]

fēmina, -ae (f) *woman* [L2]

fenestra, -ae (f) *window* [L31]

ferō, ferre, tulī, lātum (irreg. 3rd conj.) *I carry, bring (forth), bear* [W32]

ferus, -a, -um *fierce, wild* [L7]

fessus, -a, -um *tired, weary* [L20]

festīnō (1) *I hasten, hurry* [L9]

fidēs, -eī (f) *faith* [L28]

fīdus, -a, -um *faithful, trustworthy* [L7]

fīlia, -ae (f) *daughter (dat. and abl. pl. often* **fīliābus**) [L6]

fīlius, -ī (m) *son* [L4]

fīlum, -ī (n) *thread, string* [W30]

fīnis, -is (m) *end, boundary, limit* [W4]

fīō, fierī, ——, factus sum *I am made, am done, become, happen [used as present passive system of* **faciō**] [L31]

fleō, -ēre, flēvī, flētum *I weep* [L14]

flōreō, -ēre, -uī, —— *I flourish* [L17]

flōs, flōris (m) *flower* [L15]

flūmen, flūminis (n) *river* [L13]

fodiō, -ere, fōdī, fossum *I dig* [W28]

foedus, -a, -um *horrible, ugly* [L7]

folium *leaf* [W20]

fortasse *perhaps* [L26]

fortior, -tius (gen. fortioris) *braver* [W31]

fortis, -e *strong, brave* [L19]

fortissimus, -a, -um *bravest, strongest* [W32]

foveō, -ēre, fōvī, fōtum *I cherish, love, esteem* [L25]

frangō, -ere, frēgī, fractum *I break, smash, shatter* [L27]

frāter, frātris (m) *brother* [L12]

frōns, -ontis (f) *forehead* [W32]

fructus, -ūs (m) *fruit, profit* [L25]

frūmentum, -ī (n) *grain; (pl.) crops* [L15]

fugiō, -ere, fūgī, fugitum *I flee, run away* [L31]

fulgur, -uris (n) *lightning* [W25]

funda, -ae (f) *sling* [W32]

G

gaudeō, -ēre, ——, gāvīsus sum *I rejoice* [L22]

gaudium, -ī (n) *joy, happiness* [L5]

gelidus, -a, -um *cold, icy* [L31]

geminus, -ī (m) *twin* [L10]

gens, -ntis (f) *clan, tribe, nation* [L31]

genu, -ūs (n) *knee* [L25]

germāna, -ae (f) *sister* [L4]

germānus, -ī (m) *brother* [L4]

gerō, -ere, gessī, gestum *I bear, carry on;* **bellum gerō** *I wage war* [L28]

gigās, gigantis (m) *giant* [L15]

gladius, -ī (m) *sword* [L4]

glōria, -ae (f) *fame, glory* [L15]

grāmen, grāminis (n) *grass, greenery* [L13]

grātia, -ae (f) *grace, favor, kindness, thanks;* **grātiās agō (+ dat.)** *I give thanks, I thank* [L27]

grātus, -a, -um *grateful, pleasing* [L27]

grex, gregis (m) *flock, herd* [L31]

gubernō (1) *I steer, direct, govern* [L25]

H

habeō, -ēre, -uī, -itum *I have, hold* [L9]

habitō (1) *I live, dwell, inhabit* [L3]

hara, -ae (f) *pig-sty* [W25]

harēna, -ae (f) *sand, beach* [L3]

hasta, -ae (f) *spear* [L3]

herī *yesterday* [L6]

heu (ēheu) *alas! oh! (expresses grief or pain)* [L22]

hic, haec, hoc *this, (pl.) these* [L30]

Hierusalem (indecl.) *Jerusalem*

hodiē *today* [L2]

homō, hominis (m) *man, human being* [L12]

hōra, -ae (f) *hour* [L31]

horrendus, -a, -um *dreadful, awful, fearful* [L13]

hostis, -is (m) *enemy (of the state)* [L18]

hyacinthinus, -a, -um *blue, purplish-blue, violet* [L17]

hydrus, -ī (m) *sea serpent* [W12]

I

iaceō, -ēre, -uī, —— *I lie (flat), lie down* [L9]

iaciō, -ere, iēcī, iactum *I throw, cast, hurl* [L31]

iam *now, already;* **nōn iam** *no longer* [L15]

ibī *there, at that place; then* [L5]

Iēsus, -ūs (m) *Jesus* [L25]

ignis, ignis (m) *fire* [L18]

ille, illa, illud *that, (pl.) those; that famous* [L30]

impediō, -īre, -īvī, -ītum *I hinder* [L29]

improbus, -a, -um *wicked* [L29]

in (+ acc.) *into, against; (+ abl.) in, on* [L3]

Īnachus, -ī (m) *Inachus (god of the Inachus River in Argos)* [W21]

incipiō, -ere, -cēpī, -ceptum *I begin, commence* [L31]

incircumcisus, -a, -um *uncircumcised* [W32]

īnfāns, -fantis (adj. & noun, m/f) *baby, infant* [W31]

infēlix, (gen.) -līcis *unlucky, unfortunate, miserable* [L19]

infīgo, -ere, -fixī, -fixum *I fix in, fasten in* [W32]

ingēns, (gen.) -entis *huge, vast, enormous* [L19]

inimīcus, -ī (m) *(personal) enemy* [L10]

īnsula, -ae (f) *island* [L3]

inter (+ acc.) *between, among* [L19]

interficiō, -ere, -fēcī, -fectum *I kill, slay, destroy* [L31]

interim *meanwhile, in the meantime* [L9]

intrō (1) *I enter* [L9]

inveniō, -īre, -vēnī, -ventum *I come upon, find* [L29]

invicem *reciprocally (i.e., "[to] one another")* [W26]

invideō, -ēre, -vīdī, -vīsum *I envy* [W29]

Īō, -ōnis (f) *Io (a beautiful nymph and daughter of Inachus)* [W21]

īra, -ae (f) *anger* [L2]

īrātus, -a, -um *angry, wrathful* [L15]

is, ea, id *he, she, it, they; this, that* [L17]

Isai (indecl.) *Jesse* [W32]

Israhel (indecl.) *Israel* [W32]

Israhelita, -ae (m) *Israelite* [W32]

iste, ista, istud *that (of yours); such (sometimes used with tone of contempt)* [L30]

Ītalia, -ae (f) *Italy* [W8]

itaque *and ēo, therefore* [L2]

iter, itineris (n) *journey, road, route, trek* [L13]

iterum *again, a second time* [L25]

iūdex, -dicis (m) *judge* [W28]

Iūlia, -ae (f) *Iulia or Julia* [W11]

Iūlius, -iī (m) *Iulius or Julius* [W19]

iungō, -ere, iūnxī, iunctum *I join, unite, yoke* [L27]

Iūnia, -ae (f) *Iunia or Junia* [W11]

Iūno, -ōnis (f) *Juno (queen of the gods and wife of Jupiter)* [W21]

Iuppiter, Iovis (m) *Jupiter/Jove (king of the gods)* [W21]

iūstus, -a, -um *just, right, fair, righteous* [L7]

iuvenissimus, -a, -um *youngest* [W19]

iuvō, -āre, iūvī, iūtum *I help* [L22]

iūxta, (adv. & prep. + acc.) *near (to), close to/by* [L28]

L

labor, labōris (m) *work, toil, labor, hardship* [L12]

labōrō (1) *I work* [L22]

labyrinthus, -ī (m) *labyrinth, maze* [W30]

lac, lactis (n) *milk* [L13]

lacus, -ūs (m) *lake, tub, hollow* [L27]

laetus, -a, -um *happy, joyful, glad* [L7]

lapis, -idis (m) *stone* [W27]

lātus, -a, -um *wide, broad* [L20]

laudō (1) *I praise* [L1]

laurus, -ī *laurel-tree* [W20]

laus, laudis (f) *praise* [L15]

lavō, -āre, lāvī, lōtum/lavātum *I wash* [W27]

legō, -ere, lēgī, lectum *I read, choose* [L28]

leō, leōnis (m) *lion* [L12]

liber, librī (m) *book* [L11]

līberī, -ōrum (m, pl) *children* [L10]

līberō (1) *I set free* [L1]

licet *it is permitted/allowed* [W26]

limpidissimus, -a, -um *very bright, very clear* [W32]

lingua, -ae (f) *language, tongue* [L26]

littera, -ae (f) *letter of the alphabet; (pl) letter, epistle* [L26]

lītus, lītoris (n) *shore, shoreline* [L13]

longinquus, -a, -um *distant, far away* [L7]

longus, -a, -um *long* [L20]

lūceō, lūcēre, lūxī, —— *I shine, am bright* [L11]

lūdō, lūdere, lūsī, lūsum *I play, tease, trick* [L26]

lūna, -ae (f) *moon* [L2]

lux, lūcis (f) *light* [L12]

lyra, -ae (f) *lyre* [W28]

M

magister, -strī (m) *teacher (male)* [L6]

magistra, -ae (f) *teacher (female)* [L6]

magnanimus, -a, -um *brave, bold, noble* [W9]

magnoperē *greatly, very much* [L29]

magnus, -a, -um *large, big, great* [L7]

māior, māius (gen. māioris) *greater, older* [W31]

male *badly, ill, wrongly* [L1]

maledicō, -ere, -dīxī, -dictum *I speak ill, curse* [W30]

malus, -a, -um *bad, evil* [L7]

mandūcō (1) *I chew, eat* [L6]

māne *in the morning, early* [W19]

maneō, -ēre, mansī, mansum *I remain* [L10]

manus, -ūs (f) *hand* [L25]

mappa, -ae (f) *starting flag (lit., "napkin")* [W23]

mare, maris (n) *sea* [L18]

māter, mātris (f) *mother* [L12]

mātrimōnium -ī (n) *marriage* [L20]

maximus, -a, -um *greatest, oldest* [W31]

mediōcris, -e *ordinary* [L19]

medius, -a, -um *middle (of), midst (of)* [L26]

melior, -ius *better* [W28]

mensa, -ae (f) *table* [L31]

Mercurius, -ī (m) *Mercury (the messenger god)* [W21]

mereō, -ēre, -uī, -itum *I deserve, earn, am worthy of* [L15]

merīdiēs, -ēī (m) *noon* [L28]

mēta, -ae (f) *turning-post, goal* [W23]

metus, -ūs (m) *fear, dread* [L26]

meus, -a, -um *my, mine* [L11]

Midās, -ae (m) *Midas (king of Phrygia)* [W27]

mīles, mīlitis (m) *soldier* [L12]

mille *one thousand* [L21]

mīllēsimus, -a, -um *one thousandth* [L23]

minimus, -a, -um *least, younger* [W31]

Mīnōs, -ōnis (m) *Minos* [W30]

Mīnōtaurus, -ī (m) *the Minotaur* [W30]

minūtātim *gradually, bit by bit* [L20]

mīrus, -a, -um *strange, wonderful* [L7]

miser, -era, -erum *unhappy, wretched, miserable* [L7]

mītra, -ae (f) *turban* [W28]

mittō, -ere, mīsī, missum *I send, let go* [L26]

modo *only, just, merely, but* [L27]

moenia, -ium (n, pl) *fortifications, city walls* [L18]

moneō, -ēre, -uī, -itum *I warn* [L9]

mōns, montis *mountain* [L18]

mōnstrum *monster* [W30]

mordeō, -ēre, momordī, morsum *I bite, sting* [L9]

mors, mortis (f) *death* [L18]

moveō, -ēre, mōvī, mōtum *I move* [L14]

mox *soon* [L15]

mulier, mulieris (f) *woman* [L22]

multus, -a, -um *much, many* [L7]

mundus, -ī (m) *world, universe* [L6]

musicus, -ī (m) *musician* [W28]

mūtō (1) *I change* [L20]

N

nam *for* [W32]

narrō (1) *I tell, relate, recount* [L2]

naufragium, -ī (n) *wreck, crash (lit., shipwreck)* [W23]

nauta, -ae (m) *sailor* [L3]

nāvicula, -ae (f) *boat* [W31]

nāvigō (1) *I sail* [L4]

nāvis, -is (f) *ship* [L18]

nec (neque) *and not, nor;* **nec...nec** *neither....nor* [L14]

necō (1) *I kill, slay* [L1]

neque (nec) *and not, nor;* **nec...nec** *neither....nor* [L14]

nesciō, -īre, -īvī, -ītum *I do not know* [L30]

niger, -gra, -grum *(shining) black, dark-colored* [L17]

nihil, (n. indecl.) *nothing;* **(adv.)** *not at all* [L6]

nō (1) *I swim* [L14]

nōmen, nōminis (n) *name* [L13]

nōn *not* [L1]

nōnus, -a, -um *ninth* [L23]

nōs (pl.) *we* [L17]

noster, -stra, -strum *our, ours* [L11]

novem *nine* [L21]

noverca, -ae (f) *step-mother* [W22]

novus, -a, -um *new* [L26]

nox, noctis (f) *night* [L18]

nūbes, nūbis (f) *cloud, gloom* [L18]

nummus, -ī (m) *coin* [W22]

numquam *never* [L5]

nunc *now* [L1]

nuntiō (1) *I announce, declare* [L14]

nympha, -ae (f) *nymph* [W20]

O

obsideō, -ēre, -sēdī, -sessum *I besiege, remain near* [L10]

occīdō, -ere, -cīdī, -cīsum *I kill, cut down, slay* [L30]

occultō (1) *I hide, conceal* [L22]

occupō (1) *I seize* [L6]

ōceanus, -ī (m) *ocean* [L4]

octāvus, -a, -um *eighth* [L23]

octō *eight* [L21]

ōlim *once upon a time, formerly, then* [L6]

omnis, -e *every, all* [L19]

onus, oneris (n) *burden, load, weight* [L13]

oppidum, -ī (n) *town* [L5]

oppugnō (1) *I attack* [L4]

optio, optiōnis (f) *choice* [W12]

ōra, -ae (f) *shore* [L13]

ōrāculum, -ī (n) *oracle, prophecy* [W31]

orba, -ae (f) *orphan (female)* [L22]

orbus, -a, -um *deprived of parents or children, bereft* [L22]

orbus, -ī (m) *orphan (male)* [L22]

ōrō (1) *I pray, speak (takes double acc.)* [L6]

ōs, ōris (n) *mouth* [L13]

Oswaldus, -ī (m) *Oswald* [W19]

P

Pactōlus, -ī (m) *Pactolus (a river in Lydia in Asia Minor)* [W27]

paene (adv.) *almost* [L19]

palma, -ae (f) *hand* [W14]

palus, palūdis (f) *swamp* [W13]

Pān, Pānos (acc. Pāna) (m) *Pan (god of woods, shepherds, and flocks)* [W28]

pānis, -is (m) *bread* [L29]

parens, -ntis (m/f) *parent* [W11]

parō (1) *I prepare* [L14]

parvus, -a, -um *little, small, unimportant* [L7]

pascō, -ere, -pāvī, -pastum *I feed, pasture* [W32]

pastor, pastōris (m) *shepherd* [L20]

pastorālis, -e *of/belonging to a shepherd, pastoral* [W32]

pater, patris (m) *father* [L12]

patria, -ae (f) *native land* [L3]

patruēlis, -is (m/f) *cousin (on the father's side)* [L22]

patruus, -ī (m) *uncle (father's brother)* [L22]

paucī, -ae, -a (pl) *few* [L7]

pāvo, -ōnis (m) *peacock* [W21]

pāx, pācis (f) *peace* [L15]

pecūnia, -ae (f) *money* [L3]

per (+ acc.) *through* [L3]

pēra, -ae (f) *bag, satchel* [W32]

percutiō, -ere, -cussī, -cussum *I strike down, cut down* [W32]

perdō, -ere, perdidī, perditum *I destroy, ruin, lose* [L27]

perficiō, -ere, -fēci, -fectum *I complete, finish* [W23]

perīculum, -ī (n) *danger* [L5]

permittō, -ere, -mīsī, -missum *I permit, allow* [W30]

persequor, -sequī, ——, -secutus sum (deponent) *I pursue (with hostile intent), hunt down* [W32]

persuādeō, -ēre, -suāsī, -suāsum (+dat.) *I persuade* [W15]

pertūsus, -a, -um *leaky* [W29]

petō, -ere, -īvī, -ītum *I shoot* [W20]

Philistheus, -ī (m) *Philistine*

Phrygia, -ae (f) *Phrygia (a land in Asia Minor)* [W27]

pila, -ae (f) *ball* [W30]

pinguis, -e *fat* [W25]

pīrāta, -ae (m) *pirate* [L2]

piscis, -is (m) *fish* [L19]

piscor, -ārī, ——, -ātus sum (deponent) *I fish* [W29]

placidus, -a, -um *calm, quiet* [W29]

plumbeus, -a, -um *leaden, of lead* [W20]

poena, -ae (f) *penalty, punishment;* **poenās dō** *I pay the penalty* [L27]

poēta, -ae (m) *poet* [L2]

pōnō, -ere, posuī, positum *I put, place* [L26]

pōns, pontis (m) *bridge* [W19]

populus, -ī (m) *people, nation* [L11]

porcus, -ī (m) *pig* [L10]

porta, -ae (f) *door, gate* [L31]

portō (1) *I carry* [L4]

portus, -ūs (m) *harbor, port* [L25]

possum, posse, potuī, —— *I am able, can* [L11]

post (+ acc.) *after, behind* [L17]

postea *afterwards* [L28]

postnatus, -ī (m) *oldest [Won]* [W19]

postquam (conj.) *after* [W15]

potēns, (gen.) -entis *powerful* [L19]

pōtō, -āre, -āvi, pōtātum or pōtum *I drink, drink heavily* [L6]

praecīdō, -ere, -cīdī, -cīsum *I cut off, lop* [W32]

praedīcō, -ere, -dīxī, -dictum *I predict, prophesy* [W31]

praemium, -ī (n) *reward* [W27]

prīmus, -a, -um *first* [L23]

prō (+ abl.) *before, in front of; for (the sake of), instead of* [L18]

proelium, -ī (n) *battle* [L15]

prope (adv./prep. + acc.) *near, next to* [L19]

properō (1) *I hurry, rush* [L20]

propter (+ acc.) *because of, on account of, near* [L25]

provocō (1) *to challenge* [W32]

puella, -ae (f) *girl* [L3]

puer, puerī (m) *boy* [L5]

pugnō (1) *I fight* [L1]

pulcher, -chra, -chrum *beautiful, handsome* [L7]

purpureus, -a, -um *purple; dark-red, dark-violet, dark-brown* [L17]

pyra, -ae (f) *funeral pyre* [W8]

Q

quadrīgae, -ārum (f, pl) *four-horse chariot* [W23]

quam *as, than, how* [L28]

quandō *when (?), ever; since, because* [L12]

quārtus, -a, -um decimus, -a, -um *fourteenth* [L23]

quārtus, -a, -um *fourth* [L23]

quattuor *four* [L21]

quattuordecim *fourteen* [L21]

–que, (enclitic) *and* [L10]

quia (conj.) *because, since, that* [L18]

quid *what?* [W19]

quīndecim *fifteen* [L21]

quīngentēsimus, -a, -um *five hundredth* [L23]

quīngentī *five hundred* [L21]

quīnquāgēsimus, -a, -um *fiftieth* [L23]

quīnquāgintā *fifty* [L21]

quīnque *five* [L21]

quīntus, -a, -um decimus, -a, -um *fifteenth* [L23]

quīntus, -a, -um *fifth* [L23]

quis *who?* [W31]

quod *because, that* [L10]

quōmodo *how, in what way* [L25]

quoniam *because, since* [L26]

quoque *also, too* [L29]

R

rapiō, -ere, rapuī, raptum *I snatch, seize, carry (off)* [L31]

raptus, -ūs (m) *kidnapping, abduction* [W31]

reficiō, -ere, -fēcī, -fectum *I repair* [W29]

rēgia, -ae (f) *palace* [L2]

rēgīna, -ae (f) *queen* [L2]

regnō (1) *I rule, govern, reign* [L6]

regnum, -ī (n) *kingdom* [L5]

regō, -ere, rexī, rectum *I rule* [L26]

relinquō, -ere, -līquī, -lictum *I abandon, leave behind* [L28]

removeō, -ēre, -mōvī, -mōtum *I remove, take away* [L14]

repentē *suddenly* [L10]

reptō (1) *I crawl, creep* [L14]

rēs, reī (f) *thing* [L28]

respondeō, -ēre, -spondī, -sponsum *I answer, respond* [L9]

resurgō, -ere, -surrēxī, -surrēctum *I rise again* [L29]

retrō *back(ward), behind* [W23]

rēx, rēgis (m) *king* [L12]

rīdeō, -ēre, rīsī, rīsum *I laugh, smile* [L9]

rogō (1) *I ask (takes double acc. or phrase with dē)* [L6]

ruber, -bra, -brum *red, ruddy* [L17]

rūfus, -a, -um *red, ruddy* [W32]

S

sabbata, -ōrum (n, pl) *Sabbath* [W26]

saeculum, -ī (n) *generation; the spirit of the age, times* [L6]

saepe *often* [L6]

sagitta, -ae (f) *arrow* [L3]

saliō, -īre, -uī, saltum *I jump, leap* [W29]

salveō, -ēre, ——, —— *I am well;* **salvē(te),** *Good day! Be well!* [L9]

salvus, -a, -um *safe, saved, well, sound* [L25]

sanctus, -a, -um *holy, sacred, consecrated* [L25]

satis (adv. & indecl. adj./noun) *enough, sufficient(ly)* [L30]

Saul (indecl.) *Saul* [W32]

saxum, -ī (n) *rock* [L29]

sciō, -īre, sciī (scīvī), scītum *I know* [L29]

scopulus, -ī (m) *cliff* [W30]

scrībō, -ere, scripsī, scriptum *I write* [L26]

scūtum, -ī (m) *shield* [L10]

sē (acc. reflexive pronoun) *himself, herself, itself* [W8]

sēcrētum, -ī (n) *secret* [W28]

secundum (adv. & prep. + acc.) *after; according to* [L28]

secundus, -a, -um *second* [L23]

sed *but* [L1]

sēdecim *sixteen* [L21]

sedeō, -ēre, sēdī, sessum *I sit* [L9]

sella, -ae (f) *seat, chair* [L31]

semper *always* [L5]

senex, senis (m) *old man* [L14]

septem *seven* [L21]

septendecim *seventeen* [L21]

septimus, -a, -um decimus, -a, -um *seventeenth* [L23]

septimus, -a, -um *seventh* [L23]

sequor, sequī, ——, secūtus sum (deponent) *I follow* [W30]

serva, -ae (f) *female slave, servant* [L4]

servō (1) *I save* [L6]

servus, -ī (m) *male slave, servant* [L4]

sēū (sīve) *or;* **sēū…sēū** *whether…or* [L30]

sex *six* [L21]

sextus, -a, -um decimus, -a, -um *sixteenth* [L23]

sextus, -a, -um *sixth* [L23]

sī (conj.) *if* [L18]

sīca, -ae (f) *dagger* [L3]

sīcut *as, just as, like* [L20]

Sīlēnus, -ī (m) *Silenus (pudgy old fellow [usually drunk], former tutor and longtime companion of Bacchus)* [W27]

silva, -ae (f) *forest* [L3]

simulacrum, -ī (n) *statue* [W25]

sine (+ abl.) *without* [L9]

sinister, -stra, -strum *left(-handed); inauspicious* [L30]

sīve (sēū) *or;* **sīve… sīve** *whether…or* [L30]

sōl, sōlis (m) *sun* [L12]

sōlus, -a, -um *only, single* [L12]

somniō (1) *I dream* [W18]

soror, sorōris (f) *sister* [L12]

spectō (1) *I look at, watch* [L1]

spēlunca, -ae (f) *cave* [L3]

spēs, speī (f) *hope* [L28]

spīna, -ae (f) *barrier (lit., "spine," the wall dividing a race course in half lengthwise)* [W23]

spīritus, -ūs (m) *spirit, breath* [L25]

spurius, -a, -um *spurious* [W32]

statim *immediately* [L13]

stella, -ae (f) *star* [L11]

stō, stāre, stetī, statum *I stand* [L1]

stultitia, -ae (f) *foolishness, folly* [W27]

stultus, -a, -um *foolish* [L7]

stupor, -ōris (m) *amazement, astonishment* [W28]

sub (+ acc.) *under, up under, close to;* **(+ abl.)** *below, under(neath), at the foot of* [L14]

sum, esse, fuī, futūrum *I am* [L3]

super (+ acc. /+ abl.) *over, above, beyond* [L26]

superbus, -a, -um *proud, haughty* [W18]

superō (1) *I conquer, defeat* [L2]

suprā (adv. & prep. + acc.) *above, over* [L14]

surgō, -ere, surrēxī, surrēctum *I (a)rise* [L28]

suspīciōsus, -a, -um *suspicious* [W21]

susurrō (1) *I whisper* [W28]

suum negōtium agō (idiom) *I mind my own business* [W29]

suus, -a, -um (reflexive possessive adj.) *his (own), her (own), its (own)* [W31]

synagōga, -ae (f) *synagogue* [W26]

T

tabernāculum, -ī (n) *tent* [W32]

taceō, -ēre, -uī, -itum *I am silent* [W26]

tactus, -ūs (m) *touch* [W28]

tamen *yet, nevertheless, still* [L30]

tangō, -ere, tetigī, tactum *I touch, strike* [L27]

tellūs, tellūris (f) *the earth, ground, land* [L14]

tempestās, -tātis (f) *weather, storm* [L26]

templum, -ī (n) *temple, shrine* [W25]

temptō (1) *I attempt* [W27]

tempus, temporis (n) *time* [L13]

tenēbrae, -ārum (f, pl) *darkness, gloomy place, shadows* [L11]

teneō, -ēre, tenuī, tentum *I hold, possess* [L9]

terra, -ae (f) *earth, land* [L4]

terreō, -ēre, -uī, -itum *I frighten, terrify* [L9]

tertius, -a, -um decimus, -a, -um *thirteenth* [L23]

tertius, -a, -um *third* [L23]

Thēsēus, -eī (m) *Theseus* [W30]

tigris, tigridis (m/f) *tiger* [L12]

timeō, -ēre, -uī, —— *I fear* [L9]

Tmōlus, -ī (m) *Tmolus (a god and a mountain in Lydia)* [W28]

tollō, -ere, sustulī, sublātum *I lift up, raise* [W25]

tonitrus, -ūs (m) *thunder* [L25]

tonsor, -ōris (m) *barber* [W28]

torrens, -ntis (m) *a torrent, stream* [W32]

torreō, -ēre, torruī, tostum *I burn, parch, dry up* [L17]

trādō, -ere, -didī, -ditum *I hand over, surrender* [W13]

tragoedia, -ae (f) *tragedy* [W4]

trahō, -ere, trāxī, trāctum *I draw, drag* [L30]

trans (+ acc.) *across* [L11]

tredecim *thirteen* [L21]

tremō, -ere, -uī, —— *I tremble, quake* [W25]

trēs, tria *three* [L21]

tribūtum, -ī (n) *tribute, tax* [W30]

trīstis, -e *sad, gloomy, dismal* [L20]

tū (sg.) *you* [L17]

tum *then, at that time; next, thereupon* [L15]

turba, -ae (f) *crowd, mob, throng* [L2]

turris, turris (f) *tower, turret* [L18]

tuus, -a, -um *your (sg), yours* [L11]

U

ubi *where (?), when* [L12]

ubīque *everywhere* [W29]

ūllus, -a, -um *any; anyone, anything* [W27]

ululō (1) *I howl, scream* [L6]

ūnā *together, in one* [L29]

unda, -ae (f) *wave* [L10]

ūndecim *eleven* [L21]

ūndecimus, -a, -um *eleventh* [L23]

ūndēvīcēsimus, -a, -um *nineteenth* [L23]

ūndēvīgintī *nineteen* [L21]

undique *on/from all sides, from every direction* [L30]

ūnicus, -a, -um *one, only, sole* [W22]

ūnus, -a, -um *one* [L21]

urbānus, -a, -um *polite* [W29]

urbs, urbis (f) *city* [L18]

ursus, -ī (m) *bear* [W32]

uxor, -ōris (f) *wife* [L30]

V

valeō, -ēre, -uī, -itum *I am well/strong;* **valē(te)** *Goodbye! Be well!* [L9]

valles, vallis (f) *valley, vale* [L18]

vastō (1) *I devastate, lay waste* [L14]

vātēs, -is (m/f) *prophet/prophetess* [W31]

vehō, -ere, vexī, vectum *I carry, ride, convey* [L27]

vēlum, -ī (n) *sail* [W30]

venēnum, -ī (n) *poison* [L10]

veniō, -īre, vēnī, ventum *I come* [L29]

ventus, -ī (m) *wind* [W28]

verbum, -ī (n) *word* [L5]

vēritas, -tātis (f) *truth* [L27]

versus, -ūs (m) *row, line (of poetry), furrow* [L27]

vertō, -ere, vertī, versum *I turn, change* [L28]

vērus, -a, -um *true* [L22]

vesper, vesperis (m) *evening, evening star* [L14]

vester, -stra, -strum *your (pl), yours (pl)* [L11]

vestis, vestis (f) *clothing, garment* [L18]

vetus, (gen.) -teris *old* [L30]

vexō (1) *I vex, ravage, annoy* [L19]

via, -ae (f) *road, way* [L11]

vīcēsimus, -a, -um prīmus, -a, -um *twenty-first* [L23]

vīcēsimus, -a, -um *twentieth* [L23]

victōria, -ae (f) *victory* [L11]

videō, -ēre, vīdī, visum *I see* [L9]

vidua, -ae (f) *widow* [L22]

viduō (1) *I deprive of* (**viduāta, -ae** *widowed*) [W19]

vīgintī *twenty* [L21]

vīgintī ūnus, -a, -um (ūnus et vīgintī) *twenty-one* [L21]

villa, -ae (f) *farmhouse, country house* [L2]

vinciō, -īre, vinxī, vinctum *I bind, tie* [L30]

vincō, -ere, vīcī, victum *I defeat, conquer* [L26]

vīnum, -ī (n) *wine* [L5]

vir, virī (m) *man* [L4]

virgō, virginis (f) *maiden, young woman* [L12]

viridis, -e *green; fresh, young, vigorous* [L17]

virtūs, virtūtis (f) *manliness, courage, strength* [L12]

vīta, -ae *life* [L11]

vītō (1) *I avoid, shun* [L30]

vīvō, -ere, vīxī, victum *I live* [L27]

vīvus, -a, -um *living* [L20]

vocō (1) *I call, summon, invite* [L1]

volō (1) *I fly* [L10]

vōs (pl.) *you* [L17]

vox, vōcis (f) *voice* [L14]

vulnerō (1) *I wound* [L1]

vulnus, vulneris (n) *wound* [L13]

vultus, -ūs (m) *face, expression* [L25]

GRAMMATICAL CONCEPTS

1st Conjugation Verbs: L1

1st Declension Adjectives: L7

1st Declension: L2

1st Person Personal Pronoun: L17

2nd Conjugation: L9

2nd Declension Adjectives: L7

2nd Declension: Masculine, L4;
Neuter, L5

2nd Person Personal Pronoun: L17

3rd Conjugation –iō: L31

3rd Conjugation: Active, L26; Passive,
L27

3rd Declension Adjectives: L19

3rd Declension: Masculine/Feminine,
L12; Neuter, L13; i-stems, L18

3rd Person Personal Pronoun: L17

4th Conjugation: Active and Passive,
L29

4th Declension: L25

5th Declension: L28

Ablative Case: L3**; Ablative of Time
When,** L28; Ablative of Time Within
Which, L28

Accusative Case: L2

Accusative of Duration of Time: L28

Active: Present Indicative, L1;
Imperfect Indicative, L6; Future
Indicative, L6; Perfect Indicative,
L14; Pluperfect Indicative, L15;
Future Perfect Indicative, L15

Adjective Agreement: L7

Adjectives: 1st/2nd Declension, L7;
3rd Declension, L19; Demonstrative,
L30; Agreement, L7; Predicate, L7;
Substantive, L9

āiō: L14

Cardinal Numerals: L21

Case: Ablative, L3; Accusative, L2;
Dative, L2; Genitive, L3; Nominative,
L2; Vocative, L11

Complementary Infinitives: L11

Conjugation: 1st, L1; 2nd, L9; 3rd
Active, L26; 3rd Passive, L27; 4th,
L29; 3rd –iō, L31

Dative Case: L2

Declension: 1st, L2; 2nd Masculine,
L4; 2nd Neuter, L5; 3rd Masculine/
Feminine, L12; 3rd Neuter, L13; 3rd
i-stem, L18; 4th, L25; 5th, L28

Demonstratives: L30

Enclitic: definition, L10

eō: L29

faciō: L31

Fifth Declension: L28

fīō: L31

First Conjugation Verbs: L1

First Declension Adjectives: L7

First Declension: L2

First Person Personal Pronoun: L17

**Fourth Conjugation: Active and
Passive,** L29

Fourth Declension: L25

Future Active Indicative: L6

**Future Perfect Tense: Active
Indicative,** L15; Passive Indicative,
L22

Future Tense: Active Indicative, L6;
Passive Indicative, L20

Genitive Case: L3

Imperatives: L11

Imperfect Active Indicative: L6

Imperfect Tense: Active Indicative, L6

Indicative: Present Active, L1; Present
Passive, L20; Imperfect Active, L6;
Imperfect Passive, L20; Future Active,

L6; Future Passive, L20; Perfect
Active, L14; Pluperfect Active, L15;
Future Perfect Active, L15

Infinitives: Complementary, L11

Magnificat: L9

Nicene Creed: L17

Nominative Case: L2

Numbers: Cardinal, L21; Ordinal, L23

Numerals: Cardinal, L21; Ordinal, L23

Ordinal Numerals: L23

Passive: Present Indicative, L20;
Imperfect Indicative, L20; Future
Indicative, L20; Perfect Indicative,
L22; Pluperfect Indicative, L22;
Future Perfect Indicative, L22

Pater Noster: L1

Perfect Tense: Active Indicative, L24

Passive Indicative: L22

Personal Pronouns: L17

Pluperfect Tense: Active Indicative,
L15; Passive Indicative, L22

possum: **Present,** Imperfect, and
Future Tenses, L11

Postpositive: definition, L12

Predicate Adjectives: L7

Prepositions: L3

Present Active Indicative: L1

Present Tense: Active Indicative, L1

Pronouns: Personal, L17;
Demonstrative, L30

Psalmus 23: L25

Second Conjugation: L9

Second Declension Adjectives: L7

Second Declension: Masculine: L4;
Neuter, L5

Second Person Personal Pronoun: L17

Substantive Adjectives: L9

sum: **Present Tense,** L3; Imperfect
Tense, L10; Future Tense, L10

Symbolum Nicaenum: L17

Third Conjugation –iō: L31

Third Conjugation: Active, L26;
Passive, L27

Third Declension Adjectives: L19

**Third Declension: Masculine/
Feminine,** L12; Neuter, L13; i-stems,
L18

Third Person Personal Pronoun: L17

Time Constructions: L28

Vocative Case: L11

SOURCES & HELPS

Bennett, Charles E. *New Latin Grammar.* Wauconda, IL: Bolchazy-Carducci Publishers, Inc. 1998. A good resource for your grammar questions.

Biblia Sacra Vulgata. Stuttgart, Germany: Deutsche Bibelgesellschaft, 1994. I adapted a few selections from this for the Latin to English translations, as well as using Psalm 23 for the Unit 4 memorization. If you have extra time, read a bit from the Vulgate every day to improve your Latin skills.

Glare, P. G. W. *The Oxford Latin Dictionary.* Oxford: Oxford University Press, 1983. The *OLD* is of course "the" standard for all Latin dictionaries, although occasionally I have found nuggets in Lewis and Short's *A Latin Dictionary* that were not in the *OLD*.

Greenough, J. B., et al., ed. *Allen and Greenough's New Latin Grammar.* Newburyport, MA: Focus Publishing, R. Pullins & Company, Inc., 2001. A fantastic resource; I referred to it frequently regarding grammar concepts of all kinds.

Jenney, Charles Jr., et al. *Jenney's First Year Latin.* Newton, MA: Allyn and Bacon, Inc., 1987. I consulted this text for the order of teaching various grammatical concepts. I studied Latin from it back in my junior high days, and have always been fond of it (although it is a little too fond of Caesar for my liking). Although short on explanations, it contains plenty of exercises and translations to practice each concept.

LaFleur, Richard A. *Love and Transformation: An Ovid Reader.* Glenview, IL: Scott Foresman-Addison Wesley, 1999. I referred to this Latin text (in addition to online texts) for some of the myths in the Latin to English translations.

The Latin Library. http://www.thelatinlibrary.com. This website has numerous Latin texts from all time periods, and I used it for some of the passages I adapted from the Vulgate.

Latin Vulgate. http://www.latinvulgate.com. This website is helpful because it has side-by-side translations from the Vulgate. Although most of us are familiar with Biblical texts and stories, sometimes the Vulgate has completely different wording than what we are used to (see the discussion of Psalm 23 in Lesson 25 as an example).

Lee, A. G., ed. *Ovid: Metamorphoses, Book I.* Wauconda, IL: Bolchazy-Carducci Publishers, Inc., 1988. I also referred to this book (in addition to online texts) for some of the myths in the Latin to English translations.

Lewis, Charlton T., and Charles Short. *A Latin Dictionary.* Oxford: Oxford University Press, 1958. Lewis and Short's dictionary is a standard resource and has helpful examples and commentary on many entries.

Martin, Charles, trans. *Ovid: Metamorphoses.* New York: W. W. Norton & Company, 2004. I consulted this English translation as well as the Latin texts for some of the myths found in the Latin to English translations.

Simpson, D. P. *Cassell's New Latin Dictionary.* New York: Funk & Wagnall's, 1959. I picked this up at a used bookstore (always check out the language section for Latin books!), and it has an especially helpful English to Latin section.

Stelten, Leo F. *Dictionary of Ecclesiastical Latin.* Peabody, MA: Hendrickson Publishers, Inc., 1995. I consulted this dictionary for the translations adapted from the Vulgate, since some dictionaries don't include ecclesiastical words.

Wheelock, Frederic M.; revised by Richard A. LaFleur. *Wheelock's Latin,* 6th ed. rev. New York: HarperCollins Publishers, 2005. I have taught out of this book for several years and referred to it for some grammar matters as well as researching in what order grammatical concepts were presented. It is a good standard text and resource, but not the best for someone trying to teach himself Latin.

Whitaker, William. "Words." http://www.archives.nd.edu/cgi-bin/words.exe. This website (from which you can also download a program) has Latin to English and English to Latin search engines. You can type in any form of a Latin word and it will parse it for you and give you the meaning—pretty handy! All students seem to know about this, so it's best to face it head on. I told my students they were welcome to use it, but that they not become dependent upon it (and of course they shouldn't use it to "cheat" on parsing exercises). It's best to use it when you are stumped by a particular form and need to look it up. The English to Latin search can be very helpful when writing stories or sentences.

Vulgate Frequency. http://www.intratext.com/IXT/LAT0001/_FF1.HTM. This website tells you which words appear the most often in the Vulgate or various other Latin texts. Since I'm especially fond of the Vulgate and Vergil, I consulted this site to see which words needed to be incorporated into the vocabulary lists.

VERB FORMATION CHART

Which principal part is used for which tense, voice, and mood? Keep this handout all year, and fill it in as you learn the various verb forms. The principal parts of *necō* (I kill) are provided as an example.

	FIRST	SECOND	THIRD	FOURTH
	necō	necāre	necāvī	necātum
DEFINITION/ FUNCTION				
INDICATIVE				
IMPERATIVE				
INFINITIVE				
SUBJUNCTIVE				
PARTICIPLE				